Augustus Craven

Fleurange

Augustus Craven

Fleurange

ISBN/EAN: 9783741142345

Manufactured in Europe, USA, Canada, Australia, Japa

Cover: Foto ©Andreas Hilbeck / pixelio.de

Manufactured and distributed by brebook publishing software (www.brebook.com)

Augustus Craven

Fleurange

LEISURE HOUR SERIES

FLEURANGE

A NOVEL FROM THE FRENCH OF

MME. AUGUSTUS CRAVEN

AUTHOR OF "A SISTER'S STORY," "ANNE SEVERIN," ETC.

TRANSLATED BY M. M. R.

NEW YORK
HOLT & WILLIAMS
1873

FLEURANGE.

I.—THE OLD HOUSE.

" God tempers the wind to the shorn lamb."

I.

"BEAUTIFUL, young, poor, alone in Paris,—what will become of her?"

For the third time Dr. Leblanc repeated these words in the presence of his sister, Mlle. Josephine, who remained so dumb one might have believed her deaf also, had not the irregular motion of her knitting-needles, and a pause now and then in her work, accompanied by indistinct exclamations, borne testimony to a preoccupation equal at least to that of her brother.

The latter had at first manifested his by measuring with long strides the room in which they were, and now that he had taken his accustomed place at the fireside opposite his sister, he opened and shut his snuff-box with a great noise, and took pinches thence with futile profusion, inasmuch as he forgot to convey them to their destination, and tapped on the floor with his feet in a manner expressive either of real perplexity or extreme agitation.

Mlle. Josephine kept on knitting, and seemed not less absorbed than her brother. Finally she said:

"If she were only not so young and pretty!"

"And so poor, and so alone also! your remark is valuable, sister! It is evident that if she were old, ugly, rich, and surrounded by friends, the situation would be quite different. I am really obliged to you for the discovery, Josephine!"

"Do not be out of patience, brother, I only repeat what you have just said; I continue, if she were a person of different appearance—"

"Come! that's enough!"

"And another name—"

"Another name? What has that to do with it?"

"A name which was not ridiculous—"

"Ridiculous? Her father's name? It is an honorable name,—yes, noble, I believe. Poor Gerard d'Yves! He was guilty of a thousand follies, he ruined himself, and finally turned painter; but if he had been judicious, he had talent enough to have retrieved his fortunes; besides, he was well-born, and his name—"

"I am not speaking of his name, but his daughter's."

"What then?"

"Well, brother, do you consider this young girl's name can be said to be a Christian name?"

"Fleurange?—I admit that it is singular, but her father loved odd things of every kind; he heard that name in Italy—*Fior Angela*, and he translated it."

"The mother should have had more sense."

"The poor mother died at her child's birth, so she had nothing to say about it."

"Did you not tell me there was a brother of hers, a professor in some city in Germany?"

"Yes; years ago he lived in Leipsic,—but how to find him now? All the family disapproved of this marriage, which was made without the father's consent. Poor Marguerite lived but a year, and Gerard, remaining a widower, would keep up no acquaintance with his wife's family. He continued to reside in Italy, placing his daughter in some convent near Perouse, before she was six years old, and he had only just sent for her when, two months ago, he arrived here, already very ill; and here he has died, leaving the child absolutely alone in the world."

"But to separate her in this way from all her mother's relations was certainly very ill-judged. Poor Gerard had no one himself to whom he could leave her in such a case as this."

"He understood that himself, but too late; and as he felt himself growing more feeble every day, he made some attempt to learn what had become of this Ludwig Dornthal, of whom I have just spoken, the favorite brother of Marguerite. But he could ascertain nothing satisfactory. Ludwig Dornthal had married, and had left Leipsic, and gone to establish himself elsewhere in Germany, but where, no one could tell. This fruitless effort made the poor fellow's last hours most wretched. He held himself responsible, and no doubt he was so, for the frightful isolation in which he was about to leave his child; and expiated with bitter repentance the hot-tempered and inconsiderate resolve which had led him to break with those whose pardon he should rather have implored,—or, at least, should have most gratefully accepted when it was proffered to him. But such was his character, affectionate, enthusiastic, fascinating, no doubt,—but weak, violent, and unthinking; he was born neither to be happy himself, nor to cause the happiness of any one; and his daughter would have been nearly as much to be pitied had he lived, as she now is, all alone in the world."

"Poor child!" said Mlle. Josephine, raising her small black eyes, whose expression brought a ray of heaven's sunshine over the pale and wrinkled face. After a minute's silence she added: "'Heaven tempers the wind to the shorn lamb.' You will see, brother, that some good fortune will befall her; or, perhaps, we shall have some happy inspiration."

"So be it, sister, and the sooner the better, for I confess I have none! I admire your confidence."

"My confidence is in God," said Mlle. Josephine simply.

"Yes, yes! And so is mine," said the doctor. "Certainly, I believe in His mercy, in His goodness; but, in this case—"

"In this case, you would rather have the management in your own hands?"

"Well, well, Josephine, let us attend to the most pressing affairs first. It is now eight; I must positively go up and find this poor child. Even the Sister who has been there for the last few days has left her. She cannot possibly pass the night all alone up there."

"Certainly not," said Mlle. Josephine.

"For two weeks she has not been out of that little fourth-story room, except this morning to follow her poor father to the grave: and since her return from the funeral, what do you think she has been doing? See; look there!"

Mlle. Josephine took the paper that her brother held out to her, and glanced over it. It was a list of the poor artist's debts.

"They amount in all to five hundred francs, and here is the money. She asked me to pay these bills, and obtain the receipts for her."

"I see that she has destined one-fourth of this sum to the physician who attended her father," said Mlle. Josephine slowly.

"Who, in cases of this kind, of course, accepts no pay."

"Of course," repeated Mlle. Josephine; "out of this sum, then, there is a hundred and twenty-five francs to be returned to her."

"Yes, sister, and that is all her fortune."

"Then at this moment she has nothing at all?"

"Nothing."

The conversation was at this point, when some one knocked softly at the door, and almost immediately the young girl of whom they were speaking, Fleurange d'Yves, appeared.

She took one step forward, then stopped, and leaned against the wall. The doctor started from his chair.

"The poor little creature!" he said, "while we sit gossiping here, she is fainting with fatigue and weakness."

She had slid into a chair placed near the wall, and seemed utterly destitute of strength. In a second, Mlle. Josephine was at her side, and bathing with cold water her pale forehead and colorless cheeks. All the movements of the doctor's sister at once had become prompt and decided. At a sign from her brother she disappeared, and returned almost instantly bringing a vial and a glass of water.

"That is it," the doctor said, and pouring a few drops into the water, he held it to the lips of the young girl. She

it was not to trouble you in this way that I came to see you."

"Do not talk yet. Drink what I have given you."

Fleurange raised the glass to her lips, but returned it untasted to the doctor.

"I cannot," she said. "My head swims; I don't know what is the matter; perhaps it is the surprise that I have just had,—this letter that I have just received. I came to show it to you."

The doctor took the letter, but, before he began to read, he brought Fleurange to the fire, while Mlle. Josephine, guessing at her brother's wishes, placed on the table a bowl of soup, bread, and some wine.

Fleurange took the old lady's hand in both her own.

"Thanks!" she said in a low voice; "yes, I believe it was that. I am generally strong, but—"

"I dare say you have eaten nothing all day?"

"No, and I was hungry."

The doctor rubbed his spectacles and opened his snuffbox with a great noise, as the young girl made the light repast, which soon brought the color to her cheek again, or, at least, the usual color, for her face was, ordinarily, very pale. Large eyes, grave and gentle, gray rather than blue, shadowed by lashes black as her hair, made her face singular and striking. Yet, in spite of this singularity, in spite of her paleness, the delicacy of her features, and her slender figure with its willowy grace, if one had wished to describe in two words the general impression produced by the aspect of Fleurange d'Yves, one would have chosen these: simplicity and strength. Without doubt, Dr. Leblanc was right in feeling that this young and beautiful and destitute creature stood in need of protection; and yet no one could look at her without understanding that, better than any other, she would know how to protect herself.

The doctor still held her letter in his hand, and now he unfolded it. The date was Frankfort:

"MY DEAR NIECE—It was only yesterday, and by the most unforeseen accident, that we have at last learned the situation of your father, and the place of his residence. No one of us has ever seen him since his marriage with my poor sister Marguerite, twenty years ago. Y know that, at that time, there was felt in our country a terrible hatred against the French, and my father would never have consented to accept a French son-in-law. My poor sister, then, fled from the paternal roof, to marry the man she had chosen. My father was very unhappy, very angry, and at first implacable; but before her death he forgave her, although she did not know it. From that time we lost all trace of your father; we only knew that he had quitted Pisa with his child, and we had long since relinquished all hope of seeing him again, or ever knowing the daughter of my poor sister, when yesterday a stranger, passing through our city, chanced to show me a picture which he had just bought in Paris, and which was, so he told me, the work of a dying painter. This picture represented Cordelia on her knees before her father, and the name of Gerard d'Yves was inscribed upon the canvas. The painter's address was given by the purchaser, and I hasten to profit by it. I assure you, my dear child, that the relatives of your mother have not forgotten the ties which unite them to you. If ever you have need of a shelter, you will find it beneath our roof. My wife and my children already love the daughter of my poor Marguerite; they have heard of you and thought of you as a long-absent sister whose return they expect. If God restores health to your father, bring him to us; if Providence decree otherwise, come yourself, my dear child. The stranger who has put us upon your track says that the painter's daughter sat as the model for Cordelia. If this be true, it does not diminish our desire to see you. Come soon, then, my dear niece; at all events, reply speedily to this letter, and receive the assurance of your uncle's kindest regards.

"LUDWIG DORNTHAL."

"Josephine! Josephine!" cried the doctor; "here, sister, read this letter. But first embrace me. Yes, you were right. Your faith was better than my wisdom. Yes, yes! 'God tempers the wind to the shorn lamb!' Poor child! embrace me too!"

"Willingly," cried Fleurange, rising, and she threw herself, sobbing, into the doctor's arms. Fatigue, grief, the emotion caused by this unexpected and unhoped for offer of a refuge in the hour of her most extreme desolation—all united to agitate her mind, to excite her nerves, to exhaust her strength. Her heart was swelling with tears that must be shed, and they fell like rain over her clasped and icy hands, while a convulsive movement shook her whole frame, and a faint cry escaped her trembling lips.

The doctor let her weep for a long time silently, adding not to her grief by any words, nor seeking by any to repress it. Finally the paroxysm passed by, and Fleurange rose, confused.

"Again pardon me," she said; "I pain you, instead of thanking you as I ought; it is not my fault, but I believe I can promise you it shall not happen again; usually I do not weep."

She spoke with restored strength, drying her eyes, and putting her hands through her hair, which she pushed back from her forehead, and then she stood up.

"Pray where are you going?" said Mlle. Josephine, with a sort of brusque authority.

"I?" faltered Fleurange. "I am going up stairs."

"You think you are going to pass the night all alone in the little room next to—next to—"

She hesitated, and Fleurange grew pale, while her lips trembled. "What can I do?" she said. "I know it is painful, it is distressing, but I must;—besides, I am not afraid, I am under your roof."

"Very good! For the moment you are going to remain under our key," said good Mlle. Josephine, and taking possession of Fleurange, she carried her off into a little room adjoining her own, where a bed with white curtains was prepared for a young girl. The little room was papered with blue, and lighted by a brilliant fire, and had the most cheerful aspect imaginable.

"See, my child, here is your room and your bed," she exclaimed. "No thanks, and, above all, no tears! Into bed this minute, without giving yourself time to think, much less to speak! You don't believe you will fall asleep, but you are mistaken. On your knees?—that is right, but let it be a very short prayer. Now, be quiet, while I put up your long hair. And now, does your head rest well on that pillow? Yes? That is good,—now to sleep: God and the good angels watch over you!"

Mlle. Josephine drew the curtains of the little bed, and softly left the room, while the poor orphan quickly lost all recollection of the trials or the joys of the day in a deep

devoted to the discovery and the relief of the unhappy. In this case, "he that seeketh, findeth," and findeth easily; so it was rarely that a week passed away without bringing good reason to open the blue room, and give shelter there for some days, now, to some poor girl without employment or refuge,—now, to some deserted child,—now, to some convalescent, yet too feeble to return to work again. This suited the doctor. He would have been glad to add a veritable asylum to his dwelling for his poor patients, and that he was not rich enough for this, although his practice was large and his services paid as talent and celebrity deserve, was due in large measure to the fact that he gave with one hand what he received with the other, with a profusion not always conformable to prudence. When it was a question of giving, the brother and the sister were equally inconsiderate. They had invented a proverb worthy of the Bible, and it served as a rejoinder to their friends. "He who gives to others enriches himself," they used to say, and they continued to pursue fortune in this way, giving themselves up to a noble prodigality in well-doing. Fortune really had never failed them, nor had they found fulfilled the sinister prophecies of those who take for a motto quite a different proverb concerning charity,—a proverb a little too well known, and too often practised by the world. Dr. Leblanc and his sister knew not, it is true, the luxury of elegant apartments and fine equipages; they still lived in the Quartier Latin, in the same old house in which they had been born; one old servant assisted the cook, and Mlle, Josephine with her own hands aided in maintaining the neatness and order of the house. But they were lavish in their way, and many an artist aided by them, many a scholar whose education they defrayed, many a sick person, gratuitously attended and generously succored, added to the renown of this great doctor, and threw about his name an eclat which he had never sought. Simple and wise, healing the body and honoring the soul, he loved his profession as a mission received from on high, and exercised it as a sacred ministry, with fidelity and affection.

II.

When Fleurange opened her eyes the following morning it was late, for it was already broad daylight, and the month was December. She must have slept very soundly too, for she had not heard the lighting of the fire, which flamed brightly in the chimney. Her sleep had been indeed that which in youth follows long fatigue, or long-sustained effort to bear grief or anxiety in silence. The paroxysm of tears on the preceding evening, the long repose of the night had brought the two-fold solace which the exhausted strength of the young girl required, and her first sensation on waking was that of gentle content. Soon, however, her recollection became clear, and that anguish of the first waking, on the day after a great misfortune has become complete, oppressed her heart.

It is true she had scarcely known her father; the convent where she had been brought up was not even in the city in which he lived, and she had seen him but rarely during her childhood; but the days when he made his appearance at the convent had been holidays for both. It was difficult to understand how a father so glad to see his child could leave her to grow to womanhood at a distance from him. Finally came the time that was to reunite them, and, for several weeks, the father and daughter wandered about together in Italy, and while unveiling all the wonders of art to a mind naturally capable of understanding them, the artist felt his soul glow once more with all the enthusiasm of his early life. But it was the last flicker of a dying flame. Soon came illness, the sad return to Paris, the fluctuations of a malady which enfeebled at once mind and body, which separated the child from the father, even while he, yet lived and while she yet watched, day and night, at his bedside. That look which no longer answered her own, those murmured words which she could not understand—that was already to have lost him, even before the separation of death, which soon came.

"Oh father! father scarcely known, and so quickly lost!" cried Fleurange; and it may be that an involuntary reproach mingled with her grief. She could not know the sublime and paternal instinct which guided the poor artist when he sent his child away. He desired her to be strong, to be pure, to be pious; he wished her rare and beautiful mind to be trained and developed only when divine and immutable order had established itself in her soul; he wished, in a word, that she should become all that he himself was not,—and God gave His blessing to this wish.

In a beautiful locality near Perouse, he met, at the head of a simple charity-school, one of those women whom the world itself would honor and venerate, did they but reveal themselves to it. By "the world," I mean that crowd of thoughtless and satirical men and women who are hostile to all sentiments which they do not share, and, most of all, unfriendly towards the religious sentiment. And yet, after all, this "world" is suspicious rather than unjust, sceptical rather than false; if it sees the appearance of evil, it at once takes for granted the reality; if it sees the appearance of good, it assumes promptly that this appearance is deceitful; but when the good shows itself plainly, irreproachable in its simplicity and truth, visible in all its unfeigned reality, the world, even this very world, inclines towards it. The thing is rare, it is true,—much more rare than it should be, —for these faultless souls seek not to show themselves, but to remain hid; and the world seeks, not to find them out, but to deny that they exist.

Madre Madelina was one of these great souls, hidden from view. No one spoke of her, nor of her little convent designed for the education of poor children, but into which a few young girls of better class had been admitted.

Like so many Italian monasteries, it stood in a charming and poetic situation; it was not, however, one of those that are seen afar off on a hill-top, ruling some landscape that ravishes the eye and transports the soul,—a landscape which suggests to the most careless the desire to fall upon their knees, and which has inspired Christian souls with the idea of there installing prayer in its permanent sanctuary.

The convent of Santa Maria al Prato, on the contrary, was situated in a deep valley, surrounded by scenery such as that in which Perugino or Raphael have placed their

outlines are clearly sketched along the horizon; a brook, winding through the olive-woods and past those scattered dwellings that betray a people whose love for art is an instinct of their nature; the sombre foliage of a few pines and cypresses relieved against the blue of the morning sky, or, in the evening, against its crimson tints—such is the landscape whose beauty tranquillizes the soul as much as that of sublime summits exalts it, and which seems made for meditation and work, as the other is for contemplation and ecstasy.

To this retreat Providence conducted the father of Fleurange; he was guided thither perhaps by that protecting intervention which, it is sweet to believe, mothers snatched from their children may still exercise towards them. In the hands of Madre Madelina he left her, when she was five years old, and up to the time when she was eighteen he saw her but twice in the year; and yet every year he felt more and more certain that he had attained for her the object proposed. Not that Fleurange had any proof to give him of her progress, in the shape of prizes obtained or crowns conferred. The festivals at which these trophies are distributed were unknown at Santa Maria al Prato, and equally unknown were those examinations where the memory crams itself with facts for a single day, and retains them scarcely beyond the four-and-twenty hours. In truth, the endeavor had been not so much to give her varied information, as to teach her *how* to study, to give her a love for books, for industry, and for silence.

By nature she was truthful and brave; she had now become skilful and efficient. Madre Madelina had seemed to have a presentiment that this life, so sheltered in its beginning, was destined more than others to be exposed to the rude winds of destiny. She could not foresee, of course, that Fleurange would so soon be left an orphan, but the character of the father, and what she knew of his past history, made her feel that a wisdom like that of premature experience would be needful as a safeguard for the child. This, which would have been true had the father lived, was no less so now, when his early death left the young girl to herself alone.

Fleurange resisted the temptation of remaining in be

absorbed in her own sad reflections. She rose hastily, and was dressed and ready when, for the third time, Mlle. Josephine entered the room. A smile lighted up the good lady's face when she recognized the effect of a night's sleep upon her *protégée*. The latter, affectionate and grateful, and still preserving the Italian habits of her childhood, bent to kiss the hand of her benefactress.

"Let my old hand alone!" cried Mlle. Josephine, "and kiss *me*, if you please! Now we must not keep my brother waiting. It is our breakfast hour, nine o'clock, and we are never late."

Fleurange followed her hostess into the dining-room, just beyond the parlor. The furniture of these two rooms had not been renewed for more than fifty years; but nothing seemed shabby, thanks to the exquisite neatness which reigned throughout.

The doctor was already at table. Mlle. Josephine sat down opposite to him, placing Fleurange between them.

"Now you are quite restored," said the doctor, extending his hand to the young girl. "I am very glad, but for fear of a relapse I shall keep you under my eyes for some days yet; so I give you notice all is arranged, and from now till your departure you will not return to your fourth story again!"

"What can I say to you, sir? You are both so good, and I love you so much, that I accept charity from your hand without shame, and almost without pain."

"I forbid you using that disagreeable word," said Mlle. Josephine.

"But still it is charity," said Fleurange, her voice sad and firm, " for I have nothing, and this very day, to buy a morsel of bread, I must have first held out my hand for alms."

Fleurange had not yet opened her work-box, which Mlle. Josephine had brought down with her other effects, and in which she had replaced the hundred and twenty-five francs.

"Come, come, you are not so badly off as that yet, thank God! But let us speak of more important matters.

minute's silence she added: "I am going to ask him to receive me for one month."

"But from his letter I judge him disposed to offer you a hospitality much more extended than that."

"Perhaps!—I will accept it, however, only until I find a means of living without being an expense to him."

"What intentions have you then?"

"I do not know," said Fleurange, "but there are ways to earn one's living, you know: I must try and find something which I shall be able to do."

The doctor looked at her, and then he said: "There are many things which you would be able to do, and which would, notwithstanding, be impossible for you."

"Why?" asked Fleurange.

"Impossible for you at your age, and for such a girl as you are."

"Why?" repeated Fleurange.

"I will explain it to you when you have told me what you propose to do."

"Come," said Mlle. Josephine, with impatience, "there is no need of so much ceremony in saying that when one is young and pretty, she must take care what she does. If the child does not know it already, the sooner she is told it the better!"

"Young and pretty," repeated Fleurange, without the slightest embarrassment; "yes, I know that will be very troublesome in my position; it would be better to be very plain, and to be ten years older,—I have already thought of that. It is very unlucky, but what can I do?"

The doctor smiled. He had never heard a woman admit her own beauty with so little vanity. The simplicity of Fleurange, the child-like candor of her large eyes, whose expression was at the same time so grave and reflective, struck him, and his interest, which, till now, had attached itself rather to the young girl's position, centred from this moment in herself.

He replied, with a smile: "As to that, it is a misfortune to which you must resign yourself, for the next twenty years at least."

But seeing that Fleurange grew more and more serious, he added: "Never mind, keep a good heart; we shall find

Fleurange brightened. "Oh, thanks!" she cried. "I feel so much encouraged! And besides," she went on, "there are so many things that I know how to do."

"Tell us some of them," said the doctor.

"First, I think I have some skill in teaching children; I love them, and they are fond of me, and obey me willingly."

"What else?"

"I know Italian, and German (for I was resolved to speak my mother's language correctly); my father thought that I read aloud well. He had been accustomed to hear reading and declamation, and he used to say that my voice pleased him better than any other. His affection for me might have made him partial, yet, perhaps, he might have been right, and I could try."

"Hum!" said the doctor, "there is a good deal to be said on both sides of that question."

"Then I can do all kinds of work: I can sew nicely, I can wash and iron and sweep—I could even perhaps do some cooking."

The doctor again looked at the young girl's noble face, as she enumerated with so much readiness the rude and humble labors of which she believed herself capable. It was evident that she was quite in earnest: one could not doubt that she was able and willing to do all that she had said. He was greatly moved, and remained silent.

But Mlle. Josephine cried with enthusiasm: "There's what I call an education! My dear child, who taught you so many reasonable and useful things?"

Tears came to the eyes of Fleurange. "It was my dear Madre Madelina," she said.

This answer called out other questions, to which Fleurange replied, relating in detail how she had spent her childhood.

The doctor's satisfaction increased at every word of this recital, which, however, battered down two ancient prejudices of his.

Without his having an antipathy to pretty faces, they inspired in him a sort of distrust, or, at least, uneasiness, which his long experience had, no doubt, often verified amply. But in observing this young girl, so brave, yet modest, so strong, so delicate, who seemed ready so courageously to encounter the difficulties of life,—why blame her for being beautiful? why not, in a sense, forget that she was so?"

Furthermore, the doctor had a singular, and, considering his opinions generally, an inconsistent prejudice against convents. He seemed to have preserved this one point of agreement with people whom he habitually combated on all others. And now this education, which conformed not merely to all his ideas, but even to his whims, was found to be a conventual education. On this subject, as well as on others, he must modify his opinions, it seemed. He resigned himself to the necessity with a good grace.

And now the letter from Frankfort again occupied their attention. The brother and sister already began to think with regret of the departure of their young *protégée*, but still they felt that it was for her interest not to lose a moment in making herself known to this family who had so opportunely remembered her. By the advice of Mlle. Josephine, Fleurange began to write at once; the letter, short and simple, was soon finished, and she brought it to the old lady to read.

The latter began it with an air of satisfaction, which however gave place at its close to one of annoyance. "What is it?" Fleurange said. "I have made some mistake, some omission?"

"By no means: the letter could not be better, but—"

"What is it? tell me frankly, I implore you!"

"Well, it is— No, I don't dare to tell you."

"Please," Fleurange said, "tell me what offends you. There is nothing in the letter which I would not gladly alter at your advice."

"It is— But you cannot change that!"

"But tell me, dear Mlle. Josephine; you alarm me," cried Fleurange, in real anxiety.

"You cannot change your baptismal name," at last the old lady said.

"My name?" cried Fleurange, with surprise; "is it my name that displeases you so much? I am sorry,—Madre Madelina loved it so much! She said it meant the flower of angels, the most beautiful of the angels—Gabriel—whom she regarded as my patron. She called me indifferently, Fleurange or Gabrielle."

"Gabrielle!" cried Mlle. Josephine with animation. "Gabrielle! that is good! There is a name that everybody understands! Why, is that what Fleurange means? Then I beg you, I entreat you, resume that, and give the other up."

The doctor had been re-reading the letter of Professor Dornthal, which he had retained since the previous evening; he now raised his eyes, and listened attentively to the conversation, and seeing that Fleurange hesitated what reply to make to the singular request of Mlle. Josephine, he said:

"I do not understand my sister's anxiety on this subject, and my own feeling is quite opposed to hers. But it might be that the more simple of the two names would better suit the taste of the good German family who are expecting you, and Gabrielle might be more favorably received than Fleurange. Besides," he added, smiling, "your cousins across the Rhine would be sure to pronounce the name in a way which would greatly diminish its charm, and take away all meaning from the pious and poetic interpretation which you have just given it."

"It might be so," said Fleurange, smiling in turn. "At all events, I will do what you say about it."

"We will think the matter over," said the doctor; then running over the Professor's letter again:

"Do you know the name of this stranger," he said, "who, in purchasing your father's last work, has done you, unawares, so great a service?"

"No, I do not. The picture was sold, with several others, at the time when my father perceived that all hope of his recovery was gone, and that he should never be able to paint again. My poor father!" she went on, with faltering voice, "he was already very ill on the day when he made me sit, in order to finish that picture—"

Fleurange stopped suddenly, and colored. The doctor's glance seemed to question her. She went on with some embarrassment:

"The purchaser of the picture was very possibly a

stranger who came that day to the studio. At least, I have been thinking that it might be so."

"Why?"

"Because he was very enthusiastic in praise of this Cordelia, and asked permission to come and see the picture when it was finished. But my father, from that day, could never use his brushes again, and the picture was sold with the rest, just as it was."

"Was this amateur a German?"

"I do not know; he spoke French well, but with some slight accent."

"Was he a man of high rank?"

"I do not know—I have never seen any one of high rank."

"But what did this visitor seem like?—God bless him!" asked Mlle. Josephine.

His appearance was noble and dignified, his face uncommon, his voice grave and musical," replied Fleurange. "Yet, notwithstanding the gratitude I owe him, the remembrance of his visit troubles me, and makes me sad."

"Why so?" asked Mlle. Josephine.

"Because it was connected in some way with the last and fatal crisis of my father's illness. He was then so feeble, he could not endure the slightest agitation. This stranger looked attentively at me, and said something in a low voice. I do not know what he said, but it seemed to distress my father exceedingly; he sent me from the room at once. Usually he had not allowed me to be in the studio when he received visitors. In the evening he talked with me about the position in which he must leave me, and attempted to advise what I should do. But his words were incoherent, and from that day he seemed never to have his reason clearly again."

"The poor father!" said the doctor; but he dwelt no longer upon the subject which had brought about this recital. The fugitive color had vanished from the cheek of Fleurange; she was now pale and calm as before, pen in hand, ready to correct the letter in accordance with the doctor's advice. After a last deliberation between the young girl and her old friends, it was decided that the letter should be sent, bearing this signature: Gabrielle d'Yver

III.

The day when Marguerite had married Gerard d'Yves, Sigismond Dornthal had effaced from his will his daughter's name, and forbidden his family ever to mention her to him again. Soon, however, brought to milder feelings by illness, and urged by the persuasions of Ludwig, Marguerite's favorite brother, he had consented to write a few words of forgiveness and blessing, but ere the letter reached Pisa the poor young wife had breathed her last. In the transports of a grief which added to the impetuosity and inconsiderateness of his temperament, Gerard tore in pieces the letter which contained this late repentance, and answered but by these words: "It is too late!"

And thus the aged Dornthal learned of his daughter's death, and died himself, shortly after, ignorant of the birth of his grandchild, of which the brothers only heard vaguely after a time, and without Gerard's intervention. The property of the father was divided between his two sons, but Ludwig, devoted to letters, and already occupying a professor's chair at Leipsic, abandoned entirely to his elder brother the management of their common fortune, and Heinrich Dornthal became the sole head of the commercial and banking-house which their father had founded. He used the capital of his brother as his own, and made over to him regularly his share of the profits without Ludwig's participating in the slightest degree in the conduct of affairs. Ludwig, on his part, had pursued his chosen career with ability and success, and had attracted the attention of scientific men throughout all Germany. A visit made by him to a brother *savant* residing in Frankfort had resulted in his marriage to the daughter of this professor, and shortly after, relinquishing his chair at Leipsic, he had gone to reside in his wife's native city.

He now ceased to lecture publicly, but pursued his studies with ardor, and published many scientific works whose success increased his reputation every year, and added to his means, which, owing to the prosperity of the commercial house, were already large.

Such, in a few words, was the position of the foreign family who now daily expected Fleurange. A second letter replied promptly to hers; her uncle expressed with great feeling his joy at finding her at last, and invited her very specially to reach Frankfort in time to be with them at Christmas, that season so sacred in Germany to family reunions.

In order to do this, she must leave Paris, at the very latest, by the 21st of December, for at that time no less than three days and three nights were needed to make the journey to Frankfort. The doctor and Mlle. Josephine, in spite of the regret which they felt at parting with their young *protégée*, hastened her preparations for departure, for they were touched by the affection that was shown towards her. And the letters of this unknown uncle made them anticipate for her a sweet family life, from which they would not have been willing to hold her back.

Every day, however, added to the affection with which Fleurange inspired them, and to the grateful tenderness of the young girl towards her kind old friends.

"If this should last a week longer," said the doctor, "I could not endure to part with the child."

"We must send her off then as quickly as possible," replied Mlle. Josephine; "it is for her good, and we should do her wrong in detaining her."

Fleurange had nothing to say; but when the day of her departure came, her eyes resting sadly on their dear faces, she strove to repress her tears, that she might not grieve them, and silently, with their assistance, made her little preparations for the journey.

"An English proverb which I value highly," said the doctor, "places the hospitality that speeds the parting guest in the same rank with that which welcomes the coming; this is what I am practising towards you at this moment, my dear Fleurange."

Fleurange was just finishing in haste the repast, sure to be a sad one, which preceded her departure. The doctor saw that her courage was beginning to fail. For himself, he was very much affected by the sight of the pale girlish face, and by the thought of the long and solitary journey that she was about to undertake, and at the end of which those who were to receive her, kind though they might be, would be also total strangers. But he resumed, in an encouragi-

"Come, come, my child, all promises well for you there; take courage,—do not suffer yourself to be cast down!"

"You are right," Fleurange said, rising. "I have reason to thank God, I feel it, and I wish to be grateful. In any event, be sure that I shall be courageous."

It was eight o'clock in the evening; the *fiacre* which was to convey her to the *diligence* was at the door; she went down stairs accompanied by the doctor and his sister, who got into the carriage with her. The night was dark, and the snow was falling in great flakes,—the snow which the young girl, bred under Italian skies, now saw for the first time in her life. The sight caused her at once curiosity and terror. The new and the unknown seemed to crowd upon her from every side; but these two things, attractive, usually, to one at the age of Fleurange, here assumed an aspect suited rather to oppress her young heart than to encourage it. She shivered and wrapped closer about her the thick mantle which seemed altogether too light to shield her from a cold so severe, and to which she was so unused.

They were all silent for a few minutes; Fleurange held close the hand of Mlle. Josephine, and now and then lifted it to her lips, notwithstanding the effort of the latter to prevent her. On her own part, Mlle. Josephine, with not very steadfast voice, repeated good advice over and over, and made suggestions,—among others, that Fleurange must write them often and regularly. Then she slipped over the arm of the young girl a little basket in which, with thoughtful kindness, she had arranged the many trifles which might be of use on her journey, as well as more than one *souvenir* which should recall to her, in absence, her old friend.

They arrived all too soon at their destination.

"I have taken a place for you in the coupé," the doctor said; "you will be alone with one of my patients who is still very feeble, but who must go back to her husband in Germany. Her two children are with her. You will have no other companions on the journey."

"Thanks," said Fleurange, in a low voice; and she went on: "They say that the orphan's prayers bring happiness; may mine prove this true to you both!"

She could say no more; one last time she flung herself

on Mlle. Josephine's neck, and an instant later she was leaning on the doctor's arm, and they were making their way through the crowded court-yard to where the *diligence* stood. The snow embarrassed them and rendered every footstep difficult. The fellow-travellers of Fleurange had already taken their places, the horses were attached to the vehicle, and to the sound of their pawings and neighings the conductor was adding his impatient exclamations. "Now! now then! all ready!" he repeated in a rough voice. Fleurange—crowded, pushed, dizzy, and frightened—had time only to clasp the doctor's hand and to climb to her seat in the coupé. In an instant the door was closed, there was a great uproar, wheels, outcries, snapping of the whip, vociferations,—in which these words were to be distinguished, "*Adieu! au revoir! à bientôt!*" and other exclamations much less harmonious, and the heavy *diligence* was in motion. Then Fleurange, freed from all necessity of practising further self-control, gave herself the consolation of long-continued and abundant tears.

For a long time she wept, making no effort to tranquillize herself. Why make such effort? she was alone now, all alone! Never had she been completely so before. The past seemed to be utterly effaced, and the future altogether a blank. All whom she had loved since she came into the world were now separated from her either by death or limitless absence. Would it always be so with her? Was this her destiny on earth? Might she never love with security, with confidence, with repose? Should she be always removed from places and from persons so soon as her heart began to cling to either?—this loving and ardent heart, this heart which already knew how to beat so high with tenderness and enthusiasm! And while her eyes roamed through the sombre darkness without, caught by strange figures which were like phantoms clothed in white shrouds, her imagination suddenly brought back to her, as in a magic mirror, all the varied scenes of her short life: the beautiful cloister, and the terrace with its far-off view, the sweet and noble face of Madre Madelina, and then recollections of her father, the rapid vision of Italy in all its splendor, the sad and dreadful days in Paris; finally, at the saddest time of all, the beneficent appearing of those two kind friends, those friends whom she would so gladly have remained with forever, and to whom she had now just bidden adieu!

It was impossible for Fleurange at this moment to conquer these sad thoughts. At times, however, her reason reminded her of the friends to whom she was going, of the kind welcome she had reason to expect, of the goodness of Providence in opening to her such a refuge,—but in vain! Consolation seemed completely barred out from her heart, and, contrary to her wont, depression had seized upon her.

"If they are good, and if I love them," she said to herself with bitterness, "I may be sure that I shall soon be obliged to leave them! If they are not so—" and here her imagination gave itself free range, and represented her future in the most sombre colors. But this new reverie had not the clearness of the former, and soon her forebodings began to mingle in vague confusion with her recollections, until, by degrees, fatigue, the motion of the coach, and the night aiding, sleep gained upon the young traveller and transformed her musings into an agitated and indistinct dream.

Fifteen minutes later she was suddenly awakened. Something heavy had dropped against her shoulder, and then slid to her knees. She roused herself, and extending her hands in the darkness, placed them upon the long and silky hair of a child. Until this moment she had rather guessed at than perceived, in the further corner of the coupé, a young woman, pale and ill, who held with one arm the child nearest her, while the other, still younger, leaned against him. It was the second of these two children who had suddenly changed his position.

Fleurange bent over, and drew the child toward her, and placed him fully in her lap, then took the little sleepy head upon her breast, and kissed tenderly the soft cheek now so near her own.

This slight occurrence had the sudden and unforeseen effect of putting to flight all the phantoms which her imag-

slumbers, what wilt Thou not do for thy child, O my Father, Who art in Heaven!"

The snow had ceased to fall. In the sky, suddenly set free from clouds, shone out a brilliant star. In the soul of Fleurange, too, the clouds were scattered, and the mysterious light from on high was born anew. She watched the star with delight, then closed her eyes and slept quietly, the child in her arms sleeping as profoundly as herself.

IV.

It was the young girl who awoke first, when morning came, and soon after, while she was watching with admiration the beautiful child yet asleep, she saw his big eyes open wide in turn. The first expression that dawned in them was one of extreme surprise, mingled with alarm, but the look and voice of Fleurange soon reassured him; the big eyes and the half-opened mouth grew smiling; very soon the two fat arms went around her neck, and the acquaintance was made. During this time, the pale and languid young mother with difficulty shook off the stupor, rather than sleep, which oppressed her. She blushed faintly, and murmured some words of excuse, when she saw her child in the arms of the beautiful stranger. But Fleurange reassured her, protesting with an accent of undeniable truth that the child was not in the least annoying, and soon she perceived that her presence would be anything but useless to the poor convalescent; the children, wakened from the sound sleep of the night, were most unquestionably awake, and every one knows that children under these circumstances, and confined in narrow limits, soon arrive at a degree of turbulence whose only merit is that it leads to fatigue, and so to sleep again. The poor mother made feeble and fruitless efforts to restrain them. In a few minutes she fell back, not merely exhausted, but almost fainting. Fleurange drew nearer, arranged the scattered shawls into a pillow, and then, opening Mlle. Josephine's little basket, drew out a flask, whose contents, poured on a handkerchief and applied to the forehead and cheeks of the invalid, seemed greatly to refresh her.

"Thank you!" she said, "you have done me so much good! I knew that I was feeble, but I did not think I was

"Do not exert yourself," said Fleurange. "I will take care of the children."

The poor mother smiled, and put her hand to her head, indicating by this gesture the fatigue which their noise occasioned her.

And indeed at this moment the smaller of the two children was standing up on the cushion and trying to reach that net of painful memory, suspended formerly, like the sword of Damocles, over the heads of travellers, and which used to serve as a receptacle for whatever could not be stowed elsewhere. This experiment on the part of the boy was not without motive, for his brother had already tried it successfully, and had extracted through the meshes of the net-work a miniature hunting-horn, upon which at this moment he was performing a *fanfare.*

Why could he not as well attain to his drum, which he beheld up there, almost within reach, if only he could make himself just a little taller? and he looked at Fleurange with an air of entreaty, but the latter, instead of replying to his mute appeal, laughingly captured him and perched him upon her knee; then, adroitly coaxing away the bugle from the other child, she inquired if they would like to hear the beautiful story that she could tell them if they were good. In an instant, both were nestled up to her; and so, all day long, whenever their turbulence became oppressive, she was able to bring them to order and silence by the charming narratives with which her memory seemed to be supplied in inexhaustible profusion.

By night, Fleurange and the young mother had become well acquainted.

"How can I sufficiently thank you," said the young woman, "and what a happy chance it was that brought you here!"

"Do not thank me. Your boy has done me more good than I can repay."

This reply, as was natural, did not diminish the gratitude, mingled with admiration, that Fleurange had inspired in the mother's heart, and as from admiration to confidence there is but a single step, the latter soon repeated to her companion her brief story.

She had met with a serious fall some months before.

and her life had been despaired of; then her husband had brought her to Paris, to be under the charge of Dr. Leblanc, and the doctor had cured her.

"He is so skilful and so good!" she said, while the eyes of Fleurange shone with joy, that she could now talk of her dear friends again. "He is more than a physician," continued the young mother, "he is a benefactor. I have disobeyed him in coming away so soon, he said I was too feeble; I thought not, but he was right."

"Why did you do so?"

"Because my poor Wilhelm was alone, and was impatient to see me."

"Your husband?"

"Yes."

"Could he not have come for you?"

"No: he is the chief clerk with Herr Dornthal, and he would have found it very difficult to leave."

At this name Fleurange looked up in surprise.

"Herr Ludwig Dornthal?" she said.

"No, his brother, the rich banker."

"And the other, the Professor, do you know him?"

"I have never seen him, but Wilhelm knows him well; my husband is asked to the house sometimes. They never have balls, nobody in the family cares to dance. They have receptions for conversation, for music and reading; Wilhelm says they are all so clever, the daughters as well as the sons, and the mother as much as the father."

Upon receiving this little description of the family of her uncle, Fleurange felt a slight shiver run through her. She loved study much, and art still more, and had for reading a taste which it had been necessary sometimes to check; but this phrase "so clever" had something alarming about it.

"They will be formal, pedantic, tiresome, I dare say. No matter, the main thing is that they be good; I need not expect to amuse myself there!"

One night more, and one long day, which was drawing to a close, when more frequent and brilliant lights, and houses nearer together, announced that they were approaching a great city. The joy of the mother and children became demonstrative.

"He will be looking out for us!" cried the elder boy.

"Oh yes; we shall see him as soon as the coach stops, but that will not be for an hour yet," said the mother.

Soon it became, "Now, in a half-hour!"—"Now, in fifteen minutes!"—at last—"Here we are!"

Fleurange watched her travelling companions, and envied them that they, at their journey's end, were looking for a dear familiar face. She felt overpowered with sadness and a mortal timidity.

The coach stopped. As at their departure, there now ensued great uproar,—shouts of various meaning,—flickering lights, falling on everything, making nothing distinct. Fleurange, in the crowd that surrounded the vehicle, sought, but in vain, some face that might be that of her uncle.

The door was opened. A tall man, with long hair and blond beard, presented himself. Was it he? Oh no, the children's outcries of delight proclaimed to Fleurange that they beheld their father.

"Bertha! Bertha!" he exclaimed, and without even waiting to kiss his children, he pressed the two hands of his wife, and looked at her with anxiety. "You are very pale, my Bertha," he said.

"It is nothing," she answered tearfully; "it is with joy, Wilhelm; I am cured, and I am at home again!"

He extended his hands to the children to lift them out, but before leaving the coach they clung once more round the neck of Fleurange, crying, "Good-bye, good-bye!"

"Wilhelm," said their mother in a low voice, "thank this good and beautiful young lady, she has been an angel for them and for me, during our journey," and she looked gratefully and affectionately at Fleurange.

"God reward you, my beautiful and kind young lady," said the father, as he took off his hat. Then he added, with a little hesitation: "Some one is here to meet you of course, and I cannot have the honor of rendering you any service?"

"Thanks," said Fleurange hastily. "I am expected. Indeed I have relatives here."

But as she spoke, she looked about her with anxiety. In the crowd of unknown faces which surrounded her, none seemed to be seeking her out. Is there any mistake? Have they forgotten her? what shall she do?

Her travelling companions meantime have left the coach, and the happy little groups are already disappearing from sight; she follows them with her eyes, her heart aching.

At this moment dashes up a light open carriage, driven by a young man eighteen or nineteen years old. At sight of him, Bertha's husband has lifted his hat, and, in return, a cap, resting on a thick mass of light brown hair, is raised for an instant. But the new-comer does not stop—he is in great haste, quite out of breath; runs up to the door of the *diligence*, and exclaims eagerly:

"Mlle. Gabrielle?"

"It is I," says Fleurange, though confused by her new name, and by the aspect of this young man who cannot be her uncle.

"All right. Come!"

Fleurange obeyed silently, and, finding herself on solid ground, looked once more at the new-comer, who still held her hand in a firm grasp. "There is no mistake?" she said. "My uncle, M. Ludwig Dornthal, has sent for me?"

The only reply was an affirmative gesture; in another moment an order, concise and promptly obeyed, brought down from the heights of the imperial the modest luggage of Fleurange; in the twinkling of an eye it was attached behind the little carriage, into which her young guide now assisted her, wrapped her carefully in a great fur cloak which had been sent with the carriage, sprang to his seat in front, and the horse was off at as rapid a pace as that with which he had arrived.

Fleurange for a moment was almost dizzy with the rapid motion of the carriage, but soon this very motion became agreeable to her, contrasted with the heavy progress and the rude jolting of the *diligence*. The cold was extreme, but the substantial cloak with which she was wrapped prevented her from feeling it, and thus protected, the rush of keen air, far from being displeasing, caused her an unwonted animation and gayety, in spite of her sorrow for the past and her anxiety for the future. The sky overhead sparkled with stars. It was one of those brilliant winter nights such as, one loves to imagine, was that in which Christ came, and on the heights about Bethlehem the angels appeared, bringing the glad tidings to the shepherds, and singing upon earth the melodies of Heaven. Sweet and sacred night, of which this was the exact anniversary!

At the end of about twenty minutes, the little carriage slackened its speed, and the young driver turned back, and seemed to feel it a duty to give Fleurange some kind of explanation, which she, on her part, did her utmost to comprehend; but the noise of the wheels upon the pavement rendered this nearly impossible, and she could gather only these words, "my father," and a little later, "the *Christkindchen;*" after which the speed of the horse was again increased, and no further attempt at conversation followed.

Fleurange had however at least gained, flying, thus much information, that this youth was one of Professor Dornthal's sons, and that her uncle had not been able to come for her himself, being detained by something connected with the Christmas festival. Concerning her young cousin, Fleurange's first conclusions were that his manners were rather abrupt, and that he had an odd face, but that he had shown himself energetic and careful: as to his skill in driving, it was certainly admirable, and the reins could not be in better hands.

After this short interruption, they went on without slackening speed for an instant, nothwithstanding more than one *détour* through narrow and winding lanes, till they came out into a broad street, having double rows of trees, and, driving the whole length of it, stopped at the foot of a flight of steps which led up to an oaken door, ornamented with a huge brass knocker.

Some one was watching for them, for the door was flung open in an instant. Fleurange perceived that the hall was brilliantly lighted, and that there were many persons gathered. Her cousin already stood at the steps to assist her. Confused voices, having all a cordial accent of welcome, made themselves heard. A strong hand supported Fleurange as she went up the six broad stone steps, and conducted her into the vestibule. A tall woman in a gray dress, having flowers in her cap, came forward and embraced her; and a deep and sonorous voice said: "It is my turn now; I am her uncle." Fleurange lifted her eyes to a noble face which seemed far too young for its crown of white hair, and her uncle took her in his arms, murmuring with emotion the name "Marguerite." Beside him stood a lovely young girl, blonde and grave, while another, blonde like the former, but younger, removed the heavy fur cloak from the shoulders of Fleurange, and untied her hat. A boy of seven ran out into the street to aid his brother, and a little girl, four or five years old, clung to the skirt of her mother, regarding with curious and delighted eyes the newcomer.

Fleurange, dazzled by the lights, troubled by the very warm cordiality of this reception, almost fainting with emotion, could not say a single word, but her large eyes, veiled with tears, spoke better than words, while the unusual brilliancy given to her complexion by the cold night air, and her long tresses falling over her shoulders, as they took off her hat, rendered her beauty more touching than ever before, and such that it would have disarmed even the most malevolent. What then must be its effect upon those already decided in her favor?

They drew her as in triumph into a great hall, and there she was dazzled anew by what met her gaze. In the centre of the apartment rose a tree, brilliantly lighted, on which hung fruits of all kinds, playthings, flowers, and ornaments. Two chandeliers added their lustre to that which streamed from the tree; under one of them half-a-dozen children were gathered around a table loaded with cakes, and various groups of younger and older persons were scattered here and there through the hall.

In a word, Fleurange found herself suddenly, and for the first time in her life, in the midst of what seemed to her a very brilliant social assembly, where every face—first and foremost, her uncle's even—was altogether unknown to her.

The most confident young girl might have felt some embarrassment, and Fleurange was indeed overcome with timidity, when the lady whom she supposed to be her aunt kindly came to her relief and carried her off into a little parlor where only a single lamp was burning.

Crossing the hall they encountered Fleurange's youthful guide.

"Is she ill?" he asked anxiously. "Does she need

"Only rest," said the mother with a smile, and she closed the door against her son.

Fleurange sat down and took breath; not only had it been impossible for her to speak a word, up to this moment she had been unable to collect her thoughts. Now, thanks to the tranquillity of the little parlor, she grew calm and in a few minutes she was quite restored. She was young and vigorous, the fatigue of her journey was a thing she scarcely felt, and it was not her disposition to suffer long from emotion or from embarrassment, and besides, she was so happy. One single glance, quick as a flash—had it not sufficed to lift all the weight from her heart and to fill her with a transport of joy and confidence? Her uncle's voice, his words as he embraced her,—" Oh, Marguerite, it is you yourself!"—had made her so happy; then the sweet faces of those lovely young girls, the vision of the children gathered under the Christmas tree, all, even to the brusque attentions of her young cousin, had given her that delicious sensation of security, that certainty of protection, which in her recent desolation she had desired more than all else.

She raised her head and looked at her aunt, who stood silently in front of her.

Decidedly, this lady was not handsome; she was indeed of surprising plainness, and yet, even before she spoke, before she smiled, one saw plainly in this face, so destitute of charm, two things more beautiful than beauty: intelligence and goodness.

"Remain here quite still," said Madame Dornthal, using the friendly *du*, as if it were her own child. "See, look at the clock,—a quarter of an hour will be enough, but do not try to talk, only listen to what I say. You are with your family, you understand; that is, you are at home; be sure that you understand that. You must not thank us, for you are our own child. We had five children before, now we have six. That was Clement, my eldest son, who came to meet you, because this evening his father could not leave the children; and you saw Hilda and Clara, and the two little ones, Fritz and Frida, at the door; besides, there is Gabrielle, and that is all. Your uncle has so lamented his poor Marguerite. Now he has found you, and it is a day of rejoicing!"

Fleurange put her handkerchief to her eyes, and said nothing. At this moment some one knocked.
"Who is it?"
"It is I."
Clement appeared at the door.
"A cup of coffee?"
"Yes."
The cup was brought directly, and Fleurange obediently drank it.
"Now will you go to your room? Would you rather go to bed at once, or will you return to the hall where the others are?"

Fleurange said without hesitation: "I should prefer to return to the hall and see them all as soon as possible."

Madame Dornthal's kind smile brightened all her face. "You please me so much, Gabrielle," she said, "not because you are so beautiful—that is nothing; I should have loved you just as much if it had been otherwise,—but you are so unaffected, and that is just what I like. Now, let us see; it is eleven o'clock; our friends are come to take their little ones home, and my little Fritz and Frida must go to bed. But the rest of us will go, in a few minutes, to the midnight mass, and we shall not have supper till we come back. Now, choose; will you do as the children, or will you go with us?"

"With you, oh please, with you!" cried Fleurange. "I am neither ill nor tired, and I should like to go to church."

"You must be tired, although you do not feel it yet," replied Madame Dornthal; "still I think it will not hurt you, and if you like to go, you shall. Only, to save your strength, do not return now to the *salon;* remain here and rest, and wait till I come."

She left the room, and Fleurange remained quietly, only too happy to obey this benevolent will. Five minutes later the door opened; it was Clement again, holding his little brother by the hand, and carrying his little sister in his arms.

"Fritz and Frida want to bid you good-night," he said. Fritz approached with some timidity, but Fleurange spoke to him at once in that language children understand, and which can be learned and spoken only by those who lov-

them, and he was soon at his ease. Then she took the little girl, and kissed the blue eyes which, watching her still with surprise, were beginning to grow heavy, and when she returned the child to Clement the little creature was quite asleep. He received his little sister carefully, and carried her away without waking her, with an ease that showed him quite familiar with cares of this sort, as, accompanied by Fritz, he left the room.

A half-hour of repose and silence followed this interruption. It was better for Fleurange than sleep, for her excitement seemed to have taken away all need of that. Then Madame Dornthal came, with her two daughters, and Clement and his father awaited them in the vestibule. They all went on foot, for the church was near,—walking silently and thoughtfully under the starry sky, for the children's festival had not made them forget the solemnity of this grand night.

On her knees at last in the church, Fleurange felt that her full heart must find relief, and when, from sweet and solemn voices rang out, under the magnificent arches, the grand chants suited to the night, the young girl's head bent lower and lower; all the joy and the gratitude of her heart poured itself in quiet tears and most fervent thanksgiving to the Father of the fatherless.

At the conclusion of the service, one voice, more beautiful than the rest, manly yet gentle, chanted near her the psalm: *Laudate Dominum!*" Involuntarily her own joined with it, and the two voices seemed for an instant to be but a single sound.

Turning, she perceived that he who had thus sung was her cousin, Clement Dornthal.

V.

When a friendly hand aids the shipwrecked sailor to reach the shore, the man's first utterance is an expression of boundless gratitude; repose is sweet, even upon the sands, to him who has just escaped the perils of the sea; but if there is upon this shore no place which can serve as a refuge, and if he sees only in the vague rays from a far-off light-house the hope of an assured shelter, he is soon tempted to ask with anxiety whether he will have strength to reach this half-unseen light, and whether it be really his haven of rest. Such was the united gratitude and apprehension which the young orphan had experienced on the day when she had received from the good Mlle. Josephine the hospitality of the blue room, and these feelings had never left her during all the time she remained at that first halting-place of safety. But to-day, when the joyous Christmas chimes awakened her, in the great bed where she had fallen asleep only two or three hours before day, her first thought was this: "I have reached the haven at last; my God, I thank Thee!" and she arose, happy, and eager to take possession of her new life. Her first care, at the beginning of the day, was to write to Mlle. Josephine. She needed, before she could begin to enjoy her happiness, to have her old friend know about it; she felt that she could even here show her gratitude in associating Mlle. Josephine with all her own new and happy impressions. She wrote also to Madre Madelina; she was eager to unite without delay all the friends and all the happiness of the past with her present happiness and her new life.

Her aunt, on telling her the evening before that she was *at home,* seemed to have made her, as if by magic, a daughter of the house. Everything about her was new and a little strange, but everything pleased her as if it had been naturally in accordance with her tastes. And yet the sombre tapestry that covered the walls; the old *armoire* of carved wood, wherein her small belongings found ample accommodation, the high-backed chairs ranged around the room; the antique bureau in one corner; the great monumental stove, whose spectral aspect could not but surprise—all this might easily have displeased one accustomed to the gay magnificence of Italy; but in this house no sad impression could come to the young girl from external objects; the word "welcome!" seemed written upon all things as well as upon all faces, and in this gentle atmosphere she felt that all the material well-being which surrounded her was but the image of a moral well-being, much more necessary than the other to the happiness of her life.

"You must not put on your black dress to-day, Gabrielle," said one of the two blonde sisters, appearing for the third time within an hour, in Fleurange's room, and bringing this time a basket containing a dress like their own.

"Why?" Fleurange said in surprise.

"Don't you know, in Germany we lay aside black on great holidays?" replied Clara, the younger of the two. "To-day you must be dressed like us, and you will always be so, after this melancholy black is over."

The elder sister observed that their cousin made no reply; she approached her and said tenderly: "Clara has grieved you? Forgive her. She is so gay herself," added Hilda, "that she cannot understand either misfortune or sadness."

"I have no wish to remind her of them to-day," said Fleurange, "and I will do as she desires. But you, dear Hilda," she continued, observing with admiration her cousin's golden hair and serious brow, to which a queenly crown or a saintly aureole would have been equally befitting, "are you not as gay and happy as she?"

"I am happy," rejoined Hilda, "but I am not so gay."

After some further explanations, Fleurange conformed to the wish of the sisters. But when, at the hour of dinner, the beautiful Hilda, arrayed in white, brought her a garland like the one which she herself wore, and would have placed it on her head, she made a little resistance.

"As to this garland, Hilda, excuse me, will you not, from wearing it?"

"Why?"

"Because I have never worn any such ornament, and besides, after all, I cannot forget that I am a poor orphan who has no right to wear such things, or to go into society."

"But, Gabrielle, do you not know that we only celebrate these holidays among ourselves, and that we never go into society?"

"Never?"

"No, never! and you will perhaps find that very dull. Sometimes we dance here at home, and we often have music, but we never go to a ball, nor to the theatre, unless there is some very extraordinary representation, a tragedy, or some fine opera; but so rarely that it scarcely counts."

"I don't think I shall find it dull," said Fleurange; "I never went out but once, and then I am sure it was not at

"Where was that, and when?"

"At Florence, a year ago, just after my father took me away from school. They were to have a new ballet at the theatre, and he took me; then he was sorry he had done so, when he saw the effect it produced on me. Oh, Hilda, it gave me no pleasure. I could not look at it. My father took me away as soon as possible, and tried to make me forget the impression, but it remains with me still."

"You would forget it, perhaps, if you should go to hear one of our grand tragedies, or an opera of Mozart or Weber."

"Perhaps! but about this wreath. Why must one wear it without any reason?"

"We have a reason. My father likes to have us wear the flowers of the season every holiday. This poor wreath that you refuse, of holly leaves like mine—the shining Christmas holly with its glossy leaf, and its fruit as red as coral, see how well it looks in your black hair!"

So speaking, Hilda laid the garland upon her cousin's head, and, Clara appearing at this moment, hesitation was no longer possible. In a second she had taken her sister's place; the shining leaves and the red berries were arranged as a crown on the head of Fleurange, who no longer resisted, but laughed, while the mirror gave back the image of the three young girls forming a more lovely tableau than painter's fancy ever dreamed.

"See!" exclaimed Clara, "you are both of you beautiful—one like day, the other like night; and as for me," she continued, arranging her long curls in which were fastened sprays of holly, "what can I be compared to?"

"You are a flower, a star, my Clara,—you are whatever is best to look at by day or night," said Fleurange tenderly. She preferred the elder of the two sisters, but she found an irresistible charm in the younger, and could not help caressing her, with voice and look, as though she were yet a child.

"That is graceful, poetic, and well said! Thanks, my cousin Gabrielle; now I shall ask our poet to say what I am like, and we will see if he discovers the same resemblance!"

"If our poet should be absent-minded," Hilda sa

"we can put the question to somebody else who will not be so."

Clara blushed. "Come, come," she said, "no matter about me. Let us go down, Frida has come to look for us, and everybody has arrived."

And taking her little sister by the hand, she flew, rather than ran, downstairs.

"You did not tell me that any one was coming," said Fleurange.

"It is only our own people, Gabrielle, our family and our friends. Since uncle Heinrich is a widower, he always comes to us, with his son, to spend Christmas. Before, we used to meet at his house. You will see him and our handsome cousin, Felix. The rest are our friends, and will soon become yours."

Hilda paused a moment. "You know, perhaps," she resumed, "that Hansfelt is a friend and companion from childhood, of my father's?"

"Hansfelt?" cried Fleurange. "What? Karl Hansfelt, the great poet?"

We have already said that Fleurange knew her mother's language well; the verses of the author whose name had just been mentioned were at that time sufficiently celebrated for her to have read them, and indeed to have learned many of them by heart.

"And he is your friend, and I shall see him?"

"Oh yes," Hilda said, "you will see him often; and then," she added, as if a little desirous to change the subject, "you will see a young artist who is beginning to become quite distinguished. His name is Julian Steinberg, and he is a favorite pupil of Overbeck's. Clara will introduce him to you!"

Thus informed concerning the visitors whom she was about to meet, Fleurange went down with her cousin to the great *salon*, which as well as the dining-room was situated on the ground floor of the house. This apartment was often called the gallery, by reason of its form and the great number of pictures with which its oak walls were covered. Specimens from all the schools were gathered there without being in any degree confused, for the least observant eye could remark, at one end, the pictures which belonged to the Flemish school of Van Eyck and Kemling; then, between the heavy drapery of the doors and windows, on one side, fine copies and many originals from the great Italian masters; on the other, a few Spanish pictures. Finally, one entire wall of the room was reserved for that modern school, just then springing up in Germany, of which Professor Ludwig Dornthal was a most intelligent admirer and liberal patron. He had been the first to aid and encourage, at the outset of their career, those destined later to wear the highest honors, and his house was a rendezvous for many young artists who, following out the admirable allegory later conceived and executed by their great master, sought art in the reflection of a celestial ideal, rather than in a servile reproduction of earthly images.

The house occupied by Ludwig Dornthal is no longer in existence. Modern improvements have by degrees banished those old dwellings, whose time-honored aspect differs too widely from all that the eyes of a new generation desire and demand. At the date of our story, that is to say in 1823, it was already so far noticeable that they called it the Old House, and it went by no other name in the town.

But it was spacious and commodious; its quiet location and its great garden suited well the studious habits of the professor and his family; the picturesque coloring which time had given to its old stone walls was exactly to his taste; above all, hither Ludwig Dornthal had brought his wife in the first days of their union, and here all their children had been born. Hence, the house was very dear to him and to all his family, and not only was it thus dear to those who lived in it, but it was beloved by all who frequented it; and each new-comer, like Fleurange, found himself involuntarily repeating those words which are destined to be repeated—though always in vain upon this earth—when for an instant all our faculties find themselves in happy equilibrium: "It is good to be here, let us pitch our tent, and here remain."

This impression, it may be supposed, was not dependent merely upon the external aspect of the Old House; harmony reigned therein between persons and things, and from differing material the same effect was everywhere produced. Inanimate objects seem to receive and comunicate something to the life which goes on about them, and to the attentive ear this mute language makes many a strange revelation.

When Fleurange entered the *salon* she perceived that her uncle Ludwig awaited her with a certain impatience, for as soon as she appeared he approached her, and, taking her by the hand, led her to the other end of the room, where stood a person whose features bore some resemblance to his own, but whose expression was so different that the resemblance disappeared more and more as one became the better acquainted with the two brothers.

Heinrich Dornthal, for he it was, passed in the eyes of many people for a much more important man than the professor, and one who did much more honor to the family name; he was of this opinion himself, and his brother accepted tranquilly the secondary position. Ludwig recognized with admiration in his brother the science, to him occult, of transmuting a sum of money into another sum of treble value, in less time than it would take himself to write a chapter, and with a precision in the science of figures superior to that which the professor dared claim for himself in the science of dates: he willingly agreed that the banker was the great man of the family. On the other hand, the banker made no reflection to his own prejudice from the splendor that the professor's labors threw upon their name, and it did not give him the least doubt concerning their respective values. It is always so. Those devoted to material occupations disdain those who busy themselves exclusively with intellectual things, while the latter highly esteem, in the case of others, the faculties which they themselves do not possess. It is, without doubt, for this reason: the former are ignorant enough to believe that they know everything, while the latter are sufficiently wise to know what the things are which they do not understand. There existed, however, between the two brothers a sincere and solid attachment, and, different as they were, the family feeling was equally potent with each. So, when the professor presented Fleurange to his brother, saying, "This is the daughter of our sister Marguerite, and doubly now your niece, for I have adopted her as my daughter also," the banker bent down and kissed the young girl kindly enough, but he could not help saying, "One daughter more is a good deal, brother, when you already have three."

This cold and ungracious remark disconcerted Fleurange, and caused her a painful sensation of embarrassment from which she had not at all recovered, when a young man of considerable personal beauty approached her, and offered her his arm. Fleurange looked at him with astonishment. She had never been at a great dinner, and knew not the customs which, on such occasions, are common to all countries. She drew back, and opening her large eyes, said:

"But who are you, sir, and where do you wish me to go?"

At this question and slight motion of hers every one near her smiled, and she noticed that even her good uncle Ludwig seemed as much amused as the rest; then, with that simplicity which was her great charm, she began to laugh herself, so frankly that he who had been the involuntary cause of this little scene, exclaimed half aloud: "Certainly that is the sweetest *gaucherie* that ever was seen;" then, bowing low with assumed gravity, and an air at once gallant and mischievous: "*Mademoiselle*," he said, "I am called Felix Dornthal; I have the honor to be your cousin, and I offer my arm to conduct you to the dining-room, but I agree that it would have been more proper had we first been introduced to each other."

Fleurange, blushing and smiling, accepted the offered arm, and once seated at table, this new cousin beside her, and the embarrassment of the little incident dissipated, she looked around, and began to enjoy her new position.

Was it indeed herself—she who but the other day was so alone in the world? she who had looked in the face misery and destitution? she, who now found herself in the midst of a large and happy family group, herself a part of it, loved by all, loving all?—all, except the cousin who sat by her side, and who inspired her with an involuntary distrust; and yet he had just said to her a few words in Italian, pronounced with an accent so pure that it startled her with a sweet suggestion of her native land, so lately left, so dearly loved! Yet the words which Felix spoke were some compliment to which she knew not how to make reply, and, as she raised her eyes to his, she met a look which disconcerted her still more. She murmured a few words, scarce knowing what she said, then addressed herself silently to a study of the faces around her, beginning with her uncle Ludwig. In regard to him, Fleurange thought she had never seen a more noble and gentle face; it was impossible not to be struck by the great contrast existing in this regard between him and his wife, which must have been even more striking in their youth than now. While this thought occupied her, she suddenly met her aunt's look; the latter fixed her eyes on Fleurange for an instant and smiled. This look and smile seemed to reply to her thoughts, and to offer the key to the mystery, for they revealed those gifts which make the indestructible bond of true sympathy. To these gifts beauty adds nothing, or at least it only adds ornament, useless to the heart, and which the eye soon ceases to seek; for they who know what it is to love a soul, very soon learn to love the features, whatever they may be, through which that soul finds expression.

Of all the children, the only one who had not inherited the beauty of the Dornthals was Clement. More than any one of his brothers and sisters, Clement was like their mother; he had the same irregularity of feature, and the same smile. He was, however, tall and well made, his figure, though not elegant, was not ungraceful, and when the heavy masses of hair were thrown back from his forehead one could see that the brow gave a marked dignity to the face, while his eyes were keen, expressive, and intelligent. With all this, it was a matter of surprise that young Dornthal was apparently a person of so little account, and this was all the more surprising because his aptitude for art and science was so considerable, and among students he held the highest rank. But it appeared to cost him an effort to talk, and in general society he was so utterly silent that no one ever tried to converse with him. On the other hand, the father of these children could hardly conceal the secret preference and the tender pride which he felt for his eldest son; the mother had so great a confidence in Clement that she seemed rather to consult than to guide him; the sisters and brother idolized him, appealed to him in all doubtful cases; he had a way for everything, a remedy for everything, and nothing wearied his patience. For all that, he might pass, as we have said, almost unnoticed. So it was natural enough that Fleurange, continuing her inspection, scarcely remarked her cousin at all, but found her attention very much attracted by the person who sat next him.

This was a man who might be fifty years old —perhaps older even—spare in figure, with grayish hair and beard. But an indescribable something induced the beholder to watch him with interest, to ask his name; and the name suited the face so well that not unfrequently the reply would follow: "That is just as I imagined him to look!" This was in truth the exclamation of Fleurange when, in answer to her question, her cousin, Felix Dornthal, had mentioned the name of Hansfelt.

"Karl Hansfelt!" she repeated, "it is he! yes, it is indeed he!"

"Certainly, my fair cousin, it is he himself," replied Felix, in a mocking tone. "I must think myself happy that I have at last found a subject which interests you; though I confess I did not expect to be under obligations for it to old Hansfelt!"

"But isn't it natural that one should look with interest at a celebrated man, and especially one so justly famous as he is?" she said, once more lifting her eyes to her cousin's face. But she lowered them instantly, for the gaze that was fastened upon her seemed to her the most displeasing that she had ever met. This look expressed at once the most insolent admiration, and an entire absence of kindness. She wished to go on with the conversation, however, and so continued timidly:

"He is certainly a poet whose name is on every one's lips, and whose words are in every one's memory."

"As for me," said Felix Dornthal, "I am not fond of rhymers; this one, in particular, displeases me, and I regard his approaching departure without the slightest regret."

"He is going away?" said Fleurange.

"Yes. It appears that he is offered a place at court. I don't know what, but one that will give him a chance to gratify his taste for old books, and will beside—no trifle

even for a poet!—put him quite at his ease. They have
exercised a gentle violence towards him, and, ere long, the
felicity of seeing him under our roof will be snatched from
us, and forever, as it appears; for this worthy prince who
lays claim to him insists that he shall never leave the capital again."

Fleurange said nothing: her eyes were just then attracted to her cousin Hilda, who sat near enough to overhear
the conversation without being able to join it. She saw
her stoop suddenly to pick up a flower which had just fallen
from her hand, and when she raised her head Fleurange
remarked that a brilliant flush covered her face; this was
natural enough, considering the movement she had just
made, but it was less so that she should by degrees grow
very pale, and that her hand should tremble violently as
she lifted a glass of water to her lips.

Fleurange was observing this with vague disquiet, when
her attention was suddenly diverted by a question which
her Uncle Ludwig addressed to a young man who sat near
Clara, and the reply which followed took away, for the
moment, from Fleurange all thought of any other subject.

"Steinberg," the professor said, "look at my niece, and
tell me if you see the resemblance they told us of."

The young artist lifted his eyes, and looked at Fleurange with an attention which, until now, had been exclusively absorbed by his young neighbor.

Suddenly he cried out: "Certainly, I recall it perfectly, and I see that Count George was right; here is *Cordelia*, her very self, before our eyes!"

Every one looked at Fleurange, who blushed. But why
did she shiver also from head to foot? What strange min-
gling of feelings, poignant and sweet, awakened at the name
of *Cordelia?* Doubtless she could not hear mentioned
with indifference this last work of her father's, the picture
about which gathered so many painful recollections. On
the other hand, it was this same picture which had given
her uncle the clue to finding her, and appreciating at this
moment, better, than ever before, the extent of her happiness, it was perhaps natural that the name of her unknown
benefactor, suddenly pronounced in her presence, should
occasion this extreme and inexpressible emotion;—but was

Whatever might be the cause, she remained the rest of the evening troubled and absorbed in thought. She had not then deceived herself; it was indeed the stranger whom she had seen that day in the studio who had become the owner of the picture, for he not only knew that she had served as the model for *Cordelia*, but also that the likeness was accurate, and his name was Count George ! The Count ! he was then a man of high rank. What was his other name, what his nationality ? Had he gone from the city ?

These questions Fleurange desired greatly to ask, but an invincible shyness arrested them upon her lips, and the evening closed without her feeling able to bring the conversation back to the subject again. From this curiosity, again awakened, and but partially satisfied, she preserved a sort of uneasiness with which she reproached herself as a wrong and an ingratitude when, before falling asleep, she went over the events of the day, and recalled, one by one, all that had marked forever in her memory these hours when she had celebrated for the first time with her own people the great and memorable festival of Christmas.

VI.

Two months had passed since her arrival, and Fleurange had almost forgotten what the clerk's wife had said to her about her uncle's family, and the false inferences she had drawn therefrom. But it was recalled to her one morning when, according to their custom, the inmates of the Old House were gathered in a room known as the library, which adjoined the gallery, and looked into the garden. This apartment served as the professor's study, yet it was so large that it could serve for many other uses at the same time.

Fleurange was giving a writing lesson to little Frida, when, chancing to lift her eyes, she was struck with the aspect which the room presented.

The professor sat at his desk. He had just finished a paper which his wife was now reading over, and it was easy to see with what interest he, the scholar and author, awaited the judgment of her whom he thus consulted.

While this was going on at one end of the room, at the

other, Clement, standing near a black-board was giving a lesson in mathematics to his brother. The child's attention often wandered, but the patience of the young teacher was unwearied; he repeated his demonstration with clearness, without raising his voice, and finally was successful in making himself understood and obeyed. The only motion which indicated in Clement a little impatience was that with which, now and then, he threw back his hair. This gesture, which was indeed somewhat habitual to him, showed his forehead completely, and Fleurange was for an instant struck with the expression of his face as well as with the pleasant tones of his voice; but what was going on near the great round table in the middle of the room drew her attention more irresistibly.

Near this table (upon which were heaped up books, maps, and all kinds of portfolios) stood Karl Hansfelt and Hilda; the latter was leaning against a tall desk upon which lay a folio volume, and from this volume Hansfelt read aloud verses which Hilda recited after him, but he read in Greek, and she repeated in German.

Fleurange watched them with surprise for some minutes, and then she could no longer restrain an exclamation:

"It was true, Hilda," she cried, "they were right in saying that you were all students! but you exceed the rest! Do you really know Greek well enough to improvise a translation, and especially in verse?"

Hilda began to laugh; then she said, "I am not improvising. I am reciting verses that I know by heart."

"And when these verses fall from your lips, Hilda," Hansfelt said, "the author of the translation weaves strange day-dreams for himself! He will soon be far less self-satisfied," he continued sadly, and threw the book upon the table with an air of discouragement. "It is such a pity that you are what you are!"

Hilda looked surprised. "What I am?" she repeated.

"Yes, a young and beautiful girl, instead of a studious boy, who might have attached himself to my footsteps, and followed me everywhere, as the masters 'n the middle ages

"Or, indeed, if"—began Hansfelt, but he stopped suddenly, and left the sentence unfinished.

Soon the professor and his wife arose and left the room, and Hansfelt accompanied them.

And now the lesson in mathematics was finished, to the satisfaction of both master and pupil, and Fritz, seated at his brother's side in a little wagon which had meanwhile been brought round to the door, was about to receive another lesson, much more to his tastes. But before they set out they must come back for little Frida, whose attention Fleurange was now finding it hard to retain. She kissed the child, and gave her her liberty gladly, and the two young girls remained in the library alone with each other. Hilda did not change her attitude in the slightest degree.

Fleurange approached her cousin, and kneeling beside her passed one arm round Hilda's waist, then drew her hands softly down from her eyes; great tears were falling slowly upon the open page of the folio before her.

"Hilda!"

Hilda disengaged her hand from that of Fleurange, and then, without changing her position, leaned her head against the desk, and still the tears fell like rain. Silence lasted for some minutes, and then Fleurange said softly:

"Hilda, will you not speak frankly to me?"

Hilda's wet eyes were the only reply, lifted for an instant to the face of Fleurange.

"Will you tell me nothing?"

"What can I tell you? I know that you have guessed it, and you are not the only one. My mother knows, as you do, what I have never said; and perhaps my father. But both of them blame me, I see it, and it pains me. What they condemn, I know must be wrong. I want to forget it;—I want to cure myself of it;—and I cannot!"

Fleurange remained silent for a long time. "And he?" she said at last.

"He? You have just heard him speak! He does not understand." And again the tears fell fast.

"Do you think he does not love you?"

"He loves me like a child whom he has always known."

Fleurange became thoughtful; then she said slowly: "To love one who does not love you is hard for me to understand. It seems more strange than to love without any similarity in point of age."

Hilda replied simply, and the calm tone in which she spoke was strangely in contrast with the enthusiasm of her words: "I do not know if it be strange; I know not what is his age or my own; I only know that I want the right to love him, and the certainty never to leave him."

"How long has this thought been in your heart?"

"I cannot tell; it seems to me it has been so always, at least I cannot remember a time when it was otherwise. In my childhood, my greatest reward was his praise; no pleasure so great as his coming, no grief equal to his going away. Often when the other children were playing together in the garden, I would sit here in this corner, at the window, and listen while he talked with my father; and now, Gabrielle, now he will go, and I shall never see him again!"

"He has postponed his departure, has he not?"

"Yes, he will not go away till after Clara is married; he will leave us the day after her wedding."

The conversation was interrupted by the entrance of her who had just been mentioned. Clara appeared, accompanied by Julian. They had been solemnly betrothed a fortnight before, and their gayety and happiness spread to all who were in the house. Hilda dried her eyes in an instant, and, as she went forward and kissed her sister, she seemed to lay aside her own sorrow, and, in the other's joy, to become quite unmindful of the grief which weighed down her young heart.

VII.

'At Fleurange's age the heart beats a little faster when for the first time one finds one's self in presence of that unknown sentiment before which pale, in an instant, all those that have heretofore sufficed,—that sentiment which, by its mysterious promises of the future, renders the listener indifferent or ungrateful towards the sweetest delights of the past. She watched her two cousins, accordingly, with a sort of tender interest, but it was not Clara's innocent delight, and the ardent and devoted attachment of Julian;

it was the silent and inexplicable passion of Hilda, which had a strange charm for Fleurange, and, oddly enough, caused her an involuntary feeling of envy.

"Ah! yes," she thought to herself. "I can see how respect, admiration, enthusiasm can cause this great love; I understand that it must be happiness to bow before a person so much superior to one's self! Whether it is the superiority of genius, of virtue, or of courage, or perhaps even of afflictions, it must be sweet to bend lovingly before it!"

One day Fleurange was suffering her thoughts to wander at will. Leaning against the balcony, and hearing the nightingales sing, she followed with her eyes her two cousins, who were walking together in the garden. It was spring time. The marriage of Clara and Hansfelt's departure were close at hand, and these two events preoccupied diversely all the inmates of the Old House. And so Fleurange sat dreaming at the window, yet not sadly. Notwithstanding the thoughts which, like shadows eluding her grasp, sometimes swept vaguely across her mind, she felt that she was very happy. The spring air caressed her face, and the sun lighted up gayly the old furniture of her room. She looked about her contentedly, and suffered herself to be cradled in a sweet and intense feeling of comfort. Suddenly, without any external suggestion, came a keen and poignant thought across her happiness. "What if I have to leave this place also, as I have left the others, never to return?" she said to herself, half aloud, with anguish which was for a few minutes uncontrollable. She put her hand over her eyes, and strove to free herself from this nightmare which oppressed her. She was still in this attitude when she heard, under the balcony, a voice which, more than any other, displeased her.

"If only I were a poet!" said this voice, "or even if I knew any verses, it would be a good time to quote Shakspeare, 'O that I were a glove,' and the rest, whatever it is! Clement, why can't you prompt me? I am good enough at Italian, but my English is very poor."

These words were addressed to her, and it was her cousin, Felix Dornthal, who spoke. He was in the garden, and was standing, with Clement, directly in front of her balcony. The latter was looking down, but Felix had his eyes fixed upon Fleurange, with the same air of admiration that he had assumed for her from the first, and which had been the only annoyance and the only displeasure that she had encountered under her uncle's roof. She did not see Felix very often. The circle of friends who gathered two or three times a month in the *salon* of the professor was little to his nephew's taste, and if, since the arrival of Fleurange, Felix had made his appearance there more frequently, he had not had many opportunities of speaking to her, for she avoided him with a care proportioned to the increasing aversion with which he inspired her. Felix, however, had all the advantage which a handsome face and a knowledge of the world can give, and moreover, sufficient information on many literary subjects to appear a well-informed person, and sufficient assurance and *sang froid* to bring into the conversation his own opportunity to shine. He could please, he was in no danger of doubting this, and he even believed it a thing easy to do; still he took much pains to succeed. It might then seem surprising that he inspired antipathy to this degree, precisely where he most desired to produce the contrary impression.

Sympathy and antipathy are in part involuntary, and they are often entirely inexplicable. Both spring up one knows not how, and, after a time, may be so far transformed or modified that one forgets the earlier impression. Possibly it could be proved, however, that a truthful and upright heart is deceived in these impressions more rarely than others.

However this may be, and independently of this instinctive repulsion, Fleurange had good reason for disliking her cousin on account of the habit of incessant *persiflage* which was one of his most characteristic traits. For him, goodness did not seem to exist; and while talking with him, one ceased almost to believe in its existence himself. Also, he had not been able to see that Fleurange was one of those who can be wounded by a compliment as by an insult, and it needed more than one flash from her great eyes to teach him this. Finally, when, as was often the case, he suddenly stopped speaking, his silence caused anxiety; one asked one's self what caused this sudden preoccupation, and what these gloomy cares could be which weighed upon him. Some used to shake their heads, and to assert that the only son of Heinrich Dornthal ought to control far more strictly his passion for play; and the young man had at times received remonstrances from his father on this subject. But as, with all his errors and vices, Felix had a remarkable talent for business, the banker trusted his son blindly, and often said that, being perfectly satisfied with Felix in matters of importance (by which he referred to his capacity as a financier), he was very easy in regard to other things, and awaited patiently the time when a suitable marriage should bring him back "to a more regular life."

It must be owned that for several months, without his being willing to admit it, the health of the head of the house had been seriously impaired. Affairs which had been, heretofore, exclusively in his own hands were now managed by his son, and his confidence or his weakness, in this regard, had gone to an extreme unknown to any save him who was the object of it. The banker, it is true, was not without uneasiness on this subject from time to time, but Felix, with a few words, could always reassure him, and there remained in his mind only the constantly increasing desire to see his son married and brought back to a life more conformable with the serious character of the affairs that he managed so ably, but from which it was so needful that nothing should distract him. The father would have preferred that Felix should think of one of his two cousins, but the young man found them not at all to his taste, and would often say that it was not within the walls of the Old House that he would find her to whom he would sacrifice his liberty. But when Fleurange appeared there, he suddenly changed his tone, and his unconcealed admiration had already directed towards her the thoughts and hopes of the banker.

As to the professor and his wife, they did not share the paternal illusions of their brother. They would have seen with the greatest reluctance one of their own daughters entrust her fate to Felix, and they remarked with pleasure that Fleurange did not seem disposed to accept his attentions. But they observed all this in silence, the custom of parents in Germany being, upon the great question of marriage, to seek rather to follow than to guide the inclinations and wishes of their children.

We have left Felix under his cousin's balcony. He held a riding-whip in his hand.

"Putting aside poetry, which is not my strong point," he said, "my fair cousin, please listen to the prayer which I address to you in modest prose!"

Fleurange, leaning on the balcony, replied: "I listen."

"Do you observe this lovely spring day? I have my horse here; will you have yours saddled, and allow me to accompany you on a ride?"

Fleurange raised her head with an air of surprise, and made a gesture of refusal.

"No?" said Felix.

"No, certainly not. How could you think of it? what right have you to be my mentor?"

"Your mentor!" said Felix, with a scowl. "I am your cousin, that is all. Clement has had the honor of accompanying you often, and I believe my right is the same as his."

"You are mistaken," said Fleurange composedly; "Clement is my brother, and you are not."

The habitual smile of Felix, a smile at once insolent and unkind, curled his lip.

"Assuredly not," he said, "and it is a title I by no means desire, and to which I am far from laying claim, in the present case."

Fleurange blushed, and made no answer, and almost immediately, in obedience to a sign from Hilda and Clara, she left the balcony, and went to join them in the garden.

Clement had been standing silently, while this conversation went on, drawing circles in the sand with a little switch which he held.

"Her brother!" Felix repeated, in a bantering tone, when Fleurange had disappeared. "Very good, I make no objection to that. She treats you like a boy, I observe. I am sorry if it does not suit you!"

"It suits me perfectly," rejoined Clement. "I accept the title which she gives me, and I shall know how, when occasion requires, to fulfil the duties it lays upon me, and

"What rights, for instance?"

"The right to protect her, if nothing more! Boy as I am, she has granted me that, and you will see that I shall never relinquish it; I shall use it against you, Felix, most willingly, if the occasion requires."

"My fine lad, you are very important to-day! I don't generally find so much to say. Upon my word, if you were a few years older, I should believe that the great gray eyes of this scornful beauty had fascinated you in turn!"

Clement did not turn away his eyes, nor change color. "Felix," he said, "I am only nineteen, and you are ten years older, but I have an advantage over you which rarely belongs to the younger—you do not know me, but I," he went on, looking Felix in the face, "I--you know it— understand you perfectly."

As Clement spoke, Felix grew very angry; he bit his lips, and would have made some savage reply, when the three young girls appeared at the end of the walk. Felix, seeing them, turned suddenly, and springing upon his horse, was off at full speed, with a little gesture of salutation to Julian Steinberg, whom he met at the garden gate.

Fleurange and the two girls came forward together to meet Julian. "I am late," he said to Clara, "but you will know it was no fault of mine; I was detained by an unexpected meeting. Count George is here--"

"Count George von Walden?" exclaimed Clement. "The same who was here a year ago?"

"Himself," rejoined Julian, "and who showed us this beautiful Cordelia, whom you so greatly resemble, *mademoiselle*," he added, turning to Fleurange.

"And who brought us the happiness of finding her!" cried Hilda.

"But," said Clara, "since he has seen you, Gabrielle, you doubtless know him?"

Fleurange, strangely surprised, moved, and troubled, nevertheless commanded her voice sufficiently to reply: "I did not know till I came here," she said, "that he was the purchaser of the picture."

"But," persisted Clara, "you must have seen him?"

"But you ought surely to remember him, for Julian maintains that he has the most remarkable face he has ever seen."

"Yes, not only has he handsome features," said Julian, "but there is something in his face, in his whole figure, something—"

"Striking and noble," interrupted Clement: "yes, that is true."

"Certainly!" Julian resumed, "but there is even more than that; there is something extraordinary—what shall I say?—heroic, yes! that is the right word. He has the air of a hero."

"Of romance?" asked Clara, laughing.

"No, of history; if I had to paint some great general, some famous soldier of fortune, I would ask him to sit for me."

"Besides this, he loves art," Clement said.

"Yes," added Julian, "he seems to have all gifts."

"And will he remain here?" Clara asked.

"No, unfortunately, or he would be at our wedding; but he is obliged to be in Petersburg without delay."

"What! is he a Russian?" asked Clara.

"No, not entirely."

"What do you mean?"

"I mean he is a Livonian, or Courlander, I don't know exactly which. But he is a subject of the Czar, and cannot trifle with an imperial order; this obliged him to quit Florence, where he was residing, and compels him now to resume his journey so rapidly."

The conversation passed to another subject, but Fleurange heard no more. As soon as possible she escaped to her room, and, seated once more by the window, remained lost in thought. Finally she drew a little memorandum-book from her pocket, and wrote on a blank leaf the name, Count George von Walden.

VIII.

The education of Fleurange had not accustomed her to yield to her feelings readily, and it was surprising that she allowed herself so long to be overmastered by a vague

ined more unreasonable than this, whose object was so nearly a total stranger, a man with whom she had exchanged not a single word, and whom she would in all probability never see again! This was now the third time, since the day she had seen him in Paris, that he had been mentioned in her hearing, and each time she had felt a strange emotion. But, for the first time, this was easily explained by the pain of recalling her father's recent death. Then, when at the Christmas dinner, Julian Steinberg had referred to him, she could understand her own excitement by ascribing it to her naturally eager interest to know who was the owner of the picture which had played a part of so much importance in deciding her destiny. But this time, to the quick beating of the heart and the ardent curiosity with which she had listened to every word about him, followed a long reverie, which, by degrees, became strangely wild and dreamy.

"Yes, Julian is right; that is what he is like!" she said aloud. And all the heroes with whom history, poetry, and legend had peopled her imagination, passed before her in turn, each under the same aspect; then—there being no heroes without heroism, and no heroism without strife and danger—a series of frightful scenes followed one another through her thoughts. Battles, shipwrecks, desperate enterprises, dangers of every kind, wherein the same personage appeared, and in the midst of this phantasmagoria she saw herself taking a part in some strange and indistinct way in all his adventures!

A full hour had passed thus, and the sun was almost gone, when, suddenly, a habit formed in childhood came to change the current of her thoughts, and brought her to herself once more. The setting of the sun marks, in Italy, the hour for the evening prayer. Fleurange never forgot it, and each day, at this hour, a few brief words of devotion rose to her lips.

Every one knows the power of association. All have experienced this truth, that a perfume, a flower, a strain of music, some less thing even than these, may have power to awaken a crowd of images, whose connection with the trifle that has called them up can be understood by him only in whose mind they are thus reawakened. How natural and touching, then, to attach a thought of heaven to that hour which binds night and day together, to that hour when daylight is at once glowing and dying, that hour of twilight which brings labor's close, and gives leisure for long, sweet, perhaps dangerous reveries! Who can wonder that the evening prayer becomes a safeguard? Who will say that what Fleurange felt at this moment has not been so felt a thousand times by others?

A sudden breaking in of light upon her soul, a strength against earthly phantoms, an impulse towards the skies, a rapid return to the impressions of her childhood, in a word, a crowd of healthful thoughts, in place of those confused and fevered dreams that were occupying her mind—such was the effect produced at this moment upon her by the souvenir indissolubly attached to this hour of the day.

She rose resolutely; her languid attitude, her look, till now lost in space, were at once transformed. She awoke; and this waking was not again followed by dreams.

What, indeed, was it—this folly which had seized upon her? Questioning herself thus plainly, she colored with shame. These idle and absurd reveries must be combatted, must be conquered, and the first step was to cut them short. She reopened the little note-book, and commenced by tearing out the page on which was the name she had just now inscribed there; then, without further examining her thoughts, even to reproach herself with them, which would have been only another way of prolonging them, she sat down at her table, and took up a volume which lay there. It was a copy of Dante, belonging to Clement. She had promised him to mark some passages which they had read together the evening before, and to add some notes which her memory had recalled to her. She began this work immediately, and strove to become completely absorbed in her occupation.

It is often, as we all know, much easier to desist from an action than to repress a thought; perhaps this is because it is more difficult to exercise the will strongly in one case than in the other. At this moment, however, Fleurange was most eager for self-conquest, and, at the close of a half-hour's industry, she believed that she had succeeded. She might have been a good deal surer of success had she foreseen what would soon facilitate her task, and banish from her thoughts all vain illusions and vague reveries, and, above all, every opportunity for introspection.

When she had finished writing, it was already growing dark. She heard a clock strike, and was confused to see that she had so long remained alone in her room, especially on a day when, more than ever, she should have occupied herself with others. This evening, in fact, was the last that Clara was to pass at home before her marriage. This day closed, for the inmates of the Old House, a phase of cloudless happiness. One place would henceforth remain vacant, one dear face was to disappear, one beloved member of the household would go away forever. They would see her again, without doubt, but it would not be as before. Happiness awaited her, but in a new and untried life, and Clara's laughing face grew pathetic and grave while her eyes lingered tearfully on the faces of father and mother, and brothers and sisters, and looked sadly even at the old walls she was about to leave. This melancholy communicated itself to the rest, in a degree, while at the same time their preparations for the morrow spread an unwonted confusion through this house habitually so calm and so well ordered.

Fleurange, leaving her room, went down into the picture-gallery, but this apartment was deserted. Clara, no doubt, then, was with her mother, but where was Hilda? This day Fleurange knew would be the last which Hilda would spend with Hansfelt. Doubtless her cousin must be suffering deeply, and Fleurange reproached herself that she could for so long have lost sight of her. She crossed the picture-gallery and opened the door of the library, and there she found her whom she sought. Ludwig Dornthal and Hansfelt were talking together, and, near them, Hilda, pale, silent, motionless, sat listening to the conversation which went on in her presence.

Hansfelt was talking to his friend of his departure, and spoke like a man who was never to return. The subject of their conversation was nothing of greater importance than early reminiscences, their old friendship, the cessation of their long intimacy; but Hansfelt's tone was that of profound sadness, and he seemed like one overwhelmed

Ludwig, on his part, was extremely agitated, and as he talked with his friend he stole, every now and then, an anxious and restless glance at his daughter. Fleurange gently approached her; the cold hand of Hilda clasped hers.

"I am glad you have come," she said softly; "it was right that you should be here."

Fleurange dared not answer her, and scarcely ventured to look at her, fearing to increase her emotion by seeming to understand.

A jewel-case stood upon the table. "What a beautiful bracelet!" she said, glad to find something to say.

"This is the wedding present that Hansfelt has just brought Clara," said the professor.

"Yes, a present for the wedding and for adieu, that Ludwig has permitted me to offer to one of his daughters," said Hansfelt; "for the other," he continued, in a troubled voice, "the hour for a wedding-gift will doubtless soon come, but the hour for adieu is already here. Ludwig, in memory of the beautiful years in which I have seen her grow from a child to a young woman, and in memory of this last day, will you permit me to give this ring to Hilda?"

The professor said nothing.

Hansfelt continued: "In truth, a leave-taking like this is so much like death that it gives one, as that does, the right to say all. Hilda, why should I not confess it to you now in his presence? Nothing follows from it, I know. Well, then, this man, older than your father, would, perhaps, have had the folly to forget his age had he remained near you. It is better, then, that he should go away."

He took the young girl's cold hand in his.

"If he were younger," he went on, with an attempt to smile, "it is another ring than this which he might have obtained the right—"

He stopped, alarmed. Hilda's paleness grew frightful, and her head leaned against the shoulder of Fleurange. She seemed ready to faint.

"Hilda! good Heavens!"

"What the deuce, Karl!" cried the professor, rising to his feet; "you drive me to desperation! Why, man,

"I repeat it, what are your wits good for if you can't see that I shall have to give you my daughter, if I don't want to see her die of grief!"

"Ludwig!" repeated Hansfelt, quite beside himself.

"It's true! more's the pity! I am angry enough with her for it, and with you, too; but what can I do! I shall have to forgive you both, if she will be such a fool!"

"Take care! take care, Ludwig," said Hansfelt, turning pale, "there are some hopes of which one might die, if they proved false!"

"Come, come! it is not necessary that you should die, nor she either!" then taking Hilda tenderly in his arms, he whispered, "My Hilda, my child, I give my consent; be happy in your own way. Your father gives you his blessing! Come now," he added, turning to Fleurange, "come with me; we will go and find your aunt, and leave these two to their mutual explanations."

IX.

Madame Dornthal learned with emotion, but without surprise, what had just occurred. She had never deceived herself in regard to her daughter's feelings, and for a long time had sought to convince her husband; but the latter was incredulous, and persisted in declaring it impossible that his friend and contemporary, his "old Karl," could seriously touch a heart of twenty years. "It is nothing but a fancy, which will vanish the moment she sees a man near her own age, who is worthy of her."

"Perhaps, but there lies the difficulty," said the wise and clear-sighted mother. "Between you two, Hilda has accustomed herself to living in a more elevated atmosphere than that which ordinarily surrounds a young girl. Is this good fortune or ill? I cannot say, but since, in this heart of hers, which I read like an open book, I find only pure and noble sentiments, I cannot quarrel with them. Believe me, we must not think too much of our children's happiness,—and especially, we must not plan it in accordance with our own tastes. The important matter truly is, not that they should be the happiest, but that they should become all that they are capable of becoming, that their souls, which have been intrusted to us, should brinr forth their most perfect fruits. Indeed, that is the principal thing, Ludwig, is it not?"

The more worthy one is to hear words like this, the harder it is to argue against them, and the professor, already half convinced by his wife, was carried completely away from his moorings by the scene in the library, and his consent was as cordial as it was unlooked for.

But he said sadly to his wife: "And now we are to lose both at once!"

"I had rather see them happy like us, than helping to make us happy," she rejoined, with more effort to be brave than she cared to own.

All misunderstandings cleared up, all consents obtained, it was at once decided that Hansfelt's departure should be delayed a fortnight, and then, in going, he should not go alone.

The last evening which the two sisters spent together under the paternal roof became, then, doubly memorable. It passed, however, more tranquilly than one might have feared. The professor, for all that his reason had suggested to him, and for all the evident sagacity of his reflections, and the good ground of his opposition, could not look at his daughter without seeing that there was nothing evanescent or disquieting in the deep and tranquil joy that shone in her eyes; and the reflection of this joy in Hansfelt's noble face made one involuntarily understand the sentiment that he had inspired.

"Come, I must own you are a young man after all, my old Karl," cried the professor.

"Why not?" rejoined Hansfelt. "I was dead and am alive again; my life was ended, and it is beginning. What is that but to be a young man again? But it is more than that to me. It is to be better and nobler than I could have been. '*Bonheur oblige,*' no less than '*noblesse.*' What could I not do to merit mine?"

On the morrow the sun rose brilliantly, and threw about the youthful bride an augury of happiness, and many a little presage of good-luck was quoted to her all the day long by the tender superstition of the friends who surrounded her.

The procession went on foot, equally to the satisfaction of those who composed it and those who saw it pass. Clara, in white, and crowned with myrtle, was the most lovely bride that one could desire to see; but the eyes of the spectators rested, with at least equal interest, on the two young girls who walked just behind her, followed in their turn by many others, also walking two and two. These two were, of course, Hilda, radiant to-day in her blonde beauty, and Fleurange, whose dark hair and whole appearance distinguished her from the rest. She might have observed, as she passed, more than one look and word calculated to gratify self-love; but her whole attention was engrossed with the details of this wedding, the first one she had ever witnessed. So they came to the church, where a great crowd was assembled, and as the procession drew near the altar, Fleurange, whose eyes moved in every direction, met suddenly a friendly glance, and received a ceremonious bow. She made a slight inclination in return, but without recognizing the person who had saluted her. Who could he be, and who was this young and pretty woman who leaned upon his arm? She had gone a few steps, when suddenly she remembered her young travelling companion, and "Wilhelm," her uncle's clerk. It was surely he whom she had just seen, she was sure of it now, and turned to see them again. She had just taken one step towards them, when she heard some one mention the name of Felix Dornthal; and the same voice added: "They say that the young lady who just passed us is to be his wife." Some person standing next to Wilhelm had just spoken, and Fleurange understood that they alluded to her. She stopped, coloring with displeasure, and heard the reply of Wilhelm, "Would to heaven it were so!" she might save him from—" The rest did not reach her ear, for just then the crowd separated them. She no longer saw Wilhelm nor his wife, and, for the moment, she thought no longer of this little incident. The ceremony, the return, the wedding dinner, all passed with the utmost gayety. Clara took off her myrtle crown and distributed it among the young girls, wishing them all like happiness to her own. Hilda, first of all, was remembered in this distribution, and she received the spray of myrtle without embarrassment, nor was she shy of owning that for her it was something more than a presage. After her, it was the turn of Fleurange, and presently little Frida came in for her share, with the children of her own age.

"In your turn, Gabrielle!" cried Hilda, while Fleurange fastened the green spray in her belt. "You will wear the myrtle crown before long."

Fleurange shook her head, and replied with a gravity she could hardly herself explain: "Never, never, will that day come for me!"

"Why do you say that?" Hilda asked, surprised.

"I don't know," Fleurange said, laughing. Later she noticed that the myrtle had fallen from her belt; she looked for it, for her cousins had bid her wear it till the close of the day, but it could not be found.

At twilight Clara and Julian left the old house, escorted by all to the foot of the steps, and overwhelmed with felicitations and good wishes, and adieus rather tender than sad, for their departure was not to any great distance. The professor and his wife walked with them to their new home. This was a cheery and modest little house in the outskirts of the town, where, for more than a year, Julian had been preparing a home for her who now accompanied him thither. At the door the parents stood still, and refused to enter; Madame Dornthal kissed her daughter, and, as she held her in her arms, she said: "Remember that your life begins anew; keep a share of your heart for us, but let nothing ever come before the love which is your duty now!"

"God punish me," cried Julian, "if ever that duty lay heavily upon her; if ever she regret the day when my home became hers!"

For one moment the father and mother looked at them, as they stood in the doorway of their new home; they saw the bridegroom's look of reverent happiness, and, through tears, the bride's confiding glance, and so they left them to God's protection and blessing.

On the homeward walk the poor father broke the silence first: "She may some day know, when, in turn, she parts with one of her children, what we have suffered to-day!"

"Yes, Ludwig," his wife answered, brushing away her tears, "and Heaven grant that she may then find, as we do now, that there is left in her heart a sentiment stronger even than that grief, and which can help her to endure it."

They clasped each other's hands, and never, even in the beautiful days of their youth, had they felt so tenderly, so intimately united.

On reaching home they found the Old House brilliantly illuminated. The gallery and the library were filled, not as usually by the friends and family of the professor alone, but all whom the two brothers knew in the city were gathered to this entertainment; and it was in accordance with the custom of those days that the bridal pair had withdrawn before the arrival of the evening guests, it being assumed that their happiness was too profound and heartfelt to be properly associated with a scene of noisy merriment.

The sweet seriousness underlying the festivity of the day had seemed to produce an effect even upon the mocking spirit of Felix Dornthal. Or was it something in his own thoughts which sobered him? Be that as it may, he had been noted more than once for his unusual gravity, both at the church, where he arrived late, and at the wedding dinner, where, it being his duty to propose the health of Clara and Julian, he had gracefully accomplished the task, and then relapsed into complete taciturnity. A family dinner-party doubtless could be little to his taste, and perhaps it was but *ennui* which occasioned his silence. So, at least, the three girls thought, who, declaring him sulky, would have nothing more to say to him. At the close of dinner he had disappeared, and now, in all the assembly, he was nowhere to be found. His absence was remarked by many, but by none with so much impatience as by his father, who, on this day of general rejoicing, felt more strongly than ever the wish to live to be present at the marriage of Felix himself. Rendered irritable by illness, Heinrich Dornthal wearied every one with the question, "Where can he be?"

Fleurange passed at the moment when her uncle was addressing for the tenth time that remark to the young man who stood beside him, and who seemed to share his anxiety. It was Wilhelm Müller; she recognized him now at once, and with that natural grace which gave a charm to all her movements, she stepped forward to speak to the clerk and renew her acquaintance with him. A few words were exchanged, and she went on her way, while her uncle, looking after her, felt redoubled a regret which she was as far from divining as she would have been from sharing.

The piano stood open. Some one had been playing, and suddenly the desire to dance had seized upon the younger portion of the assemblage,—that desire which spreads so quickly, and which is often in youth a sort of necessary outlet for the gayety within. Everybody is musical in Germany, and Clement was preëminently so. He promptly understood the general sentiment, and took his violin. Hilda sat down at the piano. Hansfelt stood near her, and the gayety in which this evening she shared as much as any one did not inspire her, as it did them, with the desire to leave her seat. She was, therefore, in the best mood imaginable to perform the part which, with a glance, Clement had assigned her in this improvised orchestra. The brother and sister began a waltz, and they played with that talent, that cadence, that indescribable *verve* which, like the waltz itself, is peculiar to the German nation. In an instant all was animation.

Fleurange had occasionally danced with her cousins in the winter evenings, but never, as to-day, had she experienced that contagious effect produced by gayety, noise, and general excitement. Involuntarily, she rose to her feet with an ardent desire to share in it. At this moment some one said, "Will you grant me the honor of this waltz?" and the offer suited her mood so well that she had said "Yes" and was already on the floor before she really observed that her partner was Felix. Twice they made the circuit of the room, then Felix brought Fleurange back to her place; she stopped, out of breath, pale and troubled. Felix had just been saying to her words which she so gladly would have had unsaid!

Scarcely seated, Fleurange desired to rise, that she might leave the place and the apartment where he was, but she could not; the hand of Felix laid upon her own obliged her to reseat herself. Then Fleurange mastered her confusion, understanding that the moment was come when she must be calm, firm and decided; the thing is difficult only when the heart and the will are not perfectly in accord. Here this contradiction did not exist, and Fleurange awaited almost with indifference what her cousin had to say to her.

"I ask only one word," said Felix, with more emotion, and with more respect, than was customary with him, "one word, and, if you have understood me, an answer."

"I have heard you," said Fleurange.

"And understood?"

"Yes, with regret, Felix!"

"Answer me plainly, Gabrielle. Have you understood that I love you?"

Fleurange colored, and made no reply.

"That I love you so that my happiness, my future, my very life are in your hands," he continued, vehemently; "and this is true, literally true."

Fleurange looked at him coldly. "Do you wish to frighten me?" she said.

"No, I have told you the truth without thinking that I could alarm you; but since you ask me the question, I will tell you honestly: say only that you accept my hand, and whether you say it with fear or with joy, with love or with doubt, I shall be content, and ask no more than that!"

"So, then," said Fleurange slowly, "whether I esteem you or despise you, whether I love or hate you, is a matter of indifference?"

"No woman detests a man who desires to be loved by her, when that man is her husband—when he might be her tyrant and is her slave!"

"Your humility seems foolish to me, Felix, but you are frank, and I will be so too. Never, understand me well, never will I be your wife!"

Felix grew pale, and his expression changed. "Think again, Gabrielle," he said, "think again. But first listen, I will tell you something which may touch you, perhaps, more

"That is"—said Fleurange, more affected than she was willing to show, and involuntarily recalling what she had heard said in the church.

"I only ask, would you extend your hand to save him?"

He had found a way to make her hesitate, but it was only for a moment.

"We are talking in figures, I suppose," she said, "and it is the soul's danger of which you speak?"

"Yes, a danger of the soul," rejoined Felix bitterly.

"Well, then, this is my answer: in such a danger, I will not, I cannot save any one else at the cost of my own ruin."

Felix rose. "This is your last word?" he said.

"Yes, Felix, it is so, without hesitation,—not without regret if it gives you pain."

The reply was a laugh, which shocked Fleurange inexpressibly. She looked at her cousin. There was neither respect, nor sadness, nor emotion, as just now, in his face. He had resumed his habitual air of scornful raillery and supreme self-confidence.

"Thanks for your frankness, cousin," he said. "You possess in that a virtue I advise you to preserve; it does some harm to your powers of fascination, but on the other hand it will save you from some of the dangers to which your beauty may expose you. Adieu."

"Felix, give me your hand without unkindness," Fleurange said gently.

"Unkindness?" replied Felix, "oh, do not be uneasy! I am a good player, and I can bear a loss gayly. Besides, one is not unlucky always and in everything. Certain defeats, they say, insure certain other victories. Come, Gabrielle, never mind! Give me your hand, and wish me good-luck."

Before Fleurange could answer him he was gone.

"No," she replied, "only let me go out into the fresh air a moment."

Clement gave one rapid glance around the room, then followed her into the garden.

"You were dancing just now," he said.

"Yes, I was wrong to dance."

"Your partner left you before the waltz was ended?"

"Yes," Gabrielle said; and Clement remained silent some minutes; "Gabrielle," he finally exclaimed, "forgive me if I am inquisitive, but I would be so glad to ask you a question!"

"Why should you hesitate? you and I have agreed that we may always speak frankly with each other."

"Well, then, will you tell me why Felix went away?"

"I will, and you will be surprised, Clement, I think; he asked me to marry him."

"And you gave him an answer?"

"Oh yes, indeed! I said—No!"

Clement started, and Fleurange, looking up with surprise, saw in his face the joy he could not conceal.

"Well!" she said, "neither you nor I are very fond of our cousin; I see plainly you are delighted with his disappointment."

"No, I am not delighted; if he were my worst enemy I should pity him, but I am glad"—he hesitated, unlike his usual self, who went generally straight to the point; finally he added: "I am glad of a decision on your part which saves me from ever being obliged to mention his name to you again."

"What would you have done, had I said—Yes?"

"I should have done what I am very glad not to do. But let us talk no more of it."

"Now it is you who talk in riddles."

"No, for one talks in riddles when one desires finally to be understood; but, as for me, I only beg you to forget that I have said anything on the subject."

It is doubtful what reply Fleurange might have made, for Clement's language had puzzled her. But at this moment she observed the spray of myrtle that he wore in his button-hole.

"What, have you myrtle too?" she said. "I thought

Clement blushed, and withdrew the spray from his coat. "It is yours, Gabrielle; I beg your pardon," he said; "I saw it fall from your belt and I picked it up."

"It is mine, truly," she said.

"Oh yes, take it—unless," he added after a little hesitation,—"unless now you will give it to me."

"Most certainly, Clement, keep it to remember me. It is a good omen, they say, and promises you a lovely betrothed, when the time comes."

Clement gravely replaced the spray in his button-hole, saying: "Never, never, will that day come for me!"

"*Never, never!* Oh, how strange that is!" cried Fleurange.

"What?"

"Nothing."

But that which was so strange to Fleurange was this, that Clement, apropos to the same spray of myrtle, and quite unawares, had used exactly her own words of a few hours earlier.

On the whole, this evening, which had begun for her so gayly, finished in a good deal of sadness. She returned to her own room much less cheerful than she had left it, but she had this consolation, that, all day long, this strange image of Count George had kept far aloof from her mind.

X.

More than a fortnight had passed. Hilda's marriage had taken place, and she too had left her father's roof. Clara and her husband were on their way to Italy, where they designed to pass the winter, and now those who were left in the Old House underwent that depression which succeeds inevitably to the noise, stir, and agitation produced by some important event—a depression which invariably has a tone of sadness in it, even though the event itself is purely joyful.

It could not, however, be said that the marriage of her two cousins was entirely so to Fleurange. It is true she loved them enough to rejoice in their happiness with all her heart, but how large the house seemed now! the family-table how small! the library and the garden how desolate! The person least to be pitied was Fritz, for he had his brother still, and other changes meant little to him; but little Frida wept for her sisters, and attached herself to Fleurange more than ever, while the latter exerted for the child's benefit all her well-tried powers of amusing, and, for her own sake, valued highly the diversion this occasioned her.

One day, as Fleurange and Frida sat together in the young girl's room, Fleurange singing in a low tone a ballad to which Frida listened, her head resting against her cousin's shoulder, a knock at the door startled them. It was very gentle, however, and seemed to give no reasonable ground for the alarm with which Fleurange placed the child upon the floor, and rose hastily to open the door. But, when she had opened the door, the kind of presentiment which she had felt was justified.

The person who had knocked, Wilhelm Müller, her uncle's clerk,—the expression of his face,—his agitated manner,—his unexpected and unwonted appearance at her own door,—all announced to her some sad and sudden occurrence.

"Pardon, *mademoiselle*," he said hurriedly. "I did not come in search of you. but Herr Clement is out, and the Herr Professor also. Can you tell me where I may find either of them?"

"I do not know where Clement is, but my uncle and aunt have gone to the Steinbergs' house. They take care of the garden while Julian and Clara are absent."

"At the Steinbergs! It is more than an hour's walk. Oh, good heavens! what shall I do?"

"What is the matter? tell me, I beg of you! of what misfortune do you bring the news?"

"Misfortune!" exclaimed the clerk, after a little hesitation. "Yes, *mademoiselle*, it is true, a great misfortune has happened. But I must not stop a moment. I beg you to send for Herr Ludwig, and tell him that—that his brother is dying."

"Is dying!" cried Fleurange. "Then let me go to him at once, and, in the meantime, some one shall be sent to tell his brother."

"No. *mademoiselle*. oh no! do not come! I cannot

But Fleurange insisted, and had already prepared herself to accompany him, when Clement arrived. He had just come in and learned that his uncle's clerk was inquiring for him.

"Your uncle Heinrich is dying!" cried Fleurange, before he could ask; "let us go, Clement, without losing a moment, while we send for your parents."

And she hastened towards the staircase; but in the meantime Wilhelm approached the young man, and whispered a few words in his ear.

Clement grew pale, but surmounting instantly his violent and evident emotion, he took his cousin by the hand.

"Wait here," he said; "it is better that you should not go; believe me, it is better. I will send for you later." And he led her gently, but resolutely, back into her room, and went out, closing the door. In less than two minutes the street door shut with a clang, and Fleurange was left alone with little Frida, who sobbed violently, and whom she strove to calm, seeking to calm herself also, and to support with patience the torture of suspense.

It was five o'clock when Wilhelm had come to her door, and, as it was summer, it was still broad daylight; but the sun set, night came on, and still Fleurange waited for news. Frida had fallen asleep in her cousin's arms, and the latter felt herself obliged to wait, hard as it was for her, until Clement should come or send.

She had heard her cousin give orders, as he went out, to harness a horse and send for his father. She counted the minutes till they should have had time to return from Julian's house, but the time passed and they did not come. They must have gone at once to the death-bed of their brother. What could be passing there? Why had Clement forbidden her to go? Her hands clasped themselves in silent prayer, and again she listened in feverish anxiety.

Finally she heard the sound of wheels. She placed Frida, still asleep, softly upon the bed, and was about to go down, when Clement came hastily upstairs, and in another instant was in the room, and before her question was

"Oh heaven!" cried Fleurange. "My presentiment of sad tidings was indeed true!"

"Sad tidings truly," said Clement, and, in spite of himself, he seemed for an instant suffocated by emotion too violent to be controlled.

Fleurange looked at him. There must be something more in this than his grief at their uncle's death.

"Clement! what else is it? Tell me all, I implore you!"

"Yes, Gabrielle," he rejoined, resuming with an effort his calm and gentle manner. "Yes, I will tell you all. Listen, or rather read for yourself."

Fleurange took the paper which he offered her, and read as follows:

"MY FATHER:

"I have misused your confidence. I have employed your name, of which you gave me the use, to hide my losses from you; and in the hope of retrieving them, I have made one desperate venture. If I had succeeded, all would have been saved. I have failed. Ruin falls, not upon us only, but upon all whose fortune is in our hands. Adieu, you will never see me again. I shall not kill myself. About that, have no uneasiness, I will not be so cowardly. But there are lands where those who seek death, may find it. I hope to have this good fortune. May I expiate what I cannot repair!

"FELIX."

Fleurange was silent; pity united to the repulsion, now so fully justified, which she had always felt for Felix, and she had not a word to say.

"This letter," went on Clement, "imprudently given to my uncle this morning, brought on an attack of the disease to which he has been subject, and, perhaps happily for him, it proved fatal, so that he can scarcely be said to have known what the blow really was that struck him."

Fleurange herself indeed scarcely understood it. "But where is Felix?" she asked.

"He has been gone for a fortnight."

"For a fortnight!" she repeated, with a painful remembrance of their last interview.

"He left the city the day after Clara was married."

"But," she said, "that evening he spoke of an abyss; he asked me to save him. Good heavens, Clement," she

band, have saved him? Was it possible, if I had sacrificed myself, to have spared this misfortune, this ruin to you all?"

"No! The fearful appeal to chance which followed that evening had become his sole resource for safety. Why did he speak to you like that? Was it cruelty, or was it madness? I must believe he was mad. No doubt he loved you, but "— he hesitated, and then resumed with decision, "listen to me, Gabrielle, I will tell you what perhaps it might be better to conceal, only that I must justify myself, and that I ought to reassure you; and, as for him, I can no longer spare Felix;—I despise him," and Clement's eyes flashed fire, "because he sought to render me despicable like himself; because he played the accursed part of tempter towards me, who was but a child to him; because, if he could have done so, he would have drawn me with him into that fatal road whose end he has at last reached. So, my cousin, if he had succeeded in winning you, I knew him to be so utterly unworthy that I should have told you in time, for I should have remembered that you had called me brother; to denounce him was a hateful task, and oh, how glad I was to know that you had saved yourself! But now I have told you, to spare your self-reproach, and to let you know how groundless it was."

"I thank you for it; tell me again, Clement,—tell me, as in the presence of God—I need not blame myself for this?"

"Upon my honor, you need not. Believe me, I tell you the truth."

We have already said that Clement possessed a degree of firmness and good sense, which gave him great ascendency with others. When one has this by nature, circumstances mature it rapidly, and a day will often suffice to bring its complete development. For Clement, this day had now come, and henceforth no one would have dreamed of calling him again a boy.

XI.

Ruin! the word is very positive, yet very vague. The idea which it presents to the mind, though clear enough in itself, includes a crowd of ill-defined consequences which sometimes alarm even more than present ills; sometimes offer quite groundless hopes. This condition is aggravated when such a misfortune falls upon one who, by nature averse to affairs and inclined to thought and to study, has been all his life exempt from any need of acquiring business habits. Such was the nature, and such had been, till now, the position of Professor Ludwig Dornthal. Of all possible misfortunes the one which had just fallen upon him was that which he had least expected, and he lacked the capacity to understand, even more than the courage to endure it. The word ruin, also, can be taken in a comparative sense which makes it less severe, and thus did the professor understand it. He accordingly waited with a certain tranquillity and almost indifference, while Clement, aided by Wilhelm Müller, undertook the arrangement of all the disordered affairs of the banking-house.

Inexperienced though he was, the promptness and sagacity of Clement were a source of endless consolation to the head clerk.

Seeing him so ready to understand, and so firm to decide and to act, Wilhelm Müller cried despairingly in the midst of their frightful discoveries:

"Alas! alas! if only your unhappy cousin could have had your head on his shoulders!"

"My head! it's by no means so good as his," Clement said once. "Oh, no! that was not it; something else was lacking in his case. If I only had his ability! Perhaps I might be able to retrieve our fortunes if I had his head; as it is, all my talent is to know how to endure poverty. Oh, if I alone had it to suffer, how little anxiety would it occasion me!"

"Poverty!" Wilhelm said; "but you have understood what I explained to you about that?"

"About my uncle's creditors?"

"Yes, you perceive that your father is really one of the creditors, and the principal creditor in fact, and that a very large part of his fortune will be saved?"

"Yes, but at the expense of the others!"

"Not at their expense, for his rights are the same as theirs. He was not associated with his brother, but only

Clement said nothing for a few minutes. At last he resumed: "The total abandonment of my father's rights will reimburse perfectly all the creditors without exception, will it not?"

"Yes, all."

"And not one debt will be left?"

"Not one debt, and not one penny."

Clement took a paper which lay on the table, and read it through again with great attention.

"Yes," he said, rising, "I understand it perfectly. And now, Wilhelm, it is nearly four o'clock, and they are expecting me at home. In the evening I will see you again, and we will arrange matters definitely."

This conversation had taken place in a basement-room at the house of the banker which had for many years served as an office for the head-clerk, and now Wilhelm Müller clasped the young man's hand cordially, and the latter took his leave.

It was the hour of dinner, and his parents were expecting him. The habits of the household were resumed; in real life the sad routine of the day is taken up again very quickly, even though it has been disturbed by the most overwhelming affliction, and this external regularity, painful though it be, in contrast with the grief which has transformed all within, aids in restoring composure and, with it, courage and the strength to act.

The hour was past by more than fifteen minutes. Clement, who knew his father's exact habits, came straight to the dining-room when he reached home, knowing that the repast must have commenced; and finding it so, with a word of apology, he took his seat and ate his dinner silently.

The spacious and beautiful dining-room where they were now assembled was one of the most cheerful apartments in the house. Old and precious porcelain, ranged on *étagères*, lighted up the sombre panels, as did also the old portraits, originals and of great value, which formed a precious part of the professor's collection. The windows were open into the garden. The delicious verdure offered repose to the eye, the perfume from the flowers reached

service shone in the sunlight. An air of tranquil and opulent security pervaded everything.

Clement raised his eyes, and these objects, which he had seen every day from childhood, produced a new impression upon his mind. He observed to-day many a detail that had long escaped his notice, but this examination had not the effect of distracting his thoughts; on the contrary, it seemed to make them even more sad, and he was absorbed in reverie when his little sister's voice struck his ear.

"Papa," she said, "next week we are going to the sea-shore?"

"Yes, my child."

"And then we shall go and see Hilda?"

"Yes; next month she is expecting us."

"And then?"

"Oh, then we shall come home. After two months of absence, it will be quite time, I think?"

And, in fact, the professor had never been so long away from his dear abode.

These few words brought to Clement's face such an expression of pain that his mother noticed it, and her look questioned him. But Clement lowered his eyes, and dared not raise them till the sad meal was ended, and then his mother said, "Clement, I should like to speak to you," and he followed her into the garden.

"Come," she said, leading him to a remote seat, "now tell me all about it."

"Yes mother,—dear mother! It is to you that I submit the sentence which it seems to me my honor and my conscience have passed. It is from you that I am to learn if we can escape, or if we must undergo it all."

He began his story, and while she listened attentively, and without once interrupting him, he explained to his mother, in detail, the situation in which the death of his uncle and his cousin's flight had placed them. Madame Dornthal, more habituated than her husband to the details

wealthy than before; they might have to undergo very considerable privations; they would be forced to economize at a thousand points; these had been her ideas; but all these were not trials beyond her strength. Not less frequently than her husband had she too repeated that, in the calamity which had fallen upon them, the loss of money was nothing.

Now she understood that this loss was something, and was something serious, almost as much so as death, for it was the end of life, under the aspect that life had worn for her for twenty years, which she must now meet and accept in a single hour.

But the brave mother did not hesitate. She kissed her son. "Thank God," she said, "who has given me such a boy! Yes, Clement, oh yes! you are right, a thousand times over!"

"So, mother, you think as I do. The ruin of the Dornthals shall cause no other ruin?"

"No, my child!"

"Our name shall remain without reproach, and no one in the world shall have cause to curse it!"

"Oh, no, Clement; come what may!"

"Come what may!" repeated Clement, firmly; "thanks, mother, and now good-bye. I am going; it must be you, not I, who shall give this news to my father."

"Yes, Clement, it is I who must do it!"

She brushed back her son's heavy hair with her two hands, and looked at him an instant in deep and tender silence. Clement's eyes had never expressed more visibly than at this moment the firmness, the loyalty, the energy of his soul. "Yes," she thought, "of all those who have done grand deeds, and won illustrious names in this world, none had ever a braver and nobler heart than you, my child! God be praised! Your life shall be blessed, even though all that you might be, all the strength that is in you, remains hid, and is never known save to Him only!"

Such were Madame Dornthal's thoughts, while her mother's glance lingered tenderly upon Clement's face, but she said nothing. Again she kissed him and laid her hand gently upon his head as if in blessing; a few minutes passed in silence, and then Clement lifted his mother's hand reverently to his lips and bade her good-bye, and went away. He remained absent for several hours; it was nearly nine when he came in. His mother herself opened the door for him. "Well," she said, "is all arranged?"

"Yes, mother, all. Only father's signature is needed. He will give it?" said the young man, in a very low voice.

"You cannot doubt," was the reply.

"No; my poor father! but he so little expected this!"

"Yes. I feared no hesitation on his part; but the complete illusion in which he had been living was what gave me anxiety. The effect of this surprise, this shock, was what I dreaded. Oh! Clement, I cannot tell you what terror the recollection of your uncle's fate occasioned me." She ceased, and put her handkerchief to her eyes, but after a moment she added, more cheerfully: "But all is well, only for this evening we will be alone together, he and I. Give me your papers and go, dear child, to be with your brother and your little sister; I have had no time to think of them. Ah! and Gabrielle, poor girl, you must see her and tell her all. We have nothing now to conceal, and least of all from her."

And without waiting for an answer, Madame Dornthal hastily left her son and went to rejoin her husband in the library.

XII.

For a moment Clement stood, thoughtful, hesitating; before obeying his mother's request, he seemed to need a moment to collect his thoughts and to compose himself to his accustomed tranquillity. Master of himself though he seemed, he was very young for emotions such as he had that day undergone. He crossed the hall, hesitated at the stairs, then went beyond, and directly out into the garden. Till this moment he had thought only of his parents; at least, all day he had been feeling that, as soon as his father and mother knew all, and had accepted all, he should breathe freely again, and a great weight would be lifted from his heart. But the terrible revelation had been made and still he was not at peace. His heart throbbed painfully, and he felt the necessity of being in the open air. It was dark and cloudy overhead as Clement emerged into the garden, but it seemed to suit him well, and he walked the whole length of the path, then turned and paced slowly back towards the house, intending to go and find his cousin and the children, when a voice near him said " Clement ! "

" Gabrielle ! and all alone ! "

Fleurange was sitting on a bench placed against the wall of the house.

" Yes, I have been here an hour. You will tell me all that has occurred, will you not? Sit down a minute, and tell me; do not conceal anything from me now."

" That was not my intention, Gabrielle; but let us go in now, and when the children are asleep we will talk about it more fully."

" The children are already asleep, Clement; they have been so for an hour. The poor children, do you think they could keep awake till now—it is nearly ten o'clock. After dinner I took them out here, that they might disturb no one; by eight, they were tired, so I went upstairs with them, and as soon as they had fallen asleep I came down here to wait for you."

She might have talked for a much longer time, and her cousin would not have interrupted her. When she stopped, he said nothing. At last: " Thanks, Gabrielle," he murmured, " you are"—and again he stopped, for a grasp of iron seemed to be on his throat, and he felt that he should sob like a child, if he tried to speak.

With all his masculine energy, with his gravity and courage, it was a very tender heart, this of our poor Clement's! He had not lacked for firmness all the long day. Why did it seem to abandon him thus suddenly? whence came it that after having measured bravely all the results of the resolution which he had been the first to take and to propose; after having hesitated neither at the sight of his parents nor of his brothers and sisters, he was now frightened, and, as it were, overwhelmed at the thought of the completed sacrifice and of the great change that their life was about to undergo? Why?—he could not tell himself, for he was very far from understanding all that had been going on in that fairy-land of dreams, towards which the tendency of his own character and his mind, whose inner and silent recreation was found in a poetical world, strangely inclined him. Everybody knew that he had an excellent memory and knew by heart a great amount of poetry, but no one dreamed how truly poetical was his soul. Into that secret interior life of his no one, not even his mother, had penetrated. Clement's aptitude for science and history, for the positive in studies and in life, as well as his skill for the thousand things, little and great, in which he excelled, served moreover to conceal this other half of his nature. You would count on him to take good care of a horse, to set straight an account, to give a lesson in mathematics and history, to plan a party of pleasure, or a journey; these were well-known gifts of his. But the idea that he could wander into the region of poetry and imagination, there be absorbed, there lost, and pass in silence a large part of his life in that unknown land of which he never spoke; all this was ignored even by those who knew him best, and perhaps he paid but little attention, as we have said, to this habit of his own, for the very reason that, till now, dream and reality had never rudely come into collision with each other. But suddenly he perceived that, in this ideal world he had built an asylum, a palace, a throne, which he must be resigned to see cast down and broken to pieces with the rest; and the courage which had helped him to endure in all its extent the material ruin of his fortunes, failed him utterly in the presence of this ruin of his enchanted domain.

Fleurange, seeing that her cousin made no reply, waited, at first, quietly, then said, with a degree of impatience: "Come, Clement, I beg you do not keep me any longer in suspense! Of what are you afraid? I am not a child, I am even older than yourself, and I have learned long ago what is meant by trouble and affliction. Speak frankly and fearlessly; nothing can alarm me."

The energy of Fleurange revived that of her cousin, and restored to him composure and self-control. He no longer hesitated, but in a few words told her all that he had before communicated to his mother. She now learned in her turn the whole extent of the misfortune that had fallen upon them. She understood that all would be made good, the family name and honor preserved intact, but that the professor would be utterly and hopelessly ruined.

"And your father and your mother have consented to relinquish their rights?"

"Yes, without hesitation."

"Oh, dear and noble hearts!" cried Fleurange, clasping her hands in a sort of rapture. "And was it you who counselled this?"

"Yes."

"Clement, oh, my dear Clement, truly I love you as I have never before loved you!"

"Gabrielle," said Clement, in a low voice, "do not say that to me!"

"But why not," cried Fleurange, "since I feel it, and since it is true?"

"Because—because, though we blame those who are not loyal to honor and duty, there is no. reason why we should praise those who are only faithful!"

"All the same, my dear cousin; if I love you more than ever, you ought not to blame me for telling you of it; still, I will do it no more, since I displease you."

Then followed a moment of silence. Fleurange was thinking deeply. She resumed, in a sad tone: "Now that I understand all, I see how life must change for us."

"Yes, absolutely and completely," said Clement, with a dull anguish.

"This dear old house," Fleurange went on, "must we leave it?"

"Yes," replied Clement, "it must be sold, with all that it contains, for all that my father will have in beginning life anew will be the proceeds of this sale."

"To leave this house," said Fleurange slowly, "yes, I understand that it must be so, and then we must separate!"

"Oh, why, why must that be?" cried Clement with sudden eagerness, and then he added, more slowly: "True, my dear cousin, we should be very selfish to wish to keep you with us, when poverty is all that we can share with you."

"Clement," cried Fleurange, "that is unkind and unjust in you: have I deserved it?" She hesitated an instant, and then went on in a tone of the deepest feeling: "What! when I was face to face with poverty, with misery, with hanger, yes, Clement, positively hunger, your father remembered me. He sent for me, he made me at home, he gave me not only the happiness I had known before, but a thousandfold greater happiness than I had ever dreamed of. He gave me a father, when I no longer had one, a mother, sisters and brothers, that I had never possessed before. Life, youth, joy, all these words had been a blank to me: under this roof, I have learned to know their meaning, and now—now," she said, while the tears which she could not restrain interrupted her words, "it is his son, the son of this Ludwig Dornthal, who tells me that it is to fly from the misfortunes of his family that I propose to leave them!"

"Gabrielle! Gabrielle!" cried Clement, agitated in his turn, "pardon me, be merciful, stop, I implore you,—you will make me lose my reason if you address such words to me!"

Fleurange calmed herself by degrees, and soon forced herself to smile, while the great tears filled her eyes. "My poor Clement," she said, "it is permitted me this evening neither to praise nor to blame you. Very good, let us speak no more of ourselves. What I was going to say was this, that we can no longer remain idle. The dear parents," she continued, "we must aid them as best we can, and work for them!"

"Work? I shall, of course," said Clement, "but you, Gabrielle, there is no sense in that!"

"Indeed I must," replied Fleurange tranquilly. "We will think it over. I shall hope not only to be no longer an expense to them, but also to aid them in some small degree. Oh, I shall be so glad to do it; I thank Heaven that I may have the happiness of doing something at last for those to whom I owe all things. The thought almost saves me from sadness." She rose and held out to him her hand. "Good-night, cousin, to-morrow I will tell you what dreams the good angels bring me."

He took her hand silently, and she left him, without his saying a word.

The night was cloudy. During all the conversation that had taken place, if Clement had been able to see his cousin's features, it was because, himself favored by the shadow, and seated so near her, he had dared to watch her more closely than he would otherwise have done. And now, left alone under the darkening sky, himself secure from all observation, he buried his face in his hands, and gave way to the tears which seemed two hours before to suffocate him—tears of regret, of tenderness, which he could no longer control!

Ere long, however, he conquered this violent emotion, and rose to his feet, half-ashamed of his weakness. At this moment he heard a window open just above his head; it was Fleurange, and directly she came out upon the balcony. He saw plainly her white dress, and the regular contour of her face, outlined against the lighted background of the room; he saw her glance lose itself in the sombre darkness. She clasped her hands and bent her head. She was praying; all unknown to herself, she did not pray alone. On his knees in the shadow, Clement prayed with her; the place was precisely the same in which he had stood on the day when Fleurange said to Felix these words: "Clement is my brother, and you are not so!" He remembered it now, and renewed in his heart the solemn promise of being forever faithful to all that these words could imply.

XIII.

If, a month earlier, some prophet could have made known to the happy inmates of the Old House that they had now but a few weeks more to pass within its walls, this prediction would have caused them all the greatest distress, and each would have asked himself how a trial such as this could be endured. But, in even the most prosperous life, when it is in perfect order, that is to say when the duties of every day are recognized and faithfully performed, there is a latent preparation for the rudest shocks of adversity, and if indeed the day for enduring them does come, one is surprised to find that they who seemed, more than others, to know how to enjoy their good fortune, know also, with more firmness and serenity than others, how to resign it.

The trial exists, notwithstanding. It comes upon them with all its weight, but it comes alone, and unaccompanied

by those two scourges that always follow where misconduct
has preceded misfortune—ill-temper and confusion.

Neither of these evils came in, with ruin, here. Externally, the disaster was complete; within, peace and order were maintained. All decisions, however vigorous, were made calmly, and executed without haste and without delay. They did not disguise from themselves the greatness of the sacrifice which was laid upon them; they affected not an insensibility which they did not feel, but, though often with tearful eyes, they made their preparations tranquilly, as a good and valiant crew might do, if forced by shipwreck to abandon their vessel.

Thus all the necessary arrangements were made for removal from their dear home, for the sale of nearly all those books and pictures gathered by the professor with so much care and pride, and of those collections which had been his only amusement outside the cherished circle of family and friends.

From friends, too, must they now separate! When Ludwig Dornthal had announced his intention of resuming the career which, twenty years earlier, he had relinquished, proposals were made him from all sides, and chiefly from the city in which he lived. But the considerations of strict economy which must henceforth rule his life, to which were added a secret repugnance to change his position suddenly in a city where he had been so prosperous, determined him to leave Frankfort. After some hesitation, he decided to accept a modest post which was offered him in the University of Heidelberg.

Here he was able to purchase a little house, almost a cottage, it is true, but outside the city gates, on the banks of the Neckar, and surrounded by a garden. Thence he could easily go every day to the University, and the prospect of this country repose at the close of the laborious day would aid him to meet the fatigue with less discomfort. It was then decided that he should go, with his family, and establish himself there as soon as possible. Such was the plan on which he finally settled, and whose details would be arranged by degrees in the few weeks that must elapse before they should leave the Old House forever.

Clement assumed the care of preparing for the ver-

considerable sale which was to take place ; it was his wish to spare his father this sad work and to accomplish it alone, but he found himself unexpectedly aided, for Fleurange would not allow him to refuse her energetic assistance. With him she began upon the task, silently coming and going with sleeves rolled up ; her safe and steady hands moved the porcelains, arranged them, numbered them ; brought out the books in obedience to her cousin's orders, and in a thousand ways lightened his tasks ; then, in the evening, they established themselves together in the despoiled library and wrote out and copied lists, and in great catalogues inserted notes relative to the precious books and manuscripts that were about to disappear.

It was indeed an occasion that demanded the strength and activity of youth, as well as much reflection and assiduity. To say that, while thus employed, they were not sometimes fatigued, their eyes were not sometimes wet, as they handled so many objects which they should never see again, would be untruthful ; but it would be much more so to assert that Clement, despite this severe labor, felt himself, during that week, a person to be pitied.

There came indeed a day in the future when, recalling this time, it seemed to him that those hours when he saw his cousin's lovely head bent over the great catalogue, her sweet eyes now and then lifted to question him or to give him a friendly glance,—it seemed to him, I say, that these vanished hours were among the most beautiful of his life !

Finally the task approached its completion ; that day it would be finished, and they were at work together for the last time, when Fleurange looked up.

"Clement," she said, "this will very soon be done ; I have kept till this moment a secret which I have to tell you."

Clement stopped short in his work, and questioned her with a look.

"No, no," she said, "finish what you are doing, and then I will tell you."

Clement's employment was soon ended, and then Fleurange shut her great book, and resumed :

"You remember our conversation in the garden, a fortnight ago?"

"Yes, certainly I do."

"Well, after I left you, I spent the night in thinking, and finally I decided to write to the best friend I have outside this house, the only friend, indeed."

"Dr. Leblanc?" said Clement, who, of course, knew his cousin's history.

"Yes, Dr. Leblanc. I told him all that I had learned from you. I explained what the situation of my uncle and his family would be, and what an ardent desire I felt, not only to be no longer an expense to them, but to be able to fulfil towards them a daughter's duty. Their own children have other duties; they are married; as for me, I have only this, and it is so dear, so dear," said Fleurange in that voice of hers which sometimes would send her most simple words to the very bottom of the listener's heart, "that I should esteem my life happy and well employed could I consecrate myself wholly to it!"

Clement bent his head and took up a pen, as if to correct the figures of a sum on the page before him; she must not see, in his face, the effect of her words,—ah no! she must not!

"Well," he said, after a minute, "what reply did you receive from Dr. Leblanc?"

"Here is the letter, which came two days ago."

Clement took the letter, and as he read, he felt suddenly the same anguish that had seized upon him after the conversation in the garden to which Fleurange had referred.

It cost him a violent effort to control himself, and not to tear into a thousand pieces the letter he held in his hand. He succeeded, happily, for the act would have been the most insane that he had ever committed.

Nothing in the letter justified this furious passion. It ran thus:

"MY DEAR YOUNG FRIEND:

"I cannot tell you how much I am filled with admiration and with regret at the sad recital you have given me. I have long known what a man your uncle was, but I see to-day that, even among the best, there are few that resemble him, and I was never so eager as now to clasp his hand and to see him face to face. You know that such has long been my desire and my intention,—but it is now probable that I shall accomplish it sooner than I supposed, and this brings me to the second portion of your letter.

"I understand your wish, and very gladly will assist you. Besides, I have not forgotten that I promised to aid you in gaining a livelihood, if ever it should be needful. Poor child! I hoped indeed that I should never be called upon to keep this promise. But, since it is so, I ought to tell you of a letter I received only yesterday, and which, coinciding thus with your own, seems to me like a Providential indication. This letter comes from one of my patients, a Russian lady, Princess Catherine Lamianoff, who is now in Munich, where she begs me to come and see her. I have formerly attended her, and with success, and from what she tells me I believe my presence will be useful to her now. I have decided to go and spend a fortnight with her. I shall then see you, for I shall take Frankfort on my route. But first I must explain what there is of interest for you in this letter. The Princess begs me urgently to find for her a young girl of good education, and having distinguished manners, who will consent to assume the duties of her *demoiselle de compagnie*. She is much depressed, she is ill, and your residence with her will give you, not only lucrative employment, but also an opportunity to do an act of Christian charity. But in less than a week we will talk this over. Meanwhile, depend always, as you have a right to do, upon my sincere and affectionate devotion. I give you no message from my sister, who will write by the same post a long letter in agreement with the above.

"P. S.—The Princess is a widow. She has been married twice. She is very rich, and offers to the young lady whom I am to find for her, the sum of a hundred and fifty *louis* a year."

Clement was silent for a while. "And you propose to accept such an offer as that?" he said, in a tone of irritation, singularly in contrast with his habitual gentleness. "How foolish!"

"No," said Fleurange quietly, "it is not foolish. If, in conversation with Dr. Leblanc, I see no reason for declining this situation, it is impossible to see why it would be foolish to accept it!"

"Gabrielle, you must see," cried Clement in the same tone, "that this part which you propose to undertake is simply insupportable. It is my duty, and mine only, to work for my parents, my brothers and sisters and you. If you had the slightest friendship for me, you would understand that this is a favor that I ask of you, and which you have not the right to refuse me."

"Let us talk reasonably about it, Clement," said Fleurange. "When the sale shall have ended, and your parents are established in their little new home at Heidelberg, you know that the slender means which your father can command, and even what you can add to it yourself, will hardly be enough for them to live comfortably, with Frida. You will remain at Frankfort, where, young though you are, you have the choice among several employments. But Fritz?—have you forgotten what we said yesterday? Will you be able to send him to that good school of which we were speaking? No, Clement, you know that you cannot do it. While," she continued, with animation, "if this lady should be pleased with me, all except a very small portion of the sum which I receive shall be sent to my dear brothers. Fritz shall go to school, and my good aunt will be reassured not only on my account but on his. Oh see, Clement, I should be a thousand times happier thus parted from you (even though this princess should treat me like a slave) than with you, useless, idle, and contributing by my presence to your difficulties!"

Clement, his elbow on the table, his head upon his hand, remained silent.

"Come, come, do not be so displeased, my good Clement," said Fleurange in a caressing tone, and taking his hand in her own. "We shall see each other, like the school-children, in vacations. We shall reassemble every little while there by the Neckar. That will still be our home, our domestic hearth, and on *fête* days we shall gather there."

What could poor Clement say?—how frame any objections? Must he not forever deny himself the words he had hoped one day to speak? Was he not henceforth condemned to rude daily labor. Had not his life henceforth one only end, from which he must not swerve? And had it been otherwise, was he anything in her eyes but a boy? Had he not felt all the time that his dream-happiness must vanish at the first breath of reality?

He took his cousin's slender hand in both his own, and looked up simply, cordially, and naturally.

"Gabrielle," he said, "you are right; I seem ungrateful, but I am not so. God reward you! you are an angel!" And he added, so low that she did not hear him, "An angel, from whom I am more removed than from those in the skies!"

XIV.

From this time forth, Clement seemed no longer to take any interest in his cousin's project; at least, he never alluded to it, and it was discussed in his presence without his taking part in the conversation.

Madame Dornthal, capable herself of any act of self-sacrifice, was capable of the generosity, no less real, and far rarer, of accepting the sacrifice of another. She well understood the character of Fleurange, and would have been very far from depriving the latter of a joy the most exquisite that such a heart could know.

"Dear child," she said, clasping Fleurange in her arms, "yes; I accept the aid you offer us, and I thank you for it. Yes, thanks to you, I am spared much anxiety, and if Dr. Leblanc can reassure me in regard to my Gabrielle's happiness, I shall let her go without a word, that she may follow the generous impulses of her heart."

But Madame Dornthal communicated to her husband only another motive for her consent. "She will thus escape many of the privations of our new life. She will continue to enjoy the prosperity we could no longer give her. She will enjoy far more absent from us than with us, now, poor child!"

"Yes," the professor said, "it would have been indeed a pity to shut up such a young girl in a hovel; that would pain me! How many times in the past month have I rejoiced that our dear daughters are saved this! And yet," added the poor father, sighing, "it makes one so happy to see these young faces!"

"We shall see them soon, Ludwig. Hilda and Karl await us, and Clara will come in the winter, for they have engaged Julian to do a great deal in the neighborhood of Heidelberg. Oh, Ludwig! since Providence has left us so much, let us relinquish, not only without murmurs, but without regret, that which is taken from us."

Those who dream only of enriching themselves, and make this their sole affair, are no more than others secure from ruin. One may even assert that it is they whom misfortune visits most frequently. Would it not then be well to reflect a little in advance upon those conditions which can wondrously modify the features of this severe guest, and give him the aspect which now he takes under the roof of the Dornthals? True it is that for this, one must have cared for many other things than money-getting

Dr. Leblanc came, as he had promised, about ten days after his letter. His first interview with the inmates of the Old House was coincident with the last days they were to pass within its walls, and this circumstance would have made him hesitate to come, had he not been so cordially urged by the professor. For some time, they had desired to know each other, for each was, in his own sphere, a famous man; and besides this, the young girl, who had by turns owed to each of them so many obligations, served as a bond of sympathy between them. The doctor was therefore received by the uncle of Fleurange as quite other than a stranger; the tendency of their minds, the nature of their studies, and even the salient traits of their characters, were most unlike, and yet, all things rested on the same foundation with both, and through different roads they attained the same end. They ascertained at once, then, that although life, for both, had come to its decline without having brought them the accident of an interview, they had been born intimate friends.

How many friends, unknown, thus pass all their lives without meeting each other, and without suspecting the sympathies that unite them! Who knows how many ties of this sort will be discovered in heaven? Who knows if this discovery may not be one of the sweetest joys of the other life, granted more largely, perhaps, to those who, upon earth, have been most completely deprived of it!

The hospitable house was closed; the library shelves were empty, the panelled walls were despoiled of their costly and noble adornment. All was now humiliation and sacrifice, where all so lately had been content and enjoyment, and yet, it is probable that Dr. Leblanc would not have experienced so heartfelt a sensation of respect and affection, had he visited the Dornthals for the first time in the days of their prosperity.

On their side, this new friend seemed to have always held among them the place which now he occupied; and spite of the sadness of the present and of the future, Fleurange, on the eve of quitting all these friends of hers, enjoyed no less the satisfaction of seeing them united for a moment, and counted her last days spent under this roof no less happy than the rest had been.

Madame Dornthal had gathered nothing from her conversations with Dr. Leblanc of a nature to deter Fleurange from carrying out her plans. She learned that the residence of the Princess Catherine in Munich would be only temporary; that she had merely lingered there on her return from the baths, where she had passed the summer, and that she was on her way to Florence, where she owned a winter residence.

After the exchange of a few letters it was decided that Fleurange should accept the offers of the Princess, and should set out for Munich with the doctor. She would thus have the double advantage of her old friend's protection on the journey, and of his presence with her during the first days of her new career.

Meantime the days fled sadly and rapidly, and the last that they were to spend in the Old House quickly came. The last day in which their eyes could rest on those old walls, witnesses of all the happiness of the past; and this garden, and this green lawn, and these brilliant flower-beds, and these great shady alleys, where neither next spring, nor in any future spring-time, should they come to seek the dear mementoes of departed days!

Clement, silent as he often was, but with an agitation very unusual to him, was hurriedly collecting the few books that would on the morrow form part of their modest luggage. His cousin's generous offer enabled him at once to place Fritz according to his wishes, but thus he was to be still more completely alone, and though the presence of a child would be a certain care to a young man, Clement dearly loved his little brother, and had promised himself much comfort in keeping the boy with him. Now Clement had to decide upon his own future, and he made promptly the hardest choice and the one least suited to his taste, yet which offered him the prospect of being able to aid his parents at the earliest possible moment. Wilhelm Müller had suggested to him to enter a great commercial house where the intelligent and upright clerk had himself found a position similar to that which he had formerly occupied with the banker. The arrangement had been made, and though Clement's salary was at first extremely small, he had the prospect of its increase, from year to year. "And who can tell, Herr Clement," said Wilhelm, "you may some day become a partner in this house, and perhaps you may live to be as rich, as happy and prosperous as it was your original destiny to be!"

Nothing in Clement's heart responded to these encouraging presages. But none the less did he follow the advice of Müller, and he accepted furthermore the offer of the good clerk to rent to him a little room in his own house.

"My poor Herr Clement," said Wilhelm, "what I offer you is little better than an attic, but it is under our roof, and you will feel that you have friends near you; my Bertha is a good housewife, you will find her always ready to serve you, and the little ones, if they are sometimes rather noisy, will perhaps divert you from your sad thoughts."

"That is good," rejoined Clement; "your offer suits me perfectly, and I thank you with all my heart, Wilhelm." And thus the matter was arranged.

Fleurange made her appearance in the library, while Clement was busily packing his books. She came and stood by him, and by degrees, in reply to her questions, he told her all that had passed, not forgetting the good clerk's offer of a room.

"Oh! that is good," cried Fleurange; "they are excellent people, the Müllers; I know this amiable little Bertha. You must speak to her of me."

And, the name of Bertha at once suggesting the reminiscences of Fleurange's journey, they were soon talking about her arrival on Christmas Eve, the midnight service at the church, the next day's dinner-party, and all the other happy days that had followed. There was at this moment in these recollections something too poignant and tender. Fleurange soon ceased to speak, turned her head away, and took a few steps to go out, but stopped on the sill and remained leaning against the garden-window now all hung with honey-suckle. Clement drew near her, and both silently looked out into the garden, lighted by the last rays of the setting sun.

Nothing was wanting to the sad beauty of this evening; the air was never so sweet, the sky so pure, the flowers so perfumed; all things wore an unwonted loveliness to the eyes of those who looked for the last time at scenes so dear to them.

And Fleurange! how did she seem to him who knew that perhaps never again after this evening should he see her, as then she was! What did he think of the golden light on that pure brow and soft black hair? of the pale azure of those eyes, sometimes so laughing or so tender, now grave and sad, yet where feeling was conquered by the victorious will?

What were his silent thoughts we shall not say. Not less than Fleurange was he endowed with that union of gentleness and strength which makes the highest charm of any character, and that which he felt that he must conceal in his heart he could well prevent his lips from telling, or even his eyes betraying by a single glance.

So he stood quietly at her side, while his heart was a prey to that agony of suffering which, while one is young, seems to change the very aspect of nature, and render it impossible to live.

"To-morrow, to-morrow, I shall no longer see her!" he repeated to himself, with the sensation one might have in feeling the edge of the steel that shall take one's life; and with the thought, he lost even the power of enjoying the moments which were left him.

And Fleurange was thinking of the fatality which always removed her from those she loved. She recalled the day when only the thought that she might some time leave this home had caused her so sad a feeling. And now this prophetic pain was justified! the fearful dream had become a reality. One sad thought followed another through her mind. One instant later and they would have been uncontrollable, all her firmness would have melted away in a flood of tears, but an effort of her will triumphed over this emotion, or at least prevented its manifestation.

She raised her head, and waking from her reverie she turned to her cousin.

She took it, and wrote: "*To Clement.*"

"A word more," Clement said; "please write a line, a verse if you will, from our dear poet."

"What verse shall it be?" she said, turning the leaves of the book.

"Here, this one, in the second song." He pointed it out to her, and she wrote it, then read:

"To Clement:
"L'amico mio e non della Ventura."
(" My friend, not Fortune's friend.")

"That is right, thanks!" Clement said.

"The verse is sad; I would have chosen differently."

"It is well chosen for the day; now, your name."

As she was about to write, he stopped her. "Your true name," he said; "write there, this once, the other name that is yours,—the name that suits you so well,—Fleurange!"

Fleurange smiled, and shook her head.

"Oh, no!" she said; "I might have spared myself the pain of relinquishing it, and, if I had known you all before I came, I should never have thought of giving it up, but I have been so happy since I have borne the name of Gabrielle (and it was you, Clement, who first called me so), so happy! that I no longer love this other name of my sad days, and now if I should hear any one call me Fleurange, I should feel as if it brought me misfortune!"

Clement made no reply, and when she returned him the book, he held it for a moment in his hand.

"One word, Gabrielle," he said, "and it may be the last before you go. Wherever you may be, if you at any time have need of a friend,—a friend, understand me, to whom nothing will be any sacrifice, for your sake,—do not forget that your poor brother would thus devote himself, not only without effort, but with a happiness that you cannot understand!"

Clement's voice was very grave and solemn as he said these words, but they were so in harmony with all that Fleurange had become accustomed to expect from him that she was touched, but not surprised, by what he said.

"Yes, Clement," she answered simply looking at him

not a better friend in the world, than you, and I think I never shall have."

Were they sweet to him, or bitter, these words of hers? He could not tell. It was alike impossible to increase or alleviate the sadness that overwhelmed him. And yet, she still was standing near him, in all her calm and serene confidence. He had not in his heart a single sentiment that he would not share with her. She called him her friend, and knew no other in the world whom she would prefer to him! The moments, full of suffering as they were to him now, were precious, and later he reproached himself that he had not been more appreciative of them.

It was their last conversation in the Old House. Clement kept, in memory of it, the little book that she had given him, and a bit of honeysuckle that had rested against her hair.

The rest of the evening went quickly by, and in the morning, shortly after day-break, came the moment for adieu!—the moment, for the Dornthals, when they should leave their dear dwelling, hopeless of ever returning to it again; for Fleurange, of separating from all those whom she loved, and making a new step in life, more uncertain a thousandfold than the last; for Clement, of remaining alone, and supporting, as his courage could best teach him how, solitude, severe and distasteful labor, the deprivation of all the affection and the enjoyments of his childhood, and, above all, the endurance of whatever love and grief together can lay upon a heart of twenty years.

II.—THE TRIAL.

"Era già l'ora che volge il disio
Ai naviganti e intenerisce il core,
Lo di' c'han detto a' dolci amici addio!"
                                            DANTE.

XV.

IT was a beautiful night; brilliant, serene, starry; a night which the moon, now rising, would soon render light as day.

A fresh breeze filled the sails of a vessel just leaving Genoa, and bore it onward with swift and steady course.

Groups of passengers were gathered upon the deck, some talking in low tones, as befitted the twilight—others more loudly, as though it were still broad day.

Some one was playing the guitar, and another person singing to this accompaniment one of those popular airs which in Italy everybody knows, sings or hums, so long as they remain in fashion. The music was ordinary enough, yet it did not seem so, at this time and place, it went so well with the feelings of those who sailed upon this azure sea, under this sparkling sky, in sight of these charming shores, from which the vessel stands off but a little distance while making the short voyage from Genoa to Livorno.

Somewhat removed from all of these groups, and belonging to none of them, we find Fleurange sitting alone. She had come thither but a few moments before, and at first had attracted general notice, for the grace of her figure was not concealed by the cloak she wore, and the *capuchon* which half covered her head only rendered the distinguished beauty of her features more picturesque. So, among her fellow travellers, more than one would have gladly approached the place that she had selected. But, although she was alone, and had not the appearance of being under

attitude, in her evident indifference to the effect which she produced, in the very lack of timidity, which was not boldness, but resolution,—there was in all this an indefinable something which kept at a distance the most ardent admiration, and disconcerted insolence itself. Thus, in spite of many whispers, and more than one look directed towards the charming face upon which now fell the full moonlight, Fleurange remained quiet in her corner, free to give herself up to her own thoughts, without being troubled by any one, and without the least in the world troubling herself about those who were around her.

Various and manifold were the reflections that crowded upon her. A strange fate seemed to pursue her, and to break the thread of her life, each time more and more painfully. She had suffered deeply in leaving Paris, and Dr. Leblanc, and the dear Mlle. Josephine. But how much more bitter were the tears she had shed in leaving the Old House and the dear circle with whom she had known and enjoyed to the utmost the delights of home life!

After parting from them, the firmness of Fleurange, which, till now, had never failed her, seemed suddenly to give way to that degree that Dr. Leblanc resolved secretly to take her back to her family, if, after a few days at Munich, he did not find her more resigned to her fate. But Fleurange was not one to allow herself to be thus defeated, and not soon to find in herself the strength necessary to remain faithful to the part she had assumed. On reaching Munich, her resolution was strengthened by that which would have discouraged many another. They found the Princess Catherine in bed, a victim to one of her most severe attacks of illness, and it was as nurse that Fleurange took her place for the first time in the princess's household.

This illness, in the opinion of physicians, threatened no

make durable the first impression which she would produce, he sincerely hoped, in thus bringing them together, to do a service, not less to his patient, poor for all her wealth, than to his dear young *protégée*.

At all events, nothing could better distract Fleurange from the dull weight of sorrow that rested upon her, than the immediate necessity of forgetting herself, and bestowing active and assiduous cares upon another. Without doubt a series of days and nights passed, almost without repose, at the bedside of an unknown invalid, was but a sad *début* for the young girl's new life; but in the mood in which she found herself, it was the best thing for her in the world. Those qualities which make up the character of the good nurse were possessed by Fleurange to a degree which utterly astonished Dr. Leblanc: firmness, promptness, gentleness and tranquillity in all her movements, strength and skill, readiness,—nothing was wanting, and it followed at once that, to the unfailing effect of her beauty and grace, were added the quick and grateful sympathy which the sick feel for those who know how to relieve their sufferings. The princess did not cease to thank the doctor, and the latter, for his part, well content with his plan, bade adieu to Fleurange without anxiety, auguring the happiest results from the position in which he left her.

Scarcely able to travel, the Princess Catherine was anxious to leave Munich, and by slow stages had reached Genoa. Now she was going to Livorno, and thence to Florence, where she considered it her home, her health having long since obliged her to live out of Russia, or at least to be there only during that short period of the year which claims the title of summer.

Since the time when Fleurange had left her friends, this seemed to be almost the first moment when she had found herself actually alone and at liberty to think without interruption. And her first impulse led her to give herself up unrestrainedly to the dear memory of the absent ones from whom she felt every moment separated by greater and greater distance. It was indeed the hour of which the poet sings—

"The hour that brings the wanderer's thoughts

The thoughts of Fleurange lingered upon the recent past, upon the happy family-group, now scattered; upon the days so few and brief, in which it was permitted to her to make part of it; finally upon her present isolation, for, in spite of the kindness of the princess, she felt herself indeed alone. By a strange change of place, it was she, the unprotected orphan, who seemed to have become the support of her protectress, and it was the great lady, the rich princess, the poor woman, spoiled by fortune, who seemed to seek from her, consolation and solace. Without doubt, the kind heart of Fleurange found an unlooked for satisfaction in thus bestowing attentions whose success was her sole recompense. Indeed, in lavishing them she felt her affection increase for the person who was their object; but it was the sentiment that one feels for a child or for an inferior, rather than that which it would have been natural to entertain towards the person in whose service one is, and to whom one owes respect and obedience. Hence Fleurange felt alone, and the solitude was sad. And yet, in spite of herself, and (contradictory as this may seem) in spite of her melancholy, an irresistible sensation of delight at this moment made her heart beat quick.

Who does not know it? this effect of the beautiful Italian sky upon one who has seen it,—has bidden it adieu and, now, sees it again!—who has now returned, to look with rapture, as at the sight of a dear face, once more upon the gracious and sublime beauty of that glorious land? And, when the ear has been long deprived of it, who can hear again without emotion, the sweet accents of its musical speech? All these impressions Fleurange would be sure to feel. So, as the breeze died away, and the moon climbed the cloudless sky, casting over the sea a train of light which was like a pathway of diamonds, leading to some enchanted country, Fleurange, her eyes fixed upon this brilliant furrow of light, felt herself in a silent ecstasy. All sadness of past or present was effaced; and she felt only the infinite joy of living, of being young, of being there under that sky, upon that sea, near that shore, whose perfumes reached her where she was; and when she remembered that this shore was Italy, that in a few hours she would be there, a confused presentiment of happiness, some poetic vision, added with vague promises to this secret joy with which she felt herself thrilled.

Dreams! half understood dreams of youth! rarely realized in the shape in which they are formed, and which later, as the soul yields to the dangers of life, or is strengthened to resist them, transform themselves into deceiving and fatal realities, or into divine and mighty aspirations!

At this very hour what was Clement doing, as he sat at the window of his attic, and looked, also, at the starry sky? —ah, could he have followed the image which filled his thoughts, he would have been, doubtless, very near her who sailed away from him, cradled in confused dreams. His reverie was sad, but it was not vague or undecided; the future was clearly sketched out in his thoughts. Only twenty years old though he was, he felt himself capable of keeping in his heart, forever unprofaned, one cherished image. Yes, there should she dwell as in a sanctuary; and—after God—to her should be offered up the labor, the study, the poetry, the fidelity of his life! Whatever gifts he had received should be cultivated. The talent given him by the Lord should earn its other ten talents. This should be his intellectual life, after the rude tasks of the day were over. Rude tasks, yet in his eyes sacred, and fulfilled with energetic fidelity, since with him rested his parents' comfort in the future, the repose of their declining days,—and at last! Who could tell if some day— But when the sudden awaking of a forbidden hope made him start; he repressed it. Reflection and reason, a sad and unconquerable presentiment, had long since warned him that this hope was vain. And so, "to keep his love while he crushed his hope" became his sad duty; a task severe, difficult, perhaps impossible. But, at this moment, it was his dream and chimera.

XVI.

"The princess begs Mlle. Gabrielle to come below."

This message, which broke in upon her reverie, was brought to Fleurange by one of the servants of the princess. This lady's suite was composed of a German *valet de chambre*, an Italian courier, and a Russian waiting-woman.

This latter person, named Varinka, belonged literally to the princess, for she was her slave. But Varinka, she

and intelligent, like the Russians of her class, well treated by her mistress, to whom she was faithfully devoted, and wearing the cast-off clothes of the princess, attached to her position no idea whatever of humiliation. In French, she was called *Mlle. Barbe;* in Italian, *la signora Barbara,* and she considered herself, and was considered by others, a person of much elegance. Very exacting towards those beneath her, and jealous of those whom she regarded her equals, she at first proposed to herself to esteem the new *demoiselle de compagnie* of the Princess, as one of the latter; but, unconsciously to herself, Fleurange had known at once how to take the place which belonged to her, and to oblige Mlle. Barbe to assume towards her a respectful attitude. Mlle. Barbe then immediately made up her mind to detest the new-comer, but, after some careful observation, had wit enough not to do it. In truth, while the activity of Fleurange spared her a part of her former duties, and imposed upon her no new ones (for the young girl never desired assistance from any one), her influence was exercised in a manner by which every one profited as much as she did herself. When the princess emerged from those crises in which physical distress annulled for her completely all the comfort which she had taken so much pains to procure for herself, she had but a single thought, and that was, whence come these attacks of illness?—how soon will they return again?—is it possible that they can be prevented? And thus, under the influence of these engrossing ideas, her temper became capricious, uneven, and impossible to please. In this task, no one had ever succeeded so well as Fleurange, and Mlle. Barbe said to herself: "*Au fait,* she has the fatigue, and all the rest of us have the advantage of Madame's good humor!" and this simple process of reasoning decided her to live in peace with the new-comer, while she made the most of the advantages to be derived from the young lady's accommodating disposition. Thus Fleurange, in this enemy whom she had unconsciously disarmed, had given herself an ally, and almost a friend.

To tell the truth, the message of the princess, which arrived to put an end to the young girl's agreeable reverie, came simply and solely from Mlle. Barbe, who, having learned from the courier that it was delightful weather upon deck, had experienced a desire to go herself and take a promenade in the moonlight; and had to this end, forthwith despatched the courier in search of Fleurange, as we have already related. She was quite sure that Mlle. Gabrielle would come below at once, without making any inquiries. This was one of her merits in the eyes of the sagacious maid. "She attends to nobody's affairs but her own, this young girl; that is certainly very agreeable!"

Fleurange did indeed at once relinquish the place which she had chosen in the fresh air, and went down into the ladies' cabin, of which the princess had the exclusive possession. She found the invalid asleep; nevertheless she made no inquiry into the accuracy of the message by which she had been summoned, but quietly sat down, and throwing off the cloak in which she had been wrapped:

"Here, Barbe," she said, "take this cloak, if you like, and go and breathe the fresh air; it is beautiful weather this evening!"

It was by this gracious good humor that, all unawares, she had made the conquest of this person, who was naturally unfriendly towards her, and it was this, more than all her other virtues, which pleased the princess, and transformed into a lasting affection the first caprice which she had taken for the young girl.

The Princess Catherine lay upon a sofa, her head resting on numerous cushions, her feet covered by a magnificent camel's hair shawl. Despite her illness, despite her age, which had altered the outlines both of face and figure, her beauty and grace had not vanished without leaving through all her person those traces of beauty less fleeting than beauty itself. Fleurange, at this moment, watching her face by the light of a hanging lamp, could not but admire the noble brow—the character and yet the remarkable delicacy of the profile. Suddenly, while she thus observed her, with more attention than ever before, it seemed to her that these features awakened in her memory an indistinct recollection—but before she could grasp the thought which seemed to flit across her mind, the princess opened her eyes.

Seeing Fleurange near her, she smiled, and held out her beautiful hand.

"You are here, Gabrielle," she said; "so much the

"I was told you asked for me."

"No; but I am very glad you are here."

Fleurange bent her head, and kissed the hand she held in hers; she had never felt so tenderly towards the invalid before.

The princess seemed touched by it. Without saying a word, she clasped closer the hand of Fleurange. Then she fell asleep once more, while Fleurange remained, her eyes fixed upon her. An hour passed away. The princess still slept, and Fleurange rose and stole softly across the cabin and threw herself upon a sofa to sleep for the few hours that remained before, at break of day, they should arrive at Livorno.

At this period, much earlier than railways, the road from Livorno to Florence, long and dusty, was not always accomplished in a day, and it chanced that our travellers stopped at Pisa to pass the night. The princess, who had long since ceased to take an interest in the cities through which she passed in journeying, cared only to rest, and, once rested, to go on her way. But for Fleurange, it was quite a different thing. Pisa was the place of her birth. Here was buried the mother whom she had never known; here, later, her father had brought her, in the few happy days which they had spent together. What changes, since then, had passed over her young life! what suffering and what happiness had she experienced! what ties had been formed and broken, and at an age, when one thinks usually only of the future, how much there was for her in the past! Very early in the morning, long before the princess was awake, Fleurange had gone to kneel at her mother's grave. She had then turned her steps towards the Campo Santo, and slowly made the circuit of it; of all the places she had visited with her father, she best remembered this. The pictures of the Campo Santo are like a poem, which one cannot understand till one knows the language in which it is written. But this language her father had taught her, and later, those by whom she had been surrounded in Germany had not suffered her to forget it—this reminded her that her cousin, who had never visited the place, knew every picture almost as well as she herself. How he would have known how to enjoy all this beauty of nature and of art, and all this historic interest! she thought. Poor Clement! how he would have loved Italy!

She might have added that, like many Germans, he loved it already, and knew it before he had seen it,—

"Das Land wo die Citronen blüh'n"—

to them the object of a profound and lasting passion! a passion fatal when they would satisfy it by violence, and at all price possess this land too dearly loved, but destined to be in turn reciprocated when the forced and detested union once broken shall give way to a voluntary and accepted alliance.

Leaving the Campo Santo, Fleurange entered the church, that marvellous cathedral of Pisa that one can compare to no other, for, if there are others more beautiful, one doubts it, or forgets it, when one is there. Fleurange listened to the service, then remained long upon her knees, praying, thinking of all whom she loved, and looking about her without being distracted in so doing. This may seem strange to those who would restrain to a narrow and limited form the impulse of the soul towards God. It is true, however, that for the simple and well-prepared heart, the good resolve, the most ardent impulse of love towards the eternal goodness, all those fruits of prayer which we most earnestly seek, spring often from that which does not seem especially designed to produce them. But where religion and art have clasped hands, and the inspiration which has guided the painter and the architect is the same which leads the faithful to the foot of the altar, a glance cast at a fresco or a painting aids the soul, better than a sermon, to take its flight, and accomplish the act for which it is prostrated before God.

So Fleurange, upon her knees, her book closed in her hands, thought, and looked, and prayed. Among the thoughts floating through her mind was one which, more than the rest, seemed in harmony with what met her eyes: it was that of the cloister of Santa Maria, and the first friend of her childhood, whose face came to her at the moment like that of one of the saintly figures by which she was surrounded. She was beneath the same sky, near enough to her to see her again, perhaps! At this thought, her eyes grew wet with tears, and this remembrance of her childhood soon seemed to rule all the others, and to make her prayer more fervent and more absorbing.

Sweet and saintly Madre Madelina! perhaps at this very hour you were telling God about the child still so dear to you ; perhaps from afar you seconded her prayers, and by your own rendered more effectual those words of every day which Fleurange whispered before she left the church: "Our Father, lead us not into temptation, but deliver us from evil."

XVII.

For the first time since her illness the princess emerged from her languor, and recovered the faculty of speaking of something else than herself. During the latter part of their journey, Fleurange perceived that she knew well how to converse, and that the indifference which she sometimes manifested for things which seemed to her companion most worthy of interest, was not ignorance, but a simple preference for something else. She loved, as well as any one, picture-galleries, churches, works of art, rare collections ; only she liked still better shops where she could obtain for herself some portion of what she admired, and which pleased her best when she could display it as her own. She enjoyed the splendors of the Italian sky, and its delicious climate, which her health obliged her to come so far to seek, but if to these advantages had not been added that of living in a luxurious home, surrounded by elegant society she would have regarded her expatriation as an exile, but faintly alleviated by all the marvels of art and nature with which she might be surrounded.

At last the journey's end was reached. The Princess Catherine alighted at the foot of the magnificent staircase of her palace, and the pleasure of being at home again, banished, as if by enchantment, the very last traces of her recent illness.

Numerous servants relieved Fleurange of the care of the floating luggage with which the princess encumbered her carriage, and, following her protectoress, she ran quickly up the broad marble stairs which led to the first floor.

There, a great vestibule, adorned with statues, gave entrance to a suite of rooms whose splendor surprised

than one palace in Italy comparable to this in its grand proportions, its frescoes, its painted and gilded ceilings, but she had never seen anything equal to the magnificent furniture and the lavish display of the separate rooms which the princess traversed till she reached the last in which she stopped. This *salon*, not so large as the others, opened like the one which preceded it, upon a broad covered terrace, whose roof was painted in fresco; but which, filled with flowers, with rare plants, and also with seats of every form and size, was at once a garden sheltered from the sun, and an elegant ante-room attached to the apartment they had just entered, which was the princess's own room.

A table with fruit, cake, and ices stood ready. The princess threw herself upon a *chaise longue*. "We shall dine late," she said, "give me a biscuit and an ice; and eat some yourself. But first take off your hat, lay aside your travelling-bag; rest,—for it is fearfully warm this noon."

Fleurange obeyed her, and very willingly made a light repast, which the heat of the day rendered extremely acceptable.

While she ate her ice, standing, the princess broke the seals of the many notes and letters that were heaped upon a little table near her.

First she read the notes. "Well, there are more people here than I should expect at this time of year! So much the better. Let us see the cards."

She read a series of names from all the nations of the world, accompanying them by divers comments from which one might have concluded that these people whom she was so glad to meet again collectively as society, severally as individuals, were to her objects of utter indifference. At last she came to her letters.

"Ah!—at last!" she cried, tearing open a large envelope. "Let us see the date! Yes, I breathe freely again! Thank heaven, he is still there!"

She read a page of this letter, then cried: "In less than a month! What! in less than a month!"

Then she finished her reading silently, and remained a long time thoughtful and troubled.

"Ah! Gabrielle, you are there," she said, coming out

of her reverie. "Pardon me!" She rang the bell. "You shall go to your room. I advise you to lie down. I shall do so myself. We shall meet again at seven; it is my dinner hour; I expect almost no one to-day, and I shall dine in my dressing-gown."

Fleurange, thus dismissed, followed the *valet de chambre* who came at the sound of the little bell, and he conducted her through the suite of rooms and the vestibule, up the great staircase, to the second floor, where her room was. There he bowed respectfully and left her, after having called her attention to a corridor by which she could communicate with the princess without going the length of the grand apartments.

The room into which she had just been introduced was beautiful and spacious. It seemed decorated rather than furnished, for its dimensions, its paintings and gildings, would have justified a much more considerable furnishing, and a much richer, than was already there. But, such as it was, it had an agreeable aspect to the young girl. The wide, lofty window in its deep embrasure admitted floods of light, but it would have offered no view save that of the sky, if three stone steps had not rendered it easily accessible. From the summit of these steps, the eye fell upon the inner court of the palace. This court was like a cloister surrounded with graceful columns; a jet of water leaped up from a fountain of white marble placed in the centre of a carpet of turf, and surrounded by rose-laurels; birds were chirping in a great aviary. There was in this graceful and peaceful picture, surmounted by the azure dome of the sky, something which singularly invited to repose and to reverie, and there Fleurange remained at the top of the steps, without a thought of stirring, and letting her fancy wander, as it so often did, into vague space, when the appearance of a servant, bearing her trunk, warned her to descend from these heights, both literal and figurative, and proceed to the prosaic task of unpacking and arranging her possessions. As she was about to begin, she perceived that she had left her travelling-bag in the *salon*. This contained her keys; necessarily she must go in search of them; she took the shorter way which had been pointed out to her, in going, but in returning she could not resist the temptation to revisit alone, and to examine, quite at leisure, the sumptuous suite of rooms through which she had walked so hurriedly before. Slowly she paced along, stopping here and there admiring with childlike curiosity, and yet with innate appreciation of the beautiful, all the objects which were gathered there in unheard-of profusion. But for all the exquisite taste displayed, it was impossible not to remark a certain ostentation which by contrast wakened in Fleurange a thought of the dear old house she had left. The Old House, where simplicity was so well allied to the magnificence of art, where all that charmed the eye, seemed to address itself to the soul, to invite to labor, to study, to serenity, and to peace, while here all that reached the soul through the eyes allured one to idleness, luxury and pride.

The comparison made Fleurange sad. She no longer was interested in what surrounded her, and was about to regain her room by the great staircase, without making any further examination, when, crossing the vestibule, a large door in front of her drew her attention, and she could not resist the temptation to cast one glance into this apartment. She pushed the door gently open, and found herself in a room of no less vast dimensions than the others, but resembling, in its furnishing, a study rather than a drawing-room. The half-closed blinds admitted light enough to see the Hungarian leather that made the hanging of the walls, the bookcases of ebony, the furniture symmetrically arranged and covered from the dust, the tables on which books were placed in that perfect order which indicates that no hand has touched them for a long time; all manifested that this room had an inmate of its own, and had not, like the rest of the house, been put in order for its mistress. There reigned here a certain air of studious repose which was more in conformity with the real taste of Fleurange than all the splendors she had just now passed in review. She took a few steps forward, looked around her, and in order better to see the objects which in the half-light she could not well distinguish, went up to one of the windows and ventured to open the blinds. This full light falling suddenly into the darkened room, made her aware of a picture opposite her, which she had not before observed. She cast a glance at it and—what she felt is not easy to describe! She could not herself have found words to express the excess of surprise and the violent emotion which made her grow red, then pale, and tremble,— this picture which she thus suddenly saw before her, was the very one which had played a part so important in her destiny! It was her father's last work; in a word, it was that Cordelia for which she had served as model one day, and which, since that day, she could never mention without emotion.

She was for several minutes overpowered by a torrent of thoughts. These thoughts, a few months ago, by a desperate effort, had been banished. But how could she be surprised at their tumultuous return? How fail to excuse in herself the eager curiosity to know how this picture came here, and in what house she really was? She felt that she should soon understand it all, and, with beating heart, she closed the shutters, and gently left the room in which she had encountered this unexpected apparition.

She had already crossed the vestibule, and was at the foot of the grand staircase, when she met Mlle. Barbe, very busy, and in that condition of fatigue, near akin to ill-humor, which, on the day of departure or of arrival, manifests itself (and not without reason) in those upon whom rests chiefly the burden of packing and of unpacking.

Fleurange, however, stopped her, resolved to seek an explanation from the first comer.

"Barbe," she said, "I have just been over the house."

The sentence was good for a smile from Barbe, for the latter took special pride in the splendors of her mistress's palace.

"We are well accommodated, are we not?" she said, with an air of satisfaction.

"Yes, extremely well. This all belongs to the Princess, does it not?"

"Yes, from garret to cellar."

"And she lives here all alone?"

"Certainly, with the Count."

"The Count?"

"Yes, her son, who always is with her when he is in Florence. Those are his rooms," she added, designating the door which Fleurange just closed.

"Her son? that is—"

"Count George von Walden."

"Count George von Walden?" repeated Fleurange, as if in a dream.

"Eh! yes, that is the name of the first husband of the Princess; did you know it?"

"No; I have never heard of that."

"He died young. Madame was also young at that time. She mourned for him a long time, and then she married again. But she had no other children. Then the prince died too, but—"

At this moment appeared a servant, bearing an armful of packages, larger and smaller, one of which escaped from his hands. Barbe hastily left Fleurange, and went to solace her own fatigue by addressing to the awkward individual, who was much more wearied than herself, a sharp reprimand.

XVIII.

Fleurange had resumed her seat at the top of the three stairs in her window, and thence was looking down as before into the sheltered, peaceful courtyard. But what a change had come over herself in the half hour since she had left it! What a contrast between that tranquillity which then seemed so well in harmony with her own tranquil thoughts, and the agitation in which she now found herself! She strove to be composed, but for some time this was impossible. The emotion caused by this most unexpected discovery which she had just made,—was it joy, surprise, pain, or was it fear? She could not clearly see. But it was a confusion of all these different sensations, and she allowed herself to be tossed hither and thither, for some time, in a whirlwind of contradictory thoughts. By degrees they became more clear and more distinct. Fleurange recalled the day when, for the last time, she had heard the name of Count George, and she remembered the resolution which she had formed on that day.

This resolution, until now, it had been easy for her to keep, thanks to the varied events which had absorbed and distracted her attention. Now, it was her duty to remain faithful to it, in the new and dangerous position in which she found herself. It was no longer possible to forget

live under the same roof with him. But that which she must now teach herself to feel was that he would be in reality brought no nearer to her when he should be there, before her eyes, under his mother's roof, than when he dwelt for her in the world of imagination and memory. This might possibly be more difficult; in regard to it she could not tell; this however she knew, past all doubt, here lay her duty; and this point made clear, all was simplified for her.

The gentle hand which had guided her infancy had not sought to extinguish the exquisite though dangerous qualities with which she was endowed. It had made no change in the vivacity of her imagination, the ardent tenderness of her heart, and the romance of her disposition. These precious gifts Madre Madelina regarded as dangerous only in the absence of two other qualities which she cultivated in Fleurange with a care comparable to that which, in a lower sphere, is applied to the development of the human voice, and its transformation into a powerful, harmonious, almost celestial organ. However beautiful, it is well known, a voice may be, one cannot sing who does not possess perfect accuracy of tone, and strength of respiration sufficient to sustain for a considerable time the note in all its purity and without the slightest falling off. The divine harmony of human faculties depends in like manner upon the perfect accuracy of sound which the word *duty* gives back in the soul, and that strength of character which seizes and sustains it without hesitation or failure. These were the two qualities which in Fleurange ruled all the rest, and up to this time had preserved her from the dangers to which she might have been exposed by the rest.

More than two hours had thus flown by; the evening star, to Fleurange a messenger of good thoughts, rose pure and brilliant in a cloudless sky, and inspired in her the accustomed prayer, when the clock struck the hour, and rudely recalled the young girl to herself. She hurriedly opened her trunk, dressed in haste and entered the *salon* at the same moment with the princess herself.

Fleurange was dressed in simple black silk. She would have been at a loss to make an elegant toilette, but at any rate it would not have occurred to her to do so, after the intention announced by her protectress of dining that day in *robe de chambre*. She was then a little surprised at seeing that the attire thus designated was a floating robe of white cashmere, richly embroidered in gold. The headdress of the princess was a tissue of gold and lace, and she wore upon her neck six rows of magnificent pearls, which fell to her shoulders; but that which still more surprised and disconcerted the young girl was the glance of dissatisfaction which the princess cast at her as she came in. It was the first time that the kind and friendly reception to which she had been accustomed had failed her.

This was, however, not the moment to give or receive explanations, for the princess was not alone: two or three persons were present, whose names Fleurange learned later. One was an old *savant*, Don Pomponio; another, a young artist, Signor Livio; lastly, the Marquis Trombelli, who was considered a great bore. To say the truth, they occupied an inferior rank among the habitual guests of the palace, but they saved the mistress of the house from the vexation of seeing the culinary triumphs of her *chef* wasted upon the desert air, as well as from the danger of dining without a sufficient number of guests in a vast hall where a *tête-à-tête* with Fleurange would have seemed to her very dismal. She was in general by no means indifferent in regard to those who frequented her *salon*. But for her guests at table, she attached almost as much importance to their number as to their worth, and asked not much more of them than the facile talent of knowing how to appreciate the delicious viands that were set before them.

Notwithstanding the singular simplicity of her attire, Fleurange did not pass unnoticed. The *savant* talked a little more than usual, with the hope to dazzle her; the marquis eyed her on various occasions; the young artist hazarded a few complimentary remarks; but as she replied only in monosyllables, the conversation languished, the evening dragged, and the princess had already yawned more than once, when she brightened up suddenly with an exclamation of delight, as a servant announced: "The Marquis Adelardi."

The person who entered was a man of about forty.

Fleurange soon learned that he was a Milanese, and she perceived at once that he was one of those men who talk well on every subject, who are interested in all topics, whether the gossip of society, political news, or social or literary questions, and whose only fault is that they treat all subjects as of equal importance. In a moment the atmosphere of the drawing-room was changed. The Marquis Adelardi had not been there fifteen minutes before he had found means to make the most of the mediocre elements of which the circle was composed, inducing each one to talk of that which he best understood, passing from politics to history, from art to science, and showing himself capable of speaking well, if not profoundly, on every topic.

Fleurange, sitting silently with her embroidery, amused herself with this conversation, but the interest she took in it redoubled, and changed its character, when the newcomer approaching the arm-chair of the princess, asked:
"And how is George? When shall we see him again?"

The princess replied in a tone half anxious, half satisfied:
"We shall see him soon, for my letter this morning, from St. Petersburg, announces his return before the end of the month."

"Good! I miss him everywhere and always."

"And I do also, you may suppose," said the princess, playing with her pearl necklace, with a pensive air. "Still Adelardi, you know, as well as I do, that he would have done better to remain where he was till the close of the year."

"Nay, my dear princess, you must give that up; believe me, you can never make a courtier of George."

"It is not that alone—"

"Oh yes, I understand. You thought the fair Vera—"

Here the marquis leaned nearer the princess, and they exchanged in a low voice a few remarks, of which Fleurange heard only these: "And you know that is what I most desire."

It was the princess who had just spoken.

"And he?" said the marquis.

"He! You know him well!"

"But for that very reason I should not have believed him insensible to such fascinations as hers."

"Certainly not; but you can never be sure that he is not absorbed by some previous fancy which no one could foresee. And indeed I think if she had not been at court—"

Here again the princess lowered her voice.

"Be tranquil. In time, he will surrender."

"I hope so; but, meanwhile, you must agree with me that he would have done better to remain."

"Yes, and no; I am not sure that it would be very wise in him to expose himself to being compromised, as he is always in danger of being."

The princess became very grave. "In that aspect you are right," she said, "and it gives me great alarm. But I think he would become more prudent if he were obliged to be careful. That is a necessity that any one who lives in Russia at last comes to understand."

The conversation went on for some time in low tones, then the princess declaring that she was extremely fatigued, an exception was made to the accustomed rule of late hours, and all withdrew.

As Fleurange was about to do the same, the princess stopped her, and called her seriously to account for the simplicity of her toilette.

"I require," she said, "in the person who, in some sort, assists in doing the honors of my house, an elegant appearance. And I pay her in proportion," she added, with that lack of delicacy which one remarks, sometimes, even in women of high breeding, towards those who are dependent upon them.

It was not a fault that often showed itself in the princess, but ill humor unveiled this side of her character.

Fleurange colored. "Princess," she said, "I ask your pardon, but I cannot obey you. It is impossible," she repeated, while tears came to her eyes.

"What do you mean by that?"

Fleurange hesitated for a moment; then, obeying her habitual impulse to frankness and candor she related all that till now the princess had not known in regard to herself— the ruin of her family, and the motive which had decided her to accept the position which she now held.

"If I must spend for dress the money I receive from you: if I am not allowed to assist my family, save at th' risk of your displeasure, then—then—" and her voice trembled,—"alas! madam, I must go elsewhere to seek the means—"

The princess did not allow her to finish. The tones of the young girl, as she told her simple story, had made sympathy drive out displeasure, and the result of this little scene was the permission granted to Fleurange to dispose not only of part, but the whole of her salary, in accordance with her wishes, on one condition, upon which the princess insisted and to which Fleurange was forced to consent. This was that, henceforth, the princess, and the princess only, should provide for the toilette of her youthful companion.

Upon the morrow, Fleurange was furnished in profusion with all that could satisfy the wishes of her protectress, and the latter indeed seemed to take pleasure in gratifying her generosity in this way, after the lively interest which had been awakened in her mind, by the story of Fleurange. With a mixture of gratitude and of repugnance, Fleurange submitted, and sought to harmonize, as far as possible, the simplicity of her own taste with the elegance required by the taste of her mistress. But the result was, that when she again dressed to appear in the drawing-room, the effect that she produced far surpassed all that had been anticipated by the person who seemed to have attached so much importance to setting off, to the best advantage, the young girl's beauty.

Elegance and luxury, in fact, were necessary to the existence of the Princess Catherine, and, as a piece of furniture or tapestry of a certain simplicity would have been remarked as out of place in her apartments, so Fleurange's black silk dress had broken the general harmony, and had annoyed her like a flaw in a fine porcelain. But it would by no means have pleased her that Fleurange should have ceased to fill the position of *protégée* and dependent, which gratified at once her pride and her kind feelings. If the admiration which on the first appearance of the young girl was offered somewhat too lavishly, had been sought, or even accepted by her, the ill-humor of the princess would doubtless have made itself felt instantly; but the proud

homage whose incense comes to trouble the purity and dignity of the heart only when vanity has given it free access.

Now, Fleurange was not at all vain; this was one of her charms, and, at the same time, a safeguard to her.

The practised eye of the princess had soon perceived that she had no cause for anxiety in this regard, and the favor of Fleurange increased almost without limits. It was to the princess the most desirable thing in the world to add to her drawing-room the ornament of so distinguished beauty, without having any inconvienence from it, to enjoy, herself, the charm of the society of Fleurange, her usefulness in a thousand little ways, and her sweet temper, while nothing ever occurred to suggest a need of watchfulness in any respect against her. The princess could now be as idle as she desired. Fleurange wrote notes for her, arranged flowers, took up and finished what the princess had eagerly commenced and soon abandoned, but now would exhibit with pride as the fruits of her own industry. Fleurange was always there to read aloud with her charming voice, and talent as natural as it was rare, poetry in German or Italian, reviews and newspaper articles, then, on the arrival of visitors, prompt to disappear, unless expressly desired by the princess to remain with her. She thus fulfilled, unknown to herself, in simply following what seemed the way traced out for her, even to the very least wishes of her protectress, and perhaps the latter was even more grateful to her for the tact with which she could divine, than for the readiness with which she could obey.

Thus the days glided past, and it was now more than a month after their arrival in Florence. During this time, the name of Count George, a hundred times spoken in her presence, had ceased to produce upon Fleurange the effect against which her good resolution had been formed. She thought, even sometimes with a smile, that when she should know him, she would doubtless be much astonished that he could have occupied so large a space in her thoughts. "They say phantoms always vanish, when you look them in the face."

This was the thought which crossed her mind one day when she was alone in the little *salon*. The princess w out, and Fleurange sat at the embroidery-frame at work; the thought we have just recorded was suggested to her by the news received that morning of Count George's certain arrival before the close of the week.

"Yes, reality puts fancy to flight," she said to herself, following out her reverie; "and it is very likely that when I know him better—"

She was suddenly interrupted by the sound of rapid steps in the adjoining apartment. Usually, no one came from that direction unannounced. She rose in haste, intending, as usual, to leave the room, but had scarcely taken one step before she found herself face to face with the newcomer.

It was he; doubtless, *he!* Count George!

She had no time to observe what she herself felt. The effect which she produced, surprised her, or rather, frightened her, to that degree that she remained motionless, mute, overwhelmed.

"Fleurange!—great Heavens! is this possible? Is it true? Fleurange! Fleurange!" repeated, with an emotion that was deeper than joy, this voice, graven no less than these features upon the memory of her who listened.

This name, this name of childhood now half-forgotten, thus pronounced; this hand which clasped her's as that of a recovered friend, but with a look which made Fleurange instinctively withdraw her own; these rapid questions, these earnest replies, these words—eager, tender, passionate, all, in this interview, was prompt, ardent, dangerous as lightning!

But, almost at the same instant, a carriage was heard without, and before the Princess Catherine had appeared in the drawing-room, Fleurange had escaped to her own room, pale and almost fainting.

All that was unreasonable and almost mad in her thoughts of earlier days, all that, in appearance, was impossible had, in one instant, transformed itself into sudden, unforeseen, threatening reality!

What words were these to which she had just listened? What! for a year he had been pursued by thoughts of her,—he had striven to banish them, but in vain, and, at this moment, he had returned from Russia, resolved to try all means to find her again,—to see once more the face that had never been absent from his thoughts!

 Yes; this was what he had just said. And these words to which she had listened were the very counterpart of what she had herself felt, and striven against!

Poor Fleurange! was it joy that her pale and troubled face now expressed? was it a transport of pride, or of tenderness that set her heart beating? was it happiness that made her shed this torrent of tears?

Ah, no! these words so sweet to hear, when it is permitted to listen, this blessedness of being loved when one loves, which counts among the greatest in this world, these words so readily understood because they express what one has so well experienced—all that sometimes suddenly lights up a life like sunshine, had fallen upon hers with the blinding glare, the rapidity, the danger of a bolt from heaven!

XIX.

All those personal advantages which are so pleasing and so attractive, were possessed by Count George von Walden in a very high degree; and though it might not have been wise to trust entirely to his chivalrous face, and to regard his distinguished manners as the sure index of a soul exempt from selfishness, it was nevertheless impossible to see him without remarking him, or to forget him after having seen him. The very deep impression made upon Fleurange was not then so singular as it might appear, and she had more excuse than she herself imagined. The really surprising point, notwithstanding her singular loveliness, was that this impression had been reciprocal, and that, at the end of a year, it was not at all effaced.

Evidently it would not be right to compare the innocent, confused, involuntary sentiment of the young girl with that which such a man as Count George was capable of feeling. But, under the name of Cordelia, the image of Fleurange had remained present to his eyes, as well as to his imagination. He passionately desired to see her again. He promised himself that he would succeed in this without examining with what intention he formed the plan, and this tenacious resolve had influenced, more probably than he was aware, a decision to which he had recently come, and whic`

Yet, without being over-scrupulous, Count von Walden would have taken a second look before hazarding to the *demoiselle de compagnie* of his mother, a declaration like that with which he had just addressed her. But he had not the slightest expectation of finding in this Gabrielle, occasionally mentioned in his mother's letters, her whose singular name, as well as strange loveliness, had remained imprinted upon his memory, and at the moment, surprise took away all power of reflection. Then, seeing this beautiful girl grow red and pale, seeing her clear eyes grow troubled, he had, as if in spite of himself, spoken words which he would have better known how to repress, perhaps, had she known better how to dissimulate.

But, as we have said, all this passed with the rapidity of thought. Five minutes had not elapsed between the time when he suddenly appeared before Fleurange and the time when the princess, out of breath with her joy at his return and the haste with which she had ascended the stairs, fell, pale and overcome, into the arms of her son.

George carried her to her sofa, laid her tenderly upon it, then knelt at her side, and while she demanded, with a kiss between every two words, now—why he had come so soon ; now—why he had made her wait so long for him ; he, by degrees, fully recovered his self-command. After a good hour of conversation, when he found himself again alone, he asked himself whether this vision which had received him on his arrival was a reality or a dream of the imagination, and finally, whether it was a pleasure to him or not that this vision had appeared, and under his mother's roof !

During this time Fleurange also was coming to herself, but slowly, and her first sensation seemed to be a sort of terror. "O, dear friends! why have I left you?" she exclaimed aloud, with a feeling like that with which one in the midst of a tempest thinks of the sheltered haven. Even more than when in Paris, face to face with actual want, did she feel the need of protection, and even more than then, her isolation and her weakness alarmed her.

With clasped hands she sat in her room trying to compose herself, but in vain ; the emotion and the surprise had been too violent. Notwithstanding all her efforts, the remembrance of the voice, the tone she had just heard, caused her a sort of keen and painful joy which went through her heart like the thrust of a dagger.

"No, no, I must not think," she said, clasping her two hands over her forehead, as if to still the action of her mind.

Suddenly a new idea presented itself.

"What had he said to his mother? What must she think? Would she be haughty, reserved, disdainful, as she so well knew how to be? Would she give orders that her young companion on the instant should depart? What would happen?"

She was considering this new aspect of her position when, without stopping for the ordinary preliminary of a knock at the door, Barbe came in eagerly with the important air of one who brings at once a piece of news and a command.

"Mlle. Gabrielle," she said, "the princess sends me to inform you that Count George von Walden has arrived, and that there will be a great many persons at dinner; she begs you to pay especial attention to your toilette."

This message, which fell upon Fleurange's reflections like cold water upon burning coals, produced a sort of effervescence which rendered her ideas even more confused than before.

She looked at Barbe as if she did not understand her.

"You were asleep, perhaps," said the maid, observing the paleness and the frightened look of Fleurange; "are you ill?"

This question suggested to Fleurange the idea of saying "yes," and adding that she could not leave her room, and she was congratulating herself on this happy method of escaping for the moment from her difficulties, when Barbe exclaimed:

"Remain in your room! be ill! Well, well! I should think so! On a day like this! Madame would be pleased! Come, come, mademoiselle, you know that she would never permit it!"

"But when my head aches so that I can scarcely lift it?" said Fleurange.

Barbe looked at her. Fleurange was not telling an untruth; her head ached violently, she was very pale, and in her eyes and in her whole face there was something unusual; and still she was not less, but even more, beautiful than ever.

"Come, Mlle. Gabrielle, you are not very ill," said the maid, "make a little exertion; believe me, unless you do, you will see the princess coming up for you, and then you must go down."

This prospect brought Fleurange to obedience at once.

"Well, Barbe," she said, in a tone half plaintive, half impatient, "let her tell me what I am to wear then! to dress! Oh, if she knew how I detest it!"

"Come, *mademoiselle*, there are a good many who would be very glad to be in your place!" said Barbe, with vexation.

On principle, she was very ill pleased with all her mistress's liberality towards Fleurange, but she was easily pacified by the method which Fleurange knew how to adopt to her.

"Here, Barbe, take this shawl, it is for you; and come back in an hour and tell me what the princess désires me to wear; that is the easiest way for me, and saves me the difficulty of making a choice."

Barbe went away and reappeared in an hour, bringing a dress of sky-blue *crêpe* and some silver pins.

"Here, mademoiselle," she said, "this is your dress for to-day. Dress quickly, and I will help you. Let me arrange your hair. Ah! how lovely these pins will be in your black braids. Now your dress, quick! The princess is already in the drawing-room, and Count George and a great deal of company. You will be late; come, oh come, mademoiselle! what are you thinking of, sitting there when you ought to be dressed already!"

Fleurange was at once agitated and absent-minded; she walked about the room; she sat down and stood up without the slightest regard to the exhortations which were addressed to her. Finally, she gave herself up into the hands of Barbe, who, from the pure love of art, did so well that when Fleurange softly opened the door of the *salon*, seeking to glide in unperceived, a slight murmur of admiration ran through the room, and all eyes were directed towards her. This added to her distress a mortal embarrassment. If any one had asked her the color of her dress she could not have replied, but the idea crossed her mind that Barbe very possibly had arranged her toilette in some unaccustomed manner, and much more splendidly than usual, and she colored at the thought of what construction the princess might put upon her unwonted appearance.

But the princess did not seem to take the least notice of her; standing in the centre of the room in the most elegant attire, she did the honors with her usual grace.

Suddenly Fleurange heard her own name:

"Gabrielle!"

The princess called her. Fleurange advanced, but her eyes seemed veiled in a mist, for she had noticed from a distance that Count George stood at his mother's side.

"My bracelet is unfastened; will you close it, Gabrielle?" said the princess, in her usual tone of kind protection.

Fleurange bent her head and secured the clasp.

"George," said the princess, "here is Gabrielle, of whom I have spoken to you. Gabrielle, this is my son."

George bowed silently. Fleurange did the same, but some painful emotion brought the color to her face. For the first time in her life she seemed to herself to be the silent accomplice in a lie, or at least a deception, and although solaced by the certainty that the princess had not the slightest idea of what had passed two hours earlier, a flash of injured pride shot from her eyes as she lifted them, turning away her head at the same time.

Count George looked attentively at her for an instant, then became very thoughtful, and it was only with an effort that he took part in the conversation during dinner, where, seated opposite his mother, he did the honors of the table. In the evening, thanks to the Marquis Adelardi, whose friendship was very dear to him, and whose mind was sympathetic with his own, he grew animated, and shone, in turn, almost as much as his brilliant interlocutor; but he did not come near Fleurange, nor did he even seem a single time to cast a glance in the direction where she stood.

XX.

that, at her son's age, and with the character which he possessed, the presence of Fleurange under her roof could be absolutely free from danger to him. At the same time, whatever must change the daily habit of her life was extremely distasteful to her, and that which was distasteful was rarely admitted by her to be necessary, or even possible. She watched her son very carefully for a few days, and soon was thoroughly reassured, and the more, because in all his life he had used very little dissimulation towards her. Without suffering himself to be guided by his mother, he never sought to conceal from her his thoughts, and at the risk of causing her, now and then, very great displeasure, he allowed her to read to the very bottom of his heart without making any effort to withdraw himself from her penetration. Now, at this moment, the result of the observations of the princess was perfectly reassuring to her.

George spoke to Fleurange without any affectation of indifference, and equally, without any show of interest. He distinguished her in no way save by acts of politeness, which he would have performed equally towards any other person. He never attempted to approach her, and if he looked at her, and now and then spoke of her beauty, as did others, he seemed to be more cool and reserved than the rest. The princess drew her two-fold conclusion that George was absorbed in the thought of another, and, as she desired that it should be so, she readily gave herself the satisfaction of believing it, and relapsed into her former indolent life.

As to Fleurange, the effect of this attitude of Count George was singular. Naturally frank, upright, and courageous, she had an invincible repugnance towards dissimulation of every sort, and for several days, by this very fact of his showing himself in two different aspects, he lost, in

Whether that were so or not, the princess, as we have said, ceased to follow him with anxious eyes, and the young girl, liberated from the constraint which had at first oppressed her, ventured gradually to take part in general conversation, even when he was present. Soon she allowed herself to enjoy freely a mind whose brilliancy gave a new charm to every subject, and to which none seemed unknown or indifferent. In this respect, he resembled the Marquis Adelardi; but he was less cold, less sarcastic than the latter, and was never inclined, as was the marquis now and then, to quit the region of truly interesting subjects for that in which prevailed the petty slanders of the fashionable world, and the idle nothings of polite society. The two men were great friends, however, and without exactly resembling each other, were enough alike to be always pleased with each other's society and to run no risk of collisions.

One subject in particular excited the ardent interest of both. This was the subject of politics. Anywhere else, probably, such topics would have been wearisome to Fleurange, but here she could not help listening with pleasure. Count George knew how to make whatever he said sound well, and, without always perfectly understanding the case, she felt herself carried away by the haughty independence of his language, by his love for liberty, by his prompt sympathy with the weak and the oppressed. There are in politics certain leading doctrines which women readily apprehend, and their sympathy is easily granted to all causes and all opinions wherein these are found. And so listening, silent and absorbed, Fleurange felt herself at times passionately in accord with him whose eloquent words had for her a charm as powerful as it was novel.

The marquis seemed to be not less occupied with contemporary history than was his friend, and talked no less willingly than he on every topic, except when the affairs of his own country came under discussion. In that case, he became silent, and it was nearly impossible to keep up any further conversation with him.

One evening, the *salon* of the princess being, as usual, crowded, Fleurange, seated at a little table, was serving tea. This was one of her daily duties. Every one came for a cup, while a very few had seated themselves at the table. Of this number was the Marquis Adelardi, who was engaged with Don Pomponio, and a young artist, in a discussion of modern Italian art. At this moment Count George appeared; he listened silently for awhile, then joined in the conversation. A chair was vacant near Fleurange; he sat down, and for a time the discussion was pursued with much animation. Fleurange listened with downcast eyes; she said not a word, but not a word did she lose of all that went on around her. The conversation passed from Italy to Germany, and something was said of the new school of painters in the latter country. In enumerating a few of the most distinguished artists, Count George chanced to mention the name of Julian Steinberg, and added that the latter's best work was at Frankfort, in the gallery of Professor Ludwig Dornthal.

Fleurange, of course, was not unaware that the Count knew her friends, but the occasion of speaking of them had not yet offered, and the mention of their names was so unexpected that it made her start. She looked up, and could scarcely repress the exclamation that rose to her lips. This movement of hers was perceived only by him who had given cause for it. He let the conversation drop. Soon after, the others rose and left the table. He lingered an instant. "Mlle. Gabrielle," he said, "have the goodness to tell me, have I by accident grieved or offended you? It would be very far from my intention."

Fleurange interrupted him, with animation. "Oh no!" she said, "assuredly not!"

And these words were immediately followed by an explanation which the young girl gave with as much enthusiasm as frankness. Count George thus learned for the first time of her relationship to the Dornthals. But this subject once brought forward, it was followed by a new and more important revelation. Since the first day, for more than one reason, the picture of Cordelia had been mentioned neither by one nor the other. But now, her confidence sud-

awakened. memories, Fleurange ventured to tell him what an influence had been exercised upon her life by the fate which had made him possessor of her father's last picture, and in a tone of deep feeling she thanked him for the happiness which he had involuntarily conferred upon her.

She stopped suddenly, and her heart, as on the first day, beat with an emotion mingled with terror, for while she spoke, the eyes of Count George, fixed upon her own, had resumed the expression which, since that day she had not seen, and once again as then, she heard him pronounce her name with that accent she had striven to forget.

"Fleurange!—oh, what you tell me is so strange! What! This Cordelia has transformed your life as it has my own? Is it not—tell me, is it not the indication of a fate from which we ought not to seek to withdraw ourselves?"

He spoke in a low voice, and suddenly he stopped, for the quick blush had vanished, and Fleurange was growing pale as death.

We have already said the word *duty*, in this young girl's soul, gave back a tone strangely true and strong. The words she had just heard produced upon her the effect of an alarm-bell rather than the dangerous excitement which they were fitted to cause. She remained silent for one moment, while George, motionless and abashed, regarded her. But she succeeded in calming the tumultuous throbbing of her heart, and raising her beautiful eyes calmly and gravely to his, she looked at him with as much proud dignity as if she had been a queen and he some most obscure subject who had forgotten the distance that lay between them.

"Count George," she said, "I recall you to yourself; is this the language you ought to use towards an orphan girl who is under the protection and in the *service* of your mother?"

The profound respect of the look which bent before her own was a sufficient *amende* for Fleurange. But the expression of pain and of tenderness in his eyes made, perhaps, this mute response more dangerous for her to whom it was addressed, than the ardent words that had preceded it. She rose, however, at once, without adding a word,

XXI.

Count George had remained in the place where Fleurange left him, some time longer than he was aware, when he felt a light touch on the shoulder. It was Adelardi who disturbed his reverie.

"What are you thinking of, George?" he said. "You could not be more absorbed in the contemplation of this empty tea-cup if it were one of those magic vases of which we were speaking the other day, whose prophetic hieroglyphics are so interesting to your compatriots!"

The allusion referred to a superstitious *badinage* to which they attach importance in Russia, and which they observe on New Year's eve. It consists in pouring melted wax into a basin filled with cold water, making use of the designs thus produced in the water for drawing horoscopes.

Count George looked up with a smile.

"The comparison is not bad," he said, "for it is precisely about the future that I was thinking. Yes, I would gladly have my fortune told, and if I had any faith in the charm of which you speak, I should resort to it at once."

Thus speaking, he rose and looked about the drawing-room. It was brilliantly lighted and crowded. His mother, in superb evening dress, seemed to regard with satisfaction the numerous groups of elegant women, men of all ages, notabilities from every land, gathered about her this evening; and nothing justified the disgusted air of him who should have aided her in doing the honors of the house, still less his words:

"What an insupportable crowd of stupid people! If you have had enough of it, as well as myself, let us go and have a cigar in my room!"

"I agree upon the latter point. As to the other, it is your disposition at this moment which makes you take that view! Come, George," he continued, when they were established, one in an arm-chair, the other upon a lounge in the room whither we have once followed Fleurange, "come, would you like to have me, though I am no sorcerer, try my skill in predicting to you that future concerning which

"Doubtless, Adelardi, you are no sorcerer, but you would not be an Italian if you had not a certain talent for divination. I am willing; make your attempt. You know that you have long had the right to say anything you please to me!"

"Very well, I begin; but first, permit me to ask you the meaning of that curtain which, since your return, hides the picture which hangs opposite me on the wall?"

"You remember the subject which that picture represents?"

"Oh, perfectly; it represents Cordelia at the feet of the sleeping King Lear."

"And have you ever examined it carefully?"

"Yes, George, with great care. So that, no matter, I can save you the trouble of answering the question I have just put to you—I know why you hide the picture from sight."

"Well?"

"You hide it fearing that everybody will be struck by the resemblance between the picture and its model."

George did not immediately reply.

"If you have made a clever guess," said he at last, "must I tell you so?"

"Yes; in this game which we are playing, mutual frankness is essential, or we will talk of something else."

"No, Adelardi, since we have begun, we may as well go on."

"Very well, I proceed, and though you should be vexed with me, now I shall go to the end. Up to this time I admit that you have concealed very successfully the fancy that for the moment rules you. I believe myself to be the only one who has discovered it, except, perhaps, she who is its object. But on this point I am not certain. The character of that young girl is a puzzle to me."

"It is a character, in truth, Adelardi, which men like

"On this point your sagacity is not remarkable, since I myself have told you this."

"Yes, but I believed you, which another, less experienced, perhaps, would not have done. Now, then, this unexpected and surprising rencontre has given to the fascination already existing an aspect of fatality, of irresistible destiny—"

George, without interrupting him, changed color slightly, remembering the words he so lately himself had addressed to Fleurange.

"Irresistible," continued Adelardi, "that is to say, unhesitatingly, unscrupulously, remorselessly, you are about to seek to abuse that ascendency which you know only too well how to use; in a word—"

"Go on," said Count George.

"No matter—sermons are not my *forte*, and I should scarcely risk addressing one to you; but, however strange it may seem to you to hear me say this, I declare to you, that to lay a snare for this noble creature, or even but to seek to harm by a word, that aureole of honor and of innocence with which she is surrounded, would be in my eyes an infamy—"

"Of which you believe me capable! Thanks, Adelardi!"

"Very well, George, swear to me that you have no such thought!"

"No thought of what?"

"Of her."

"Of her? I cannot swear to you that. But I am astonished that you should think me utterly incapable of the respect that you, careless though you are, cannot help feeling in this case yourself!"

"Well then, what *are* your intentions?"

George made no reply whatever, and after a minute's grave silence, Adelardi resumed, very seriously:

"My dear friend, inasmuch as I am forty years of age —that is to say, your senior by nearly fifteen years—I think I have a right to say to you that if, between an infamy and a folly, the folly is preferable, it would be well, nevertheless, to reflect that the shorter they are, the better, and that an irreparable folly is the very worst of all."

"Let us not forget our *rôles*, Adelardi; I have neither

confessions nor revelations to make to you; you have no advice to give to me. You have undertaken, not to tell me what I ought to do, but to predict for me what I shall do."

"Very well, this is my horoscope, dictated, I will own, quite as much by what I desire as by what I foresee: you will escape from the folly which entices you, and you will observe faithfully the promise that binds you."

The face of the young man darkened.

"A promise which my mother had doubtless charged you to recall to my mind—"

"No, I speak as a friend, and upon my own instance solely. If I spoke at your mother's request, I should be perfectly willing to admit that I did so."

"It is very certain that she charges herself with that duty quite often enough. This supposed promise has become one of her fixed ideas."

"*Supposed* promise?"

"Yes, supposed; for it is a subject upon which I have never at any time spoken positively."

"Never spoken positively? Come, George, be honest, or let us cease talking."

"No, let us go on; I feel the need sometimes, of speaking from my heart. Very well, two years ago,—yes, I confess it,—when I first met Vera von Limingen I was struck by her beauty, and still more was I fascinated by her intellect, and if I had then remained near her, possibly I should soon have found it difficult to leave her. In that case, without doubt, at the present time my destiny would have been fixed. I should have assumed the yoke, and not only should I be a married man, but I should have the advantage of being a court-personage, clothed with some of those dignities to which the husband of a maid of honor might well aspire."

"But, my dear friend, when you consider that this maid of honor is rich, noble, and one of the prettiest girls at court; furthermore, that you were at that time wild about her, and that she herself made no mystery of her preference for you, I do not see that this was a very sad and dreadful extremity!"

"No, I do not say that it was; if I had never quitted St. Petersburg, possibly there might have been happiness for me, under conditions like these. Now, luckily or unluckily, having breathed a different air, I can live in that no longer. A thousand sentiments, sympathies, opinions, which have by degrees become my own, would make me to-day regard the gold chain of a place at court as the worst of slaveries. That alone would have been sufficient to have silenced upon my lips the words that Vera perhaps expected, but which she is perfectly aware I have never uttered. As to the suppositions of the world, what has that to do with it?"

"But you will admit that this was not the only cause of your separation?"

"No, if you choose to call it separation. This motive was not, or, at least, is not, the only one."

"I had no doubt of it, and frankly I cannot tell you which of these two motives I deplore most!"

"To tell the truth, Adelardi," said George, impatiently, "I really cannot understand your solicitude in regard to me. You told me yourself one day that the manner in which most marriages are made in Italy has decided you to remain a bachelor, and now I find you as much scandalized at the prospect of seeing me choose, a little outside of social *convenances*, a wife to my liking, as the Marquis Trombelli himself could be!"

Adelardi smiled.

"That's not all, and what follows is even more unaccountable. I am not contented and charmed with the political *régime* under which Heaven has caused me to be born, and it is you, Adelardi, you, who are astonished and disturbed by this! Whereupon I inquire of you, in turn, why you do not return to Milan, there to enjoy, as a faithful subject, the paternal rule under which it is permitted you to live?"

The amused expression of the marquiss's face changed suddenly, and became grave, and even sombre.

"Stop, George," he said.

"Forgive me, Adelardi; but it is impossible for me to believe that there are any subjects upon which you and I are not agreed."

Adelardi was silent for a few minutes, then with an effort he replied:

"Listen to me, George; my affection for you is most sincere, and you would not doubt it if you knew what it costs me to remain in the region into which our conversation has brought us; but it may not be useless for you to hear me; let me then say two words on a subject which usually I avoid, having, as you know, sufficient self-control to remain silent, although not sufficient to speak with coolness. Years ago, when I was a younger man than you are now, I felt even to frenzy that passion which those only know whose native land is enslaved. Yes," he continued, with unwonted emotion, "one's country, happy, glorious, honored and powerful, is without doubt the object of a worship that no noble heart can refuse; but to feel that worship transformed into an angry and sorrowful passion one must see his country broken and humiliated, must behold her in the dust, and trodden underfoot; it must be that her name be effaced from the memory of all, that even the right to hear it, nay, even, the very right to live, be refused her?"

"Yes, truly, Adelardi," cried George, earnestly, "I understand that grief!—I understand it but too well! Yet Italy is not the only oppressed country in Europe, and chance which has made a man belong to one of the tyrant nations, does not force him to share its excesses, does not deny him, I imagine, the right to lament over them."

"I will answer you in a moment. Now, George, suffer me to finish what I have to say, for this subject must, never again be named. Under the influence of this passion, like so many others, alas! of my own age, my own rank, and my own country, I yielded to the folly of criminal attempts, or at least I seemed so to do, and like many others, better men than I, and a vast number far worse, I underwent, as you know, successively, imprisonment, confiscation, exile. I do not regret what I have endured, for when one can no longer serve his country, there is a kind of sad pleasure in suffering for her; but what I do regret is that I deserved what I endured."

"Deserved?"

"Yes; for I was once a member of one of those organizations which devour us. Naturally, like others, I found myself excusable, the attraction that draws us seems so irresistible! the end that we pursue seems so noble! Yes

The marquis paused abruptly and he seemed scarcely able to continue.

"Yes," he finally resumed, " I assure you of this: there is neither strength, nor honor, nor virtue, nor loyalty, nor probity, nor anything which renders a man worthy of respect or esteem ; *nothing*, I assure you, which can resist the poisoned air that one breathes in those accursed regions. My punishment was late, for I was not denounced till after I had left them; but it was just, for I had been through them!"

Surprised and affected, George listened silently.

"The act of my life for which I most applaud myself," resumed Adelardi, "the act which required more courage than to have affronted death a thousand times in other ways—this act was that of separating myself with decision, with contempt, with horror, from all those to whom I had been a moment before allied!"

He paced the room with agitation as he spoke.

"From that time," he resumed, "I have passed through many dangers, of which I will not speak, and have undergone many sufferings, of which you already know. Now, I live here, away from my native city, separated from all my own family, and persuaded that the day which is to change the destiny of Italy will not rise for this generation, —certain, however, that her most deadly foes are not her masters, not even the most rigorous of them, but those false and perfidious friends whom she calls her brothers, her heroes, and, sometimes, her martyrs!"

The marquis returned to his seat beside Count George, and, grasping his friend's hand, "That is enough in regard to myself," he said. "Now to return to you, whose situation you must agree it is absurd to compare with mine."

"It is true, and yet, Adelardi, you wish to regenerate your country, and I wish to transform mine!"

"Yes, but for all the shadows that darken his reign, the sovereign who rules you to-day will live in history, you may be certain, as one of the noblest and most humane representatives of that absolute power which it is so difficult to wield aright."

"Yes, and it is precisely that which discourages me; to realize my dream, the successor of Alexander I. should have all his virtues, and none of his faults, and you must acknowledge that the future seems to promise us nothing like that."

"Do not commence to draw horoscopes on this subject, but listen to one last word of advice. Notwithstanding your dreams and aspirations, your opinions, and your exalted sympathies, I am very sure nothing will ever induce you to take part in any unlawful enterprise in your own country. Well, then, George, listen to a converted conspirator: avoid all intercourse with those who, less scrupulous than you about their acts, make use of the same language as yourself; and believe me further, it is infinitely annoying when one is overtaken by punishment, to feel that one has deserved it by his own imprudence and folly, and that one has no one but himself to blame."

Their long conversation had led them far away from the point of departure. It was now too late to return thither. But the Marquis Adelardi resolved that, opportunity favoring, he would return to it again, and obtain the complete confidence of George. He well understood the immediate danger, and he felt it his duty as a friend to strive to avert it. But, with all his fine perspicacity, he did not see that she who had brought this danger, knew better than any other how to turn it away.

XXII.

At the same time that this conversation was going on, Fleurange was sitting in the place of which we already know, at the top of the stone steps in her window, watching the great shadow of the columns creep forward in the moonlight, listening to the sound of the fountain, which alone broke the stillness of the night, and breathing the vague perfume of the orange-flowers which scented the air.

Many months had passed since that day when the secret dream, hidden deep in her thoughts, had seemed for an instant to transform itself into reality—reality which vanished, it is true, almost as soon as seen; now, she was again suffering from excitement and agitation, but very differently of what did she now think, sitting there in the moonlight? and why did her eyes rove so sadly over every familiar object, while the night was so brilliant and perfumed, and the words were yet vibrating in her ears which, in spite of herself, made her heart beat with a triumphant joy? of what did she think?—do you care to know?—whither was she at that moment transported by one of those impulses of the imagination which can neither be explained nor controlled? Was it to the *Casino*, where the preceding evening Count George had lingered so long on horseback beside his mother's carriage? was it to one of those picture-galleries, where more than once he had pointed out to her the wonders hidden from the superficial eye, but so well understood by her to whom they were revealed? or was it to the drawing-room which she had just quitted, and was she thinking now of that last look, from which she had turned away her eyes? No; the place at this moment present to her memory was the garden of the Old House, the hour that she recalled was the last one that she had spent there! Just so brilliant was the moonlight then! the air was soft, the flowers shed their fragrance! but the word *adieu* seemed inscribed everywhere, and transformed into sadness all the beauty of the evening. Adieu, without hope, and without return! and at this moment it was repeated to her, with even sadder accent by the different splendor of this Italian night,—Adieu!—again adieu? yes, adieu!

She must leave this place, now become too dear,—must break this too perilous spell; all this was clear and evident.

One moment,—one moment only,—she suffered her thoughts to linger upon the happiness from which she must fly. She permitted her imagination to paint it for her just as it might be if nothing forbade it; and with a clearness and a sincerity in which there was no exaggerated feeling, she recognized the truth that she would gladly have bought this happiness at the price of any sacrifice, save that which her conscience forbade her to make. Yes, to be able to live without remorse in his presence, to be his wife, and if, by some impossible good fortune, his mother should consent! —ah! to win this destiny she felt that she should fear nothing, that she should accept with delight, poverty, the

In reading these words, many persons of experience will smile and say that these are imaginary sacrifices which youth, under the influence of passion, very readily lays upon itself, but which happily are seldom brought to the test in after life. We grant this, and, not stopping longer to consider the improbable future to which Fleurange thus appealed, we will at least maintain that, without waiting for these imaginary trials, she disposed herself bravely to meet that one which in reality was offered to her. Now these experienced persons will agree that this was the most difficult of all. First, because it was real, and not imaginary; and then, because it is always easier to make, for love's sake, great sacrifices, than to relinquish the love itself, which makes them so light, and often so dear.

Yes; there could be hesitation no longer, the thread of her life must be once more broken. And this time, what loss and pain! She must go, never to return. After what had passed, self-deception and security were no longer possible for her. In remaining, she would be false to all the duties which rested upon her, and to all the gratitude which she owed the princess. Yes, she must go,— but whither? and under what pretext? Alas! and her *brothers*—was it needful to relinquish the sweet happiness of aiding them, a happiness whose means the princess took pleasure in providing! But this last thought came to strengthen all the rest; in return for so much kindness, should she cause her vexation and grief? no!—not even anxiety and displeasure. At all hazards, she must go; the princess must not know the cause of her departure, and yet her consent must be obtained. This was a great difficulty, for she foresaw, on her part, a very decided opposition.

"What shall I do! what shall I do!" repeated poor Fleurange, in her perplexity. "Oh God, do Thou assist me, for what I seek is to do Thy will,—what I desire, is to know it!"

While the young girl thus thought and struggled and prayed, the hours sped by. Already she had once left her window, but feeling that she could not sleep, she only laid aside her evening dress, and put on a *robe de chambre;* then scarcely observing that the night was far advanced she returned to the place which she had left, and the reverie which she had broken off.

Suddenly she heard steps in the corridor which led to the private staircase, and some one knocked hastily at her door.

She opened it instantly.

It was Barbe. "What?" she said, with an air of surprise, "are you still awake at this hour?"

"Yes," said Fleurange. "I was not sleepy, and—"

Barbe interrupted her.

"So much the better," she said, "for the princess is ill, and desires you to come to her instantly. Come, come quickly, *mademoiselle*, for, as you know, I am so frightened when I see her in this condition, that I lose my wits completely."

Fleurange was at the end of the corridor before Barbe had ceased speaking, and, in another minute, was at the bedside of her mistress. It evidently was the commencement of one of those severe and painful attacks to which the Princess Catherine was subject.

She had not had one since their arrival in Florence; at the instant, all Dr. Leblanc's advice and directions returned to the mind of Fleurange. Her whole appearance changed. Instead of waiting to obey, it was she who suddenly gave orders; to her every one yielded obedience, and soon her calm firmness partially appeased the terror which, in this house, at once seized on all, when illness (and illness in this frightful form) invaded the luxurious comfort with which they were surrounded. From this terror, George himself was not exempt: he had been the first to reach his mother's bedside, and now he was supporting her head, and endeavoring to hold her hands, which were agitated by a convulsive motion; but, little habituated to the sight, he trembled in spite of himself, and his habitual courage here failed utterly to be of use to him.

Fleurange observed this, and made a sign to him to yield his place to her, or rather she took it without his being able to prevent her, and he now stood motionless beside the bed, while with extraordinary strength and skill she succeeded in subduing the fearful paroxysm.

"Speak to her again," George said. "When she hears your voice, or your hand rests on hers, she seems to become more calm at once."

"Do not be anxious," said Fleurange, "and leave her with me. Leave me here alone, I implore you."

Thus adjured, George went away from the bedside, but he did not leave the room, and remained leaning against the wall in the shadow, and watching from this distance, by the light of a shaded lamp, his mother's altered countenance. Every lingering trace of beauty, preserved usually by the most refined arts of the toilette, had suddenly vanished. In an hour she had grown ten years older. Frightful spasms passed across her face, and her eyes, which roved wildly in every direction, seemed to pass in review, with an air of reproach, all these objects accummalated for her comfort, which were now so powerless to give her a moment's ease.

The spectacle caused George to shudder. Yet he was reckoned, not only among men of acknowledged bravery, but among those whose temerity amounted even to rashness. A thousand times had he defied death, and affronted perils for no other cause than that they were such. This kind of courage has nothing in common, however, with that which leads one calmly to look on suffering and death—not under that aspect with which the very enthusiasm even that hurries us towards them can invest these objects of terror, but as they present themselves to us on beds of pain, as they lie in wait for us ourselves!

From them, thus presented, George turned away with absolute horror; he recoiled from them with all the sensitiveness of a nature noble and refined, indeed, but enfeebled by pleasure and self-indulgence, and which would always be more capable of brilliant acts of heroism than of unobserved sacrifices.

Notwithstanding his real affection for his mother, it is very probable therefore that he would not long have endured the distress of seeing her suffer, had not the lugubrious gleam of the shaded lamp enabled him to discern the face and the motions of her who had so efficiently replaced him in the sick room. He therefore remained where he was, watching with admiration the calm and simple attitudes of Fleurange. She had already sent away several of the women, whose services were superfluous, and, by degrees, order and tranquillity were re-established around her. Barbe went and came, in a great flutter, with manifest goodwill, but never able to control the terror with which the illness of her mistress invariably inspired her. In this regard, Barbe had never felt the least displeasure at the intervention of Fleurange, and it was now with secret joy that she received orders from the latter to leave the room.

"It is nearly four o'clock," said Fleurange, as she glanced at the magnificent clock opposite her. "She is now a little easier; go and sleep, Barbe."

"And you, mademoiselle!"

"I shall remain; I shall not go before seven; at that hour the physician will return. After his visit I will go and lie down, and you shall take my place."

This order, calm and definite, was not one of those that Barbe needed to receive a second time. She hastened to draw up an arm-chair for the young girl; she brought a table for the remedies of which there might be need, and went out, never dreaming but that she left Fleurange alone with the princess.

George for a moment hesitated; to abandon Fleurange to that solitary watch was almost an act of cowardice; to remain near her thus unknown to herself was almost an act of treachery. He decided to emerge from his corner, and very softly he drew near the bed.

At the sound of his footsteps, Fleurange quickly turned her head with a start of surprise. The motion, slight though it was, awakened the sufferer. Her distress recommenced, and the spasms, scarcely controlled, were renewed more violently than before. For a few moments, the presence of George and his assistance were not useless to the young girl, but while she preserved her composure, his was lost completely, and it seemed as if it were impossible for him to endure the sight of this suffering which he could not alleviate.

"My mother! my poor mother!" he cried in agony,

"Gabrielle! Gabrielle!" murmured the sufferer, in an agitated voice.

Fleurange passed her arm under the head of her mistress, and sustained her with one hand, while with the other she clasped her icy hands.

"Oh Gabrielle! do not leave me! do not ever leave me!" continued the Princess in a voice scarcely audible.

Fleurange hid her face in the pillow against which she was leaning, while another voice repeated close beside her, in the lowest whisper:

"Ah no! never!"

After an instant, she raised her head.

"Leave us now, Count George," she said. "I ask you to do it."

There was an irresistible authority in her tone. George, however, hesitated for an instant, and she repeated: "I ask you to do it," and, in spite of himself, he obeyed as if it had been a command.

But as soon as he was out of the sick-room, he felt relieved, like a man to whom restraint, even the most transient, was insupportable. He needed to breathe the fresh air. He went through the *salon* and out upon the terrace.

Daybreak was beginning to brighten in the east. He took a few steps, breathing the fragrant air with delight, then stood with folded arms for a long time, and watched the pure blue of the sky assume the first tints of dawn. Without being aware of it, he hastened to efface the impression which the scene just now before his eyes had caused him.

His nature was affectionate, and, as we have said, brave. It would have been highly unjust to doubt this, but he felt an incessant need of finding in external objects the gratification of this capacity for enjoyment which was the most strongly-marked part of his nature, and which rendered him keenly sensitive to painful or unpleasant impressions. There was nothing degrading or unworthy in his tastes; what attracted George was always truly beautiful and charming and interesting. Vice, like ugliness, was repugnant to him, but so also was suffering, illness, pain. He ignored absolutely the mysterious and divine power which can trans-

This way of being free and independent was unknown to him—to him, who attached so much value to liberty and independence!—and, when this is the case, there remains hidden in characters which are otherwise generous, a secret germ of weakness and self-love, which will suddenly manifest itself, to one's surprise, even in the case of those who have shown themselves capable of the most impassioned sentiments, and have given proof of the most impetuous courage.

XXIII.

The following days were marked by the progress, the apogee, and the decline of the Princess's disorder. Soon the effects of care and medicine became visible, and convalescence fairly commenced. And now it became the most difficult time of all for those who surrounded the invalid, the time when the presence of Fleurange was more than ever necessary. From the very first her judgment and gentle firmness had controlled everything, and had yielded prompt obedience, not excluding the patient herself, who was not in a condition to resist. But, with returning strength the latter at once resumed the exercise of a capricious and obstinate self-will, and it was precisely at this phase of the preceding attack that the young girl had made conquest of the favor which she now enjoyed. Fleurange felt that it would have been a thousand times easier to have quitted her when she was almost unconscious, than at this moment, when her mistress could not do without her, and claimed her services at every hour. She could spare the princess the trouble of writing a letter, or receiving a visit. She alone could arrange her books, her flowers, the thousand trifles which surrounded her, to the liking of the difficult eyes, and the capricious taste. Finally, and above all, it was thanks to her that the evening glided by without weariness, while the physician still forbade the *salon* to be reopened, and condemned the princess to receive none but her most intimate friends.

It was at this hour that Fleurange was called to read aloud, and her voice and accent lent a charm to the reading, of which the critical taste of the princess never grew weary.

"Truly, Gabrielle," she said one evening, as the young

girl finished a selection which the princess had herself chosen, "it is an exquisite pleasure to hear you read. George, pay a little attention to what we are doing here, if you please; lay aside that review which absorbs you, and come nearer. She has just read me the sonnet of Dante,

"Tanto gentile et tanto onesta pare
La Donna mia—"

in a way that it is worth your while to listen to."

There was a moment's silence. A great screen hid the light from the eyes of the princess: the other side of this rampart sat Fleurange. She blushed, for she was perfectly aware that it was not upon the book which he pretended to read, that the young man's eyes had been fixed for the last few minutes.

"I have not been so inattentive as you suppose, mother," George said at last. "Those verses would attract my notice at any time."

And he repeated half aloud:

'E da per gli occhi una dolcezza al core,
Ch' intender non la può chi non la prova.'

George approached the table, and the expression of his eyes did not allow Fleurange to deceive herself concerning the application which he made of the lines.

Alas! for a month had she been forced to accept, to enjoy, let us own it—the presence of him whom she had resolved to flee, and she had been obliged to dismiss from her mind all thought of her own position, outside of the duties which it imposed upon her. Her will, however, had not known an instant's weakness. Every day, no doubt, the sacrifice grew more difficult, but, from that very fact, more necessary. What she sought was still the hour and the means of accomplishing it.

The princess Catherine was now in full convalescence, and could well endure the annoyance which Fleurange felt obliged to cause her. On the same evening, therefore, when the little scene occurred which we have related above, she had resolved to grant but one day longer to the considerations which had heretofore retarded her act. Longer to remain where she was, would be, she felt, henceforth a

Another thing upon which she had resolved was to confide all to her good friend, Dr. Leblanc. He was at this very time, in accordance with a promise made the preceding year, paying a visit to her friends in their new home in Heidelberg. Better than any one else, he understood her position in the household of the princess, and could aid her in leaving it. Better than any other, he could prepare the way for her return to her family without betraying this motive which she was so anxious to conceal; but to mention Count George, even to the doctor, was very hard for Fleurange. The unfinished letter still awaited its conclusion, and yet she felt that the hour for delay was past.

She had replaced the book upon the table, and was sitting silently, absorbed in thought. The princess was following out the ideas suggested to her by what Fleurange had read, and Count George, at intervals replying absent-mindedly to his mother's observations, was trying to catch a glimpse of the downcast eyes which so carefully avoided his own.

At this moment an unexpected message came to surprise all three. The *valet de chambre*, who was also the porter, announced to Mlle. Gabrielle that a young man was in the vestibule and desired to speak to her.

"A young man!"—the princess and her son made this exclamation at the same moment and quite as earnestly as did Fleurange.

"A young man!" she repeated; "did you ask his name?"

"Yes."

The *valet de chambre* had asked, but he had forgotten it completely, and stammered some names as unintelligible as they were unknown to Fleurange.

She rose. "I will go and see who it can be," she said.

George had already risen, while the princess exclaimed that Fleurange should not go down alone, so late as it was; that ill-disposed persons often introduced themselves thus in the evening; that the day before, in broad daylight, an unknown man had entered a shop, and while no one was looking—

And the princess grew quite agitated over this little occurrence.

"If you will permit me, *mademoiselle*," George said, "I will go and see who the person is. Wait a moment, and I will bring you word."

Fleurange offered no objections. She knew no one, and expected no one, and was quite persuaded there must be some mistake.

George was not gone two minutes; when he returned his face showed much pleasure.

"It is a young man," he said, "and it is you, *mademoiselle*, whom he desires to see, but I have had my share of the pleasure also, in shaking hands with Julian Steinberg! He and his wife have just arrived in town."

"Julian! Julian and Clara!" cried Fleurange, with rapture; she sprang forward, for an instant forgetting the princess, and George, and all other things, in her unexpected happiness at seeing these beloved faces again.

Count George stopped her. "Excuse me, *mademoiselle*," he said, "Steinberg only desired to know when his wife could see you. I thought it was the best way to say that my carriage, which is below, will take you at once to the hotel where they are staying, and he hastened away to tell her, without a moment's delay, that they are to have the happiness of seeing you this evening."

"Oh! how kind you are!" cried Fleurange, "and how many thanks I owe you."

But she suddenly remembered that the princess did not much enjoy anything unless she had the initiative, and, in no case, could ever quite forget herself.

Before the cloud began to gather on her brow, Fleurange hastened to her side.

"Count George is extremely kind," she said, "but it would be better to wait till to-morrow, do you not think so, princess? It is but nine o'clock; you will need me still for an hour?"

The princess was already half disarmed by these words. She was entirely so by the grace with which her son declared that he should be vexed if she showed too clearly that she regarded him incapable of taking Mlle. Gabrielle's place for a single hour.

"Come, mother," he said, "you can endure my reading to you, can you not? I am perfectly aware it will not be th same thing. But if the contrast displeases you, could we not pass a few minutes together to our mutual satisfaction? how long is it since I have lost the gift of making my conversation agreeable to you for an hour?"

These words, spoken with a caressing grace as he came and knelt by his mother's chair, touched the weakest and the most tender spot in this maternal heart. The princess idolized her son; he was the joy and the pride of her existence. But though he showed her all possible deference and tenderness, he perpetually escaped her.

This woman, so imperious towards everybody, found herself almost powerless in the case of her son, and sought to acquire an ascendency over him by the use of all her tact and skill, as though this ascendency had not been her natural right. Since his last return, George had been more reserved than was his wont; until this moment he had been able to evade all the efforts of his mother to bring about one of those frank conversations in which he would sometimes open his heart to her, and which compensated her most amply for the longer or shorter periods of reserve which had preceded them.

And now she laid her hand tenderly upon the handsome head bent towards her, and said with a smile:

"Bad child! you know what argument to use!"

Then turning to Fleurange she said: "Go, if you like; I am quite willing; go and welcome your cousin. I will do without you for the moment. You may go, but come back in an hour. I shall expect you at ten," she added, looking at the clock.

The permission was not very graciously given, but Fleurange availed herself of it most gladly; but she did not leave the room without involuntarily repaying with a glance him who had so well known how to guess her wish and had so adroitly seconded it.

XXIV.

Fleurange took time only to wrap herself in a great white *burnous*, whose hood she threw over her head, and sprang into the carriage which awaited her. It seemed to her as though heaven had sent her aid at the hour of her greatest need. She knew not in what manner, but she felt that in some way the presence of her cousin would facilitate her resolution. At all events, she was now no longer alone and one of the difficulties which had been in her way, had vanished.

These thoughts occupied her mind to the exclusion of all others, during the brief drive from the palace to the hotel. But, on arriving, on seeing Clara once more, everything disappeared, save the sweet memory of the past, the Old House, the home-fireside, the changes that had come since these two had last seen one another,—all returned with poignant intensity, and it was with tearful joy that they fell into each other's arms.

After the first emotion had somewhat abated, the two cousins looked at one another; though little more than a year had passed since their separation, great changes had passed over both.

Clara was not less fresh or less pretty than heretofore, but the beautiful baby whose birth had delayed for some months their return to Germany, seemed to have added to her girlish loveliness that something grave which comes with a mother's joy, and crowns the beauty of other days with a splendid stateliness unknown before.

As to Fleurange, it would have been more difficult to say what had transformed her. Was it the elegance of her toilette, with which the princess would never dispense, even when they were alone? was it the high society, in which she now lived? was it her greater paleness and that dejected air which gave that gentleness to her face, that new grace to her figure, to all her person, that charm even more striking than heretofore? Fleurange had suffered too much, and at too early an age, for her face to have ever reflected the careless gayety of youth. But still, after a few weeks passed under her uncle's roof, wh more radiant smile had lighted up the old house, what more joyous voice than that of Gabrielle had made it resound?

At this moment, her pale and noble features wore a look of premature gravity. Her expression of tranquil decision no longer betrayed that enthusiasm and excitement which once made her face at times so brilliant, and gave to her gray eyes the vivid splendor of black. Without having grown a day older, you would say she had acquired the experience of maturity, and that she had measured life without having taken a step further into it.

Clara and Julian, regarding her with a sort of disturbed admiration, abstained from questioning her. Something warned them that Fleurange would prefer not to be obliged to answer anything, and, indeed, her own questions prevented theirs. Those names dear to all three were mentioned in succession, and repeated over and over, while for a few minutes everything was illuminated in the sweet light of that far-off home fireside, her separation from which the young girl, through all her more recent emotions, had never failed to feel.

All was going well with these dear absent ones. Comfort, peace, and even something of luxury had reappeared under their roof, thanks to the energy and good sense of Clement.

"Dear Clement!" Clara repeated, with tears in her eyes; "he is like an earthly Providence to them all! God bless and recompense him—this dear brother!"

Then the travellers spoke of themselves. They were now only passing through Florence, where they had already spent much time; after a little detour to visit Perouse, and a few more of those places so dear to artists, they were to resume their homeward way. Already impatiently expected at Heidelberg, they were to remain there for the succeeding year, Julian having to make good the time that their delightful journey had cost them, and to undertake without delay the work that had been assigned to him.

Perouse!—hardly had they mentioned this name when a sudden idea presented itself to the mind of Fleurange.— On the way to Perouse, one must pass near Santa Maria al

Prato. Could she not accompany them thus far? could she not go and take refuge in the advice, the tenderness, the support of Madre Madelina? And thus guided, should she not be sure of taking the right course amid her perplexities? If courage were wanting, where would she find it more surely than with her, the very thought of whom brought new strength and vigor to her soul? if she needed consolation, who better than Madre Madelina could impart it? Yes, the opportunity was providential, she must hasten to avail herself of it, and without for the moment saying anything about departure and definitive separation, the consent of the princess must be asked and obtained to make that little journey, and to be absent, first, for a few days.

This plan sketched, Fleurange breathed freely, as though a weight had been lifted from her heart, and, the hour not yet expired, she took leave of her cousin, after making an engagement for the coming day, and returned in the carriage which had brought her.

It was the month of May. The spring-time, and the spring-time of Florence, was in the air. The carriage of Count George was an open *calèche*. At the moment that she took her seat, a passer-by, struck no doubt by her beauty, threw her one of those great bouquets, which, in this city of flowers, are at this season in everybody's hands: Fleurange, not even turning her head to see who offered her this discreet homage, had accepted it without scruple, and now with delight, she inhaled its fragrance. She experienced at the same moment, an unwonted gratification in the caresses of the fresh, sweet night air, in finding herself for an instant alone, with uncovered head, under the pure and brilliant sky. After the long constraint she had undergone, after so many days and nights passed in a room whither air and light could scarcely penetrate, this moment of liberty was a moral and a physical solace, of which, unknown to herself, she had imperious need. Further, through all the anxiety of care which she lavished upon her mistress, one idea, or rather, one grief had not ceased to pursue her, and she had practised without respite, a perpetual renunciation of the enjoyment of an affection whose mute or murmured expression had taken within the last few weeks, a thousand opportunities to make itself heard or divined. She found another solace, therefore, at this moment in saying to herself that this strife was about to cease, that a way to escape being open to her, there needed effort, courage, self control, but a few days longer, and then, she would only be obliged to suffer, and no longer to fear, for herself and for others.

The night drive was all too quickly ended. The horses went like the wind, and a few minutes brought her to the foot of the great marble stair-case. She ascended it slowly, and slowly went down the great *salons* towards the one where she had left the princess and her son. This room, as we know, the last of the *suite*, opened like the one which preceded it, upon the terrace which formed also an exterior communication between the two.

Reaching this last *salon* Fleurange stood for a moment; she feared that her mistress might have retired, and no longer expected or wanted her. But this was not the case. Count George was still with his mother. Fleurange heard distinctly the sound of their voices; thanks to the spring warmth of the evening, all the windows were wide open, and she passed out upon the terrace, there to await the close of their conversation. The hour fixed by the princess, ten o'clock, had not yet struck.

Scarcely however did she find herself there before she regretted it, for she perceived that, in spite of herself, she heard from this point, not only the voices of those who were talking, but every word that they said. She turned to go back, when her attention was arrested, and she found herself, as it were, fastened to the spot, by a word which reached her ear, and made her start.

The word was this: "Cordelia,"—and almost at the same instant she heard her own name. Her name! Not Gabrielle, by which only had she been known in this house, but that other name of her childhood, that name unknown to any one here in Florence, save to him who at this instant uttered it,—and with what feeling!

"Fleurange!" said Count George. "Yes, mother, this name which has escaped my lips in speaking of her, this name, strange as her beauty, and belonging, like the charm with which she is endowed, to her only in all the world—is the one by which her father called her when I saw her before me, more charming a thousand times than this Cordelia for which she was the model—"

Fleurange heard no more,—for a few minutes, it seemed to her that she should faint, and it was a violent effort of her will that saved her from falling to the ground, overcome with surprise and emotion.

Was it indeed he whose voice she had just heard? was it indeed his mother to whom he spoke? What madness could lead him to use language like this to her, thus brave the princess,—her, whom the slightest contradiction often threw into a violent paroxysm of impatience and anger?—her, who would not endure from any one the least resistance!—What would she say? What reply was Fleurange about to hear?

She no longer thought of stirring from the spot, she had no idea if she did well or ill to listen; she had but one thought, to hear what her mistress would reply, and to act in accordance with it. Who could tell? perhaps after hearing it, she might leave this place, never again to appear in her presence; already the confused idea crossed her mind, to re-descend the palace stair-case, and to go her way, in the street, and in the darkness, alone and on foot, to Julian and Clara.

At this moment, after a long silence, she heard the voice of the princess; to her great surprise this sad and agitated voice betrayed no passion; its effect was only the more profound upon her who listened with beating heart.

"So then, George," she said, "you wish to occasion me the greatest disappointment that a son can cause his mother?—Your promise, upon which I relied with so much confidence, you now desire to violate?"

"Mother, I have already told you, my word has never been given."

"Enough, George! Thanks for your frankness,—do not spoil it by a lie. If not to *her*, you break your word to me, to me, your mother. That is enough, I think, to give me some cause to reproach you!"

"Mother!"—and George rose with an impatient air,

occurred that some violent and sudden emotion would banish in an instant the last traces of a long attack of illness.

She put one arm around her son's neck and drew him towards her.

"George," she said to him, when he had resumed his place at her side, "I ought never again to trust any of your promises; but yet there is one I beg you to make me."

"Say on, mother."

"You will not commit this folly, without giving yourself time to reflect."

"I promise you."

"Listen to me further. Swear to me that you will not do it without obtaining my consent."

George hesitated.

"That would be a very serious promise," he said, in a caressing voice, "were I not sure that in the end you would refuse nothing to your spoilt child."

"George, George," his mother cried eagerly, an accent of acute pain betraying itself in her voice, "do not make me repent of my tenderness. Your promise?"

"Well then, mother, I confess I should hesitate perhaps for my own part to give it,—but, without having ever questioned her, without even knowing, in fact, how I might be received—"

The princess shrugged her shoulders.

"However it may be as to that," resumed George, "I am convinced about this consent—she would be less ready than I to dispense with it; and, in this regard, my obedience is in the keeping of a far stronger will than mine."

The princess, at first, looked surprised; then she said, after a moment's reflection:

"Perhaps you may be right. However, your hand upon this promise."

George bent down, and kissed his mother's hand, and clasped it in his own.

"There it is," he said, "my promise! Upon my honor!"

"That is well, my child; leave me now. Gabrielle will come in, and it is better she should not find you here."

George rose, and after having again kissed his mother, he left the room.

As soon as she was alone, the princess threw herself upon her *chaise longue*, and hiding her face in her hands, burst into violent sobbing.

XXV.

One moment Fleurange hesitated; then she followed her natural impulse. Resolutely she came in through the terrace-window, and when the princess lifted her head, she saw standing before her the young girl wrapped in the white *burnous*, the bouquet still in her hand.

Although the princess was expecting her, this sudden appearance surprised her to that degree that she looked at the young girl for one instant in utter silence, as though she had been a supernatural vision. But only for an instant. Fleurange perceived that the passion, suppressed in the presence of her son, was now about to break forth.

The tears of the princess had ceased to flow, and her eyes expressed at once anger and disdain. She rose quickly, and severe words were about to second the imperious gesture with which one hand designated the door, already, even, the other hand was laid rudely upon the shoulder of the young girl, when, without arrogance and without fear, the latter looked her in the face.

The expression in the large eyes of Fleurange was at that moment such that one could compare it to nothing but that magnetic gaze which conquers sometimes, we are told, the fury of unreasoning creatures. No language could have told so plainly the integrity and purity of her soul. Through all her faults, the nobility which existed in the soul of the princess was touched by this look, and responded to it. She turned away her eyes, and fell back in a sitting posture upon the *chaise longue;* she suffered Fleurange to possess herself of those two hands whose gesture was but a moment since so menacing, and to hold them some instants clasped in her own: there was a great silence.

Finally, with a voice calm and gentle, Fleurange said:
" Princess, I was upon the terrace, and I heard all."

A new flash of indignation awakened in the eyes of

her mistress, and her mouth resumed its expression of scorn.

The young girl colored faintly.

"You will readily see that I did not come with the intention of listening to your conversation," she resumed. "But, having heard my own name, I remained. It was wrong, I know, but time and reflection were wanting to prevent it. Pardon me; and forgive me also," she added, in an agitated voice, "the moment's displeasure that Count George has just caused you, on my account;"

"The moment's displeasure!" repeated the princess in a cold and ironical tone.

"At least," continued Fleurange, "you will have had but for a moment the pain of thinking that this idea, this folly of which you have just heard, could be serious enough to grieve or disturb you."

"Gabrielle!"

"Permit me to speak, princess, later you shall reply. My heart is so full of gratitude towards you—"

"Do not mention your gratitude towards me," cried the princess, interrupting her, and breaking out into a violent passion anew; "it is precisely because I believed myself to have some rights, that I am wounded so deeply, and after I have loved you so much, I am tempted to hate you. It is your perfidy, your ingratitude—"

"I am neither false nor ungrateful," said Fleurange, growing paler, "suffer me to prove it to you; it is for your own sake I ask it, even more than mine."

The princess again grew calm, as if appeased by this sweet voice, and seemed to resign herself to let Fleurange go on; she rested her head upon her hand, and listened motionless.

"No," Fleurange repeated, "I am neither false nor ungrateful, and to spare you this vexation or any other, God knows I would willingly suffer!—I thought at first," she continued, "that I would go at once, that I would fly, I would deliver you from my presence, and from the anxiety it might cause you. But princess, it must be done in a better way; he must be led to forget me. On this account it is not best that I should disappear in any romantic manner."

"What do you mean to say?" said the princess with surprise.

"Of course I must go, but not in any way that will give him the idea of following me. The less he is opposed upon this subject, the more rapidly my image will be effaced from his mind."

"You understand him well," said the princess, more and more astonished, "and you speak of it coolly enough," she added. "This poor George, you do not love him then at all?"

And this mother, just now so irritated at the presumption of her *protégée*, was on the point of becoming angry at her indifference.

A quick and violent color spread over the face of Fleurange; her eyes filled with tears: "I do not love him!" she murmured in a stifled voice, "Ah, Heaven have mercy!"

But she recovered her self-control almost instantly, while the princess more touched than she was willing to show, became attentive and ended by perceiving the importance of that which she was about to hear.

Fleurange then rapidly explained her plan; it was the same that she had formed an hour before, during her visit to her cousin; only at that time she had wished to hide from the princess the motive and the duration of her absence. All now became more easy: she should go to Perouse with the Steinbergs; while there she should find a pretext for prolonging her absence, the only points of importance being that the princess should seem to expect her speedy return, and above all that she should manifest no anxiety in regard to her son's fulfilment of his promise.

"As regards this promise," continued Fleurange, not without a certain just pride, "I may dare to say that in

George to submission, no maternal authority would have succeeded in constraining him thereto. Whatever it might cost her to acknowledge this, she could not disguise from herself that if this two-fold wound to pride and affection was spared her, she owed it not only to the generous disinterestedness of her whom she had just treated with so much *hauteur*, but also to her admirable good sense; yes, she was perfectly right in thinking that it would not be enough to suddenly disappear, to be, so to speak, carried off from George. The princess, better than any one else knew to what degree of tenacity such contradiction as this would lead her son, and it was precisely this knowledge of his character, and this only, which just now had given her strength to control herself before him. Fleurange had suggested the best, and in fact, the only method; thanks to that, the future might be saved! George was extremely changeful, the princess hoped much from this, provided that on the one hand, he should be withdrawn from the fatal charm of the presence of Fleurange, and that, on the other, the *prestige* of some great obstacle to be overcome should cease apparently to exist between them. Nothing was ever more skillful than the counsel given against herself by this young girl. The woman of the world understood and valued it. She saw the object reappear for which she had so long striven; and, in the hope of attaining that, she accepted, without remorse, the necessity of treading under foot the noble heart which thus sacrificed itself; it must even be owned that if any thing did occupy her mind, outside of the present danger, it was not the broken life of Gabrielle, but the habitudes of her own life deranged, and her own comfort disturbed by this unhappy event. Nevertheless, when they parted, at the conclusion of this long interview, the princess clasped Fleurange in her arms, in a transport of tenderness, and when the latter found herself in her own room, she felt for a moment almost completely happy. She held all deceit in such horror that the great step she had just taken, in its courageous frankness, seemed to have consoled her heart.

She was still in that enthusiastic condition of mind which follows the accomplishment of some great effort, when, entering her room she threw down the bouquet which till now she had held in her hand. At this moment a paper which she had not observed, detached itself and fell to the floor; she picked it up with some surprise, opened it mechanically, saw an unknown handwriting, and read, without understanding at first its meaning:

"To live, unable to make amends; to suffer, unable to expiate; is this a punishment of earth or of hell? Not far from you, a man thus lives and suffers: *you who pray, pray for him!*"

Fleurange read and re-read two or three times these words, without attaching any meaning to them: suddenly she started, trembling from head to foot. These last words were the refrain of a romance sung one of those evenings in the Old House, in presence of the only man in the world who could apply to himself the other words which she had just read.

But was it possible, great Heavens! that this was he? Could it be that it was Felix, her guilty and unhappy cousin, who had written them?—he, who, this very evening, had placed them in this bouquet! Was it his hand which had thrown it?

At the thought she shuddered, as though the ghost of one already dead had passed near her.

But was it only some mystification? The ruin of the house of Dornthal was not an unknown story to the gay world in Florence. Had some one wished to frighten or tease her? She lost herself in conjecture concerning this unexpected event.

How emerge from this uncertainty? How even mention the subject, without awakening an unpleasant memory, or making a painful revelation?

Suddenly she remembered the presence of Julian in the city, and this thought tranquilized her. Julian would assist her in the discovery of the truth, and better than any other he would know how to avoid doing harm by his inquiries to the unhappy man, who perhaps at this moment was hiding near them his blighted and dishonored life.

XXVI.

If, on the preceding evening, any one had predicted to the princess Catherine that her charming companion was about to be taken from her, the news might have sufficed to throw her back into that alarming condition whence, thanks to the young girl's devotion, she had but just emerged. But an interest more powerful than her fancy for Gabrielle was now at stake, and her self-love vanished, or rather was transformed, in presence of the danger which she reproached herself that she had not sooner recognized, and which threatened an essential part of her happiness, as well as the accomplishment of one of her dearest wishes.

Not to be unjust towards the princess, it must be owned that the wish was a reasonable one, and that, in the determination with which she pursued it she gave proof of true maternal clear-sightedness, as well as of wordly wisdom. We must say also that the plan in question had reference to the will, in her eyes sacred, of the adored husband of her youth, whose memory hovered always over that remote past, when life at its outset was for her better and more simple, and promised to be quite other than that which succeeding years had made it. Later, when, a widow, beautiful, rich, and still young, she had appeared in the high society of St. Petersburg, she had only herself for guide, and against the tendencies of a light and frivolous nature she had no curb but her own pride. Amid all the intoxications of this second period, she had however respected that limit beyond which the opinion of the fashionable world itself is changed, and still lavishing its incense and its flattery, denies its respect. This limit she was saved from the risk of crossing, above all by her pride, the leading trait in her character, which everywhere and always sought the highest place, and which, after having preserved to her life a sort of dignity, alone guided her in the choice of a second husband. She now believed herself happy, having attained rank, honors and fortune, but quickly perceived that she was paying for these advantages too dearly, and perhaps she might have less patiently endured the test of a badly assorted union than of the independence which had preceded it, if—at the end of two years—death had not restored to her this independence.

Henceforward, nothing came to disturb the brilliant and prosperous current of a life in which, in spite of generous instincts and a tolerably well-cultivated mind, all was frivolity, save her affection for her son. And this very affection, ardent and passionate though it was, lacked that which gives a mother's love the majesty of authority. This charming boy, who, from his earliest years, possessed all the grace that an ardent and affectionate nature could add to rare intelligence and uncommon beauty, fully satisfied that maternal pride which, in proud natures, is the most powerful of all emotions. The princess, glorying in her handsome boy, did not perceive that she was only adored, and never obeyed; and the years glided by till that period,

"*Ove uom s'innamora.*"

Then the princess Catherine began to see that she had no empire whatever over this idolized son, and that she required much prudence and address to escape from what would have been for her the most cruel of all failures: for she now felt for him all the ambitions of her own life, more keenly than she had ever experienced them for herself.

And now the ardent desire re-awakened in her to see realized a wish formed by the father of George, when the latter was but an infant in his cradle. Count von Walden had a neighbor in Livonia, a brother in arms, and a dear and intimate friend, by name Count von Liningen. Both noble, among the most noble in the province, rich, and possessors of contiguous domains, they promised them-

dered her mistress of all the estates. But, in awaiting the time when she could take possession of her fortune, the young heiress was sent to St. Petersburg, and had there been brought up in profound seclusion by one of her aunts who had long since retired from society.

The Princess Catherine had always preserved a respectful memory of a wish, which on his death-bed, Count von Walden had commended to her, but this memory assumed in her eyes a new and very different aspect, when, towards the time of which we are speaking, the youthful Vera suddenly emerged from her seclusion, and was presented at court. The effect which the young girl produced, the immediate favor with which she was received, the place which was granted her among the maids of honor of the empress, gave to this *début* a distinction of which the princess regretted deeply George had not been a witness; but he had been gone from St. Petersburg many months, and was making his first visit in Paris. During his absence his mother had neglected no opportunity of forming the intimate acquaintance of the young maid of honor; this was rendered easy, besides, by the ancient ties of friendship between the two families, and these were now renewed with a degree of fervor on both sides that augured well to the princess for the renewal of this project formed in the infancy of the two young people, who, since then, had never seen one another. Her impatience for his return increased. Vera seemed to her made to captivate her son; and as to George, his mother could never be anxious about the effect that he would produce.

At last he came, and indeed all seemed to go well for the plan of the princess. George was very much struck, almost fascinated. The beautiful Vera was still more so, but the princess, carried away by the ardor with which she desired this marriage, committed the indiscretion of speaking of it to her son, with an earnestness which had an effect precisely opposite to that which she desired to produce. George had not returned from Paris in exactly the right mood to accept, upon the instant, the idea of losing his liberty, and being forever bound. He put himself on his guard; the words which Vera perhaps already expected, hesitated upon his lips and changed into idle flatteries. His mother, without abandoning her dream, understood that she must postpone its realization. They were both young, however; her woman's and mother's eye was not deceived in regard to the impression made by her son. She believed that she could trust to the durability of the sentiment he had occasioned, and in time she had no doubt that George would return of his own free will to the feet of her whom the mother regarded as his destiny, and the more since in one of their conversations he had admitted that no woman had ever pleased him so well, and had almost promised his mother that he would never offer his hand to any one else.

Affairs therefore remained in this position. George returned to Paris, and afterwards to Italy, where his mother made it her home. But we know how, in this state of affairs, the sudden sight of Fleurange, and still other influences, had by degrees drawn away his mind and his heart in a direction very different from that which his mother sought to give them. At his last visit in St. Petersburg (during which time Fleurange had come to stay with the princess) the latter had the two-fold displeasure of learning that her son had avoided Vera as far as possible, and that this indifference so wounding to the young girl, had been ascribed by many to the political opinions which people imputed to George with a malevolence that greatly disquieted his mother. Any one who knows Russia, knows that, at that time, to lose the master's favor was no light misfortune. If the insolent utterance of a period earlier, though yet recent, was no longer exactly true, if the emperor had ceased to say that a man was something only *when* he spoke to him, and *while* he spoke to him, many at St. Petersburg conducted themselves as though this were the truth, and the princess could not have faced for her son with any resignation the position of a man in disgrace at court. And yet the imprudence and rashness of his language kept her constantly uneasy in this regard. It was therefore with an ardor almost like a maternal instinct of approaching danger that she desired his union with Vera, which would have permitted him at will to reside at court or to leave it; but in this latter case to go and occupy the position which their united rank and fortune would assure to them in Livonia, a position in comparison with which even court favor would have become insignificant.

"Oh, why is it not already a certainty?" cried the princess, with an impatience that was mingled with anguish; "why is he not already thus sheltered from all which I dread!"

And then, contrary to the counsels of her better judgment, she allowed herself, in her intercourse with her son, to enter upon a subject which, in the interest of her own plans, she should never have mentioned. Thus against her intention she stimulated a resistance, whose real cause, which she as yet did not at all perceive, was growing clearer to himself every day.

One can now understand the effect which had been produced upon the princess by the confidence into which George had suffered himself to be drawn in an excess of capricious *abandon*. At heart he was not at all afraid of his mother, and although he would probably never, of his own free will, have put her indulgence to so hard a test, he was convinced that whatever repugnance she might at first feel to his designs, a little persistence on his own part must, sooner or later, conquer it.

For nearly four months it is true, he had practised a quite unwonted art of dissimulation in respect to the attraction which he felt, but it was that he might not disquiet his mother, nor the young girl herself, nor cause himself to be deprived of her charming presence, while as yet he was uncertain what his real plans might be. These plans he now believed himself fully to understand. Under the increasing empire of the impulse which he now felt, the remembrance of Vera faded daily, and the future as well as the present, seemed to belong to her, who, for the moment, filled his existence. He decided then, upon a sudden impulse, to suffer his mother to understand fully what was going on in his heart.

Notwithstanding her inexpressible alarm, the princess had self-control enough to receive this disturbing confidence with apparent calmness, and to hide from her son the truth that this was the saddest disappointment of her life.

At first sight, all seemed lost. The beauty, the charm of Gabrielle,—who knew them, who appreciated them better than herself? What could she do against a fascination so powerful, and no doubt so long exerted, all unknown to the too-credulous mother? What folly, and what imprudence had been hers! What fatal confidence! The only danger of which she could have dreamed, the virtue of Fleurange had prevented her from apprehending. But who could have expected to find in the young girl such unheard-of ambition, such an extreme of madness?

Never had such a storm raged in her heart,—never such hatred succeeded to such affection but, before her anger had time to break forth, all these sentiments had assumed new forms, more surprising and unforeseen than their first.

The enemy became her ally. This person, against whom she felt that she should not be able to contend, came to aid her to contend against herself! And George was restored to her by the hand which could so easily make prize of him past rescue!

In presence of a danger so great, and a succor so unexpected, all the considerations which would before have made her regret the departure of Gabrielle, now united to hasten it, without losing from sight however the importance, so justly pointed out by herself, of doing nothing which might lead George to connect this departure with the confession he had just made to his mother, or giving to it the aspect of a final separation.

The interest at stake was of supreme importance, and there was no danger now that the princess Catherine would be wanting in address, or maternal prudence, or even, if need be, in diplomatic skill.

XXVII.

To say the truth, all now seemed to favor the project which she had at heart, and the opportune arrival of Julian and Clara supplied naturally a pretext which at another time it might have been difficult to find, without ex-

Accordingly, when on the morrow, in the presence of all, Fleurange timidly expressed the desire to accompany her cousin as far as Perouse, the marquis Adelardi, who chanced to be present, declared that this excursion would do her all the good in the world, and begged the princess to grant to her young *protégée* these few days of vacation, of which her exhausted strength stood in need. To these persuasions, George added his own, and the princess then seemed to yield to their prayers, yet rather through complaisance to them than indulgence to Fleurange.

Since the preceding evening, she had preserved towards her son an attitude of sad gravity which did not permit George to forget that he was in disgrace. Nor did she seek to disguise a certain coldness towards Fleurange, which he would naturally attribute to those confidential revelations of his, in which the young girl played so prominent a part.

The *rôle* of the princess was not to permit any one to observe the secret security which her conversation with Fleurange had occasioned her. So George understood, as the result of the whole matter, these two things: that his mother was displeased with him; this displeasure he had anticipated; that she repressed her resentment, and continued to treat Fleurange with kindness; this amiability touched him. He understood, furthermore, that she relied upon his word; he was grateful to her for this confidence.

Everything thus arranged itself in the most natural manner; a fortnight was fixed as the limit of this projected excursion. The Steinbergs, deceived like the rest, welcomed, with as much delight as surprise, the prospect of a pleasure which they would not have ventured to expect, and all was thus settled in furtherance of the will of the princess, without her having the air of doing anything but gratifying the wishes of those who surrounded her.

The Steinbergs were to set off on the morrow. Their last day was to be devoted to revisiting many museums, and, finally, to a walk to San Miniato, which concluded the programme.

Fleurange had no hesitation in proposing to accompany them. A feverish agitation rendered inaction insupportable. She dreaded finding herself alone for an instant with George, and she was very sure that his mother would gladly dispense with her services upon this last day. The consent of the princess proved not difficult to obtain, and towards noon Fleurange set off with Julian and Clara for the Pitti palace.

After having visited this gallery, and several others, they continued their drive, and finally stopped at the foot of the ascent which leads to San Miniato. There they alighted.

As they slowly ascended the steep path-way, Fleurange drew from her pocket the paper which had fallen out of her bouquet on the preceding evening, and gave it to Julian to read, mentioning to him at the same time the suspicion to which it had given rise in her mind.

"It is strange," said the latter, with a thoughtful air, while he examined attentively the lines which he had just read. "Nothing would be more painful, at the present moment, than the re-appearance of Felix among us, and yet I have already experienced a certain degree of anxiety on that subject, which the sight of this paper renews."

"You had already suspected his return to Europe?"

"Yes, but the indication was very slight, and, without this new incident, I should not have mentioned it to you at all. Some months ago, at Bologna, where I went to make a study which I required, there fell under my eye, in the library where I was taking notes, a bit of work which attracted my attention. It was a question of some contested point of history, in regard to which several extracts from some curious manuscripts belonging to this library had been transcribed; the page was open before me, the work had been recently interrupted. I was reading with interest and attention, when I was completely distracted

scrawl where no handwriting was recognizable. I put some questions to the librarian: he replied that the work was done for some distinguished Florentine gentleman, whom he did not know, that the copyist was an Italian, Fabiano Dini by name."

"And is that all?" said Fleurange. "Did you ascertain nothing more positive than this?"

"Nothing. On the morrow the half-finished work had been taken away, and during the rest of my stay in Bologna, the copyist never re-appeared again in the library. I kept the scrawled paper which had so excited my curiosity, and after a while, I thought no more of it. Leave me these lines now, that I may compare them with the others."

"Is it indeed he, or is all this mere accident?"

"Who can tell us?. It might be he, for you know that in Italian he is a perfect adept; but it might also be some companion of his, who knew his history. All that we have ever been able to discover in regard to him is that he went to America, with a party of unfortunates—Italians, Poles, and Germans, all, more or less, banished from their country for good reasons."

The laughing face of Clara grew sad during this recital, and Fleurange felt an additional melancholy oppress her heart. The vague awakening of these most sombre recollections seemed to her to add a presage of sadness to the already sad realities of this day.

She was silent, however. Her cousin for the present must know neither the cause, nor the real duration of the journey which she proposed to undertake with them tomorrow, and, on all accounts, it was better for herself to distract her thoughts from it as far as possible. Consequently, after entering the church of San Miniato, for some time she strove to occupy herself with the frescoes, the pictures and the mosaics, and to listen with attention to the explanations that Julian gave them of some of the symbols that are repeated there,—Christian hieroglyphics which those only know how to comprehend, who seek in art something beyond the form that strikes their eyes!

They had spent nearly an hour in this way, without remarking the passage of time, or noticing that the church was growing dark. Finally they were ready to go, and at the moment when they crossed the threshold, they found themselves suddenly face to face with Count George, who was coming in, accompanied by Adelardi. He knew, he gayly assured them, that their expedition was to terminate at San Miniato, and he had proposed to his friend to come and meet them there.

"We did not consider ourselves unworthy," he said, "of hearing what Steinberg would have to say to you here; unhappily, we are too late."

While he was speaking, Fleurange, agitated and alarmed, had made an involuntary movement to draw back into the shadow of the church. But daylight was fading rapidly, and all agreed that it was needful to return at once to the carriage which awaited them below. She went out with the others, and although she was the last, George had delayed also, and before she could avoid him, he had offered her his arm. Adelardi was already with Clara, and Julian walked beside them, and thus they began to descend slowly this charming hill-side, admiring as they went the prospect, one of the most beautiful in Florence, over which at this moment the sun cast its last soft rays.

George slackened his pace so that the others soon had left them behind, and he thus found himself, in a degree alone with Fleurange; they were both silent. Though differing widely in nature, the emotion of both was extreme.

In her case, all that the consciousness of a last farewell could add to the deep though repressed affection which she felt for him, was making this hour the sweetest and yet the most painful of her life.

As for him, on the contrary, he felt himself released from his former constraint by the species of explanation which he had had with his mother, and since moreover he was by no means *naïf* enough, or unskilled enough in reading a woman's heart, not to have understood what was going on in that one whose beatings he seemed at this moment to hear, he believed himself at liberty to speak more openly than he had ever before done.

"Fleurange!" he said to her suddenly.

She started, and would have withdrawn the hand which

"No, no," he said, "leave me your hand, and let me call you by that name. *Me* only," he added, softly. "Oh! let me keep it for myself,—you are not unwilling, surely?"

He held closer the hand which was in his, and kissed it.

Across the words which he said, a certain ill-disguised confidence was discerned by Fleurange. But, alas! had she at that moment dared to be herself, she would not have dreamed of taking offense at this. Yes, she loved him, and of this he had no doubt, so much was plain. What matter! it would have been a consolation to her to confess it frankly, openly,—to own it to every one as well as to himself. Without doubt, this security of his was a trifle too apparent, but she would so quickly have forgiven that! She would have been so happy to tell him that he was not deceived, and that her whole life should prove it to him; that would have been the true cry of her heart, if, at this dangerous hour, the clear light of her conscience had for an instant ceased to shine.

But it was not so.

"*Monsieur le Comte—*" she said, after a long silence.

"George! oh, say George!" he cried passionately. "Let me hear you, were it but for a single time, call me by my name!"

Poor Fleurange! She disengaged her hand from his arm, and walked forward more rapidly, striving to calm the violent throbbing of her heart. He followed her, and almost immediately resuming her self-command, "I believed," she said, "and indeed I hoped also, that I should never hear you speak to me again like this."

"You hoped it! Tell me then that I am deceived, that I have been presumptuous, and a fool! That I was quite wrong in thinking I could read in your eyes anything but the most profound indifference!"

She made no answer.

"Fleurange!" he continued eagerly, "this silence grieves and chills me; have I not at least the right to expect that you should answer me?"

"But have you the right to ask the question? Ah, how much more noble and generous you would be, if you knew how to remember better what you are, and what I am!"

"Fleurange," said Count George, with a tone of sincerity and of gravity, far more dangerous to hear than that of passion, "you are my wife if you consent to be, if you accept this hand which I offer you."

"With your mother's consent?" Fleurange said, speaking slowly and in a low voice; "do you dare affirm this to me?"

George, after a moment's hesitation, replied: "No; not to-day, but she will give this consent of hers,—that I affirm to you!"

Fleurange hesitated in her turn; she knew, past all doubt, to what degree this hope was a chimera; but she was speaking to him for the last time. Upon the morrow, distance, absence, time, all the separations of life would commence between them, never to be ended. There was no longer danger in saying the truth, the truth, alas! of so little importance now, and which, possibly, might second the duty she had undertaken to fulfil quite as well as denial.

"Well then," she said, simply, "yes; why should I conceal it? If all were to alter for us in life, if by a chance impossible to conceive, your mother were to say to me: Gabrielle, be my daughter, I gladly consent to it; oh then!—what I should answer you, you know without my saying it, and you know, just as well, that, until that day, I shall never listen to you."

"But that day," exclaimed George vehemently, "time will bring it, and will bring it promptly!"

"Time?" said Fleurange, "perhaps. Who knows what time can bring?—and who knows," she added, "if with time, the obstacle would not come from yourself!"

She had striven to speak these last words jestingly, but having uttered them, she stopped short, while the shadow of the great cypress-trees that darkened the road hindered George from seeing the tears that fell like rain.

She walked hastily forward to come up with Julian; George followed her in a few minutes, and all three rejoined the others, and went on some time without speaking. The daylight was fading more and more, and they walked cautiously, approaching the bottom of the slope.

They were almost there, and but a few steps distant

from their carriage, when two persons, walking rapidly, and talking with each other, passed without observing them. But those who were going down the hill, under the shadow of the cypress trees, perceived the faces of the other two, and a like emotion startled at once Julian and the two cousins. In one of the two men they had all recognized Felix.

Adelardi, on his part, seemed surprised and troubled. George, however, after having followed with his eyes these two passers-by, separated from the group of which he made part, and approaching these persons, stopped one of them; they exchanged a few words in a low voice, and then the two men continued their ascent, while George returned to those whom he had left.

"To whom were you speaking—if the question is not indiscreet?" said Adelardi.

"Oh, not at all," replied George without hesitation. "It is Fabiano Dini, of whom I have spoken to you, and who is useful to me as a very skilful agent in the purchase of various curiosities, and who assists me also in any little historical researches I may have in hand. He has been away, and is just returned. I had a word or two to say to him."

"He was in very bad company then," said Adelardi, gravely.

The two ladies were already in the carriage. Julian, obliged to follow them, heard no more.

XXVIII.

More than twenty-four hours had rolled by. Fleurange was already far away, and the occurrences of the foregoing days seemed to become for her only the shifting scenes of a troubled dream. The conversation between Count George and his mother, which she had overheard from the terrace, that which she had herself had with the princess, the interview at San Miniato, the mysterious bouquet and the re-appearance of Felix,—by turns these all came back to her, and were in their turn effaced by the thought of the last adieu which had followed them.

Yes, she had said adieu forever, while he, smiling, bade her good-bye for a few days, and his mother, graciously giving her hand to her young *protégée* continued up to the last moment to sustain her part in the little drama which only she and Fleurange understood. Nor did Fleurange fail in hers; yet, as she kissed the hand of the princess, and said good-bye, there was a something in her tones which the latter could not have failed to understand. She kissed the young girl at parting with an involuntary tenderness, and even emotion which might seem strange considering that the absence was to be of so short duration. George observed it, and was more re-assured than ever, and when Fleurange had gone, what he felt, really more than he did sadness, was the need of finding some distraction to save him from the insupportable *ennui* which her absence caused him.

And now Fleurange, alone with Julian in the *coupé* of the *vetturino*, which she shared with him, while Clara and the baby and the little Italian serving-maid occupied the interior, was striving for the mastery over her torturing thoughts. The restraint and weariness of still concealing somewhat, more antipathetic to her nature than to that of any other person, must still a little longer be endured. She was to diverge at Passignano for Santa Maria, while they were not to reach the convent till two days later, and she had decided not to announce to the Steinbergs that she was going further with them, till, on their return from Perouse, they should stop to say a last good-bye. By that time her plans in respect to the future would have been more fully matured. Vague ideas floated through her mind, and doubts, which she herself scarcely understood. She needed the penetrating gaze of her mother-friend to help her disentangle this confusion of thought and feeling. Until then silence was best.

Her conversation with Julian turned therefore mainly upon their chance meeting with their unhappy cousin.

"I have thought it over carefully," said Steinberg, "and it seems to me that it is impossible to take a single step without running the risk of doing him some serious harm."

"And it seems as if he were doing well, now," Fleu-

"Yes, and for that very reason it is most important that nothing should be said about his past life. Count George would scarcely have employed him, unless he had been well recommended."

Fleurange was silent. The truth was, she had often heard Count George reproached for his indifference concerning the character and position of those whom he employed in making his collections, or in carrying out inquiries upon matters of interest to him. "What consequence can it be to me," he used to say, "as regards their private life, for the work which I give them to do? If they are intelligent and skilful, that is enough for me, and for copying an inscription, or transcribing a page from a manuscript, I had much rather pay a clever rascal than an honest blunderer."

Without knowing why, this association between Felix and Count George inspired her with involuntary terror. How to express her fear she knew not, but she had a great desire to put the latter upon his guard. Yet, to do this without bringing harm to Felix was impossible, and so the fearful gloom which overhung the idea of her cousin now transformed itself into a painful presentiment, and added one sombre shade the more to the sadness which she in vain strove to conceal.

After a long silence she resumed: "The Marquis Adelardi seemed to know the man who accompanied Felix, the evening when we met him."

"Yes, and seemed to think ill of him."

"Had you the opportunity to question him further on the subject?"

"I tried to do so during the evening, but he seemed reluctant to answer me; and, for my part, I felt obliged to be so careful that I really learned but little."

Julian reflected an instant, and then remarked suddenly: "The Marquis Adelardi, as I heard in Bologna, was at one time a conspirator!"

"A conspirator! This gentle and admirable marquis? It is impossible, Julian."

Julian smiled. "Come, Gabrielle, do not be so frightened. I did not say he was a criminal. But I was thinking that, during that part of his life in which he was mixed up with the revolutionary troubles in Italy, he must have known many a suspicious character, and that this person whom we saw with Felix, very likely was one of these."

For the moment Fleurange was silent, and the conversation ended there. These last words of Julian had added a new anxiety to all the other painful impressions, some vague, others well-defined, which weighed down her heart and mind. She pitied Felix, but still more she feared him. The strange note which she had received seemed now to be only a rash bravado,—an attempt to frighten, or to interest her,—an irresistible inclination to produce an effect, to which he had yielded, at the risk of being discovered. The contact of this bold and restless spirit with such a man as Count George was sure to result in harm to the latter; never, it seemed to her, had so much weighed upon her at once, never had the clouds so threatened from all parts of the sky.

At last they reached Passignano, and she left her companions, and took her place in a little country vehicle to be carried to the monastery. The supposed shortness of her absence had justified her in leaving in the charge of Barbe all the dresses and ornaments added by the princess to her modest wardrobe, so that the little portmanteau which she had brought to Florence was all her luggage. This was now promptly handed up to the driver, who placed it on the seat by his side, and so the last stage of the journey began.

The road led up hill, but so insensibly, that it was only to be perceived by the increased beauty of the view which unfolded more and more under the eye. Far off, the Lake of Thrasymene sparkled like cloth of silver in the sun; nearer, the little Sanguinetto, of which Byron speaks, bearing yet, through two-and-twenty centuries, the name given in memory of that fearful conflict which made its waters red, winds through the plain which was the scene of the battle. History relates that, during that famous day, absorbed by the fury of the strife, neither the Romans nor their adversaries were aware of an earthquake which shook the ground beneath their feet. Scarcely to-day would our poor Fleurange have been conscious of a like convulsion of nature, so absorbed was she in the strife of a different character, waged between her upright will and her heart's eager longing.

In the complete solitude in which she now, for the first time in many months, found herself, she seemed to recover her liberty of thought, and, freed from the necessity of striving longer against whatever might weaken her courage, she allowed herself for the first time to look back, and to live over again in imagination the events of the last six months. She leaned her tired head against the cushion, closed her eyes, and suffered memory to bring before her, one by one, those dear yet fruitless recollections. Once more she saw him whom, henceforward, she must never see; she heard anew each word that had been spoken by that voice which she must nevermore hear; she answered him, with all that she had so often restrained herself from saying. The dangerous dream lasted long, and was followed by a sad awaking, and disturbed to its very depths that inner tranquility which she had preserved—with difficulty, it is true, but as really as her external composure—during the days of trial through which she had just passed. "It is all over now!" she murmured, with a suppressed, despairing cry, "it is all past, and I shall never see him again!"

Suddenly she heard a bell which tinkled musically at no great distance, and whose tones awakened a whole world of kindred impressions.

She lifted her head eagerly and looked about her. She was in a road bordered by great acacia trees, and where it turned, just beyond, there were pine trees, and some rustic houses. Passing these, a voice cried: "*Evviva la Signorina!*" and, a little further, "*La Madona vi accompagna!*" and then,—they were passing under a ruined arch that seemed a vestige of antiquity; still the bell kept on ringing, but more distinctly, for they drew near the church—

"What!" she cried, clasping her hands, "What! already?—We are here!"

At the end of the lane, the vehicle turned to the left, passed the church, and stopped before a little door whose carved stone embrasure was surmounted by a statue of Christ, at the feet of which were legible, cut in high relief, these words in Latin: "Come unto me, all ye that labor and are heavy laden, and I will give you rest."·

Fleurange had sprung to the ground, and was just hastening to ring the bell, when the door opened. A gentle word of surprise and welcome received her. She answered with a smile, but ran past without stopping, for, at the far end of the cloister she perceived in the distance her whom she had come to seek. It was the hour of noon; the little ones were coming out of school, *Madre* Madelina was looking at them as they went, addressing some pleasant word to this one or that, when the new-comer appeared suddenly among them, and threw the little world into disorder. *Madre* Madelina was surprised,—looked for an instant with a disturbed air at her who had come without permission thus to interrupt the order of the day and the place,—looked again,—hesitated, then opened her arms, with an exclamation of delight: "*Fior angela mia!* dear lamb, returned to the fold!"—and the child, at home again, falling into the mother's arms, forgot, for an instant, the fatigue, the dangers, the sufferings of the road, and all the thorns with which her bleeding feet had been torn.

XXIX.

The church was dark and cool, filled with perfume from the fresh flowers which adorned the altar, and from the incense burned there in the morning. The young girl and the *religieuse* remained for a few moments kneeling; for both, it was the best preliminary of their re-union. First, to thank God, and to call in as third in their happy meeting, the Supreme Friend who "is LOVE!"

At a sign from *Madre* Madelina, Fleurange soon rose and followed her into a little well-known room upon the ground floor, known as "the garden-parlor." Like all the other convent parlors, this one had no furniture except a square table in the centre of the room, a row of straw-bottomed chairs surrounding it, a book-case surmounted by a great crucifix, and against the wall opposite, a little figure of the Virgin, at whose feet was placed a vase filled with flowers. The only difference between th:-

and the other parlors was in the outlook through the great arched window, on the one side; on the other, through the open door into the garden. The lovely landscape of which we have already spoken, bounded at the horizon by grand and graceful mountain-outlines, had for its foreground masses of flowers showing the most careful cultivation; on the right, were the cloister-arches; at the left, the thick shadow of a little grove of orange-trees, now in full blossom; beyond were the vines and fruit trees and vegetables which supplied the little convent with the largest share of its food. Doves were flying back and forth, between the cloister and the garden, and, in the hours of silence, not a sound save their cooings was to be heard in all the peaceful little domain. But in recreation time, the cloister and the garden rang with children's voices and laughter, and the parlor of mother Madelina was not always as quiet as at the moment when she led Fleurange into it.

The door once closed, the *religieuse* took in her two hands the head of the young girl, and looked tenderly and questioningly into her face, as though seeking to read the very depths of her soul.

Madre Madelina was a person about fifty years of age. In her youth, she had been very beautiful, and her regular and noble features were set off to great advantage by the white band and wrimple which framed them, and from which her long black veil fell in heavy folds to the ground. Her large soft dark eyes had that wondrous expression, found sometimes in eyes which have no other beauty, and which belongs only to those within which shines that mysterious and ineffable joy of which Bossuet says, "it is *incompatible* with other joys; it must be tasted singly if at all." Such was the look expressive of divine joy, and more than human peace, which was at this moment fixed upon Fleurange. The clear eyes of the young girl did not seek to evade it; they remained fastened upon those of *Madre* Madelina. Only the color came over her face, then vanished, leaving her paler than before.

"Poor child! poor child!" said *Madre* Madelina at last, after this long and silent study. "Alas! she has suffered so much! and yet dear Lord! no harm has come to her!"

With the right hand she made a little sign of the cross upon the brow, and then upon the lips of Fleurange, and then said smiling:

"The angel Gabriel, to whom I entrusted her at parting—a faithful guardian and faithfully obeyed—has brought her safe to me again."

Whether Fleurange at this moment failed to possess her wonted self-control or whether, in the presence of *Madre* Madelina, she no longer sought to restrain herself while the latter watched her without asking a question, she gave way suddenly to a flood of tears.

"Yes, I know," *Madre* Madelina said. "There have been great efforts to make, to conquer one's self, to act, to speak, without tears! My poor child has succeeded. Now, she is tired. But," she went on, more gently, "it is to the weary that the good rest is promised, and here, especially, here, where we now are, this rest awaits those who come to ask it of Him who alone gives it to any!"

"Come," she resumed in a firmer tone, after Fleurange had long wept in silence; "come, my Gabrielle, lift up your heart—this heart which suffers so much! Let us try to lift it a little above this suffering, suffering which contains the germ of so great joy," she murmured to herself, "while the pleasures of earth contain the germ of so much suffering! Come, my child, come and follow me."

The last words had an air of gentle authority. Fleurange rose, and obeyed without a word.

Madre Madelina preceded her, and leading her across the garden now exposed to all the ardor of the sun, conducted her into the little grove, where the shade was so dense that it was cool, even at noonday. A little chapel stood within this peaceful place, where, later in the day, the children gathered to say a prayer together. Now it was all vacant.

Madre Madelina seated herself on a low bench outside the chapel, and drew Fleurange close beside her.

"Come," she said, "now tell me all that I know, and all that I do not know."

The words were needless; Fleurange had not come with the intention of keeping back a single thought. She began her story, and in accordance with the wish of *Madre*

Madelina, she commenced with the day following her departure from the convent.

She told of her first journey in Italy, with its novelty and delight; the sad days in Paris; the home in Germany, with its quiet happiness, then the misfortunes of her family, and her departure; then of Florence, with its charm, its danger, its cruel torture, its fearful temptation.

For the first time in her life, she did not hesitate to speak the name of Count George, and without concealment or evasion, she put in words all that this name awakened in her: all! from the unreasoning dreams which had preceded their first meeting, to the conversation which had preceded their final parting, to that very day's reverie, broken only by the sound of the convent-bell; all was related simply, sincerely, without instinctive effort to escape from advice, without excuse framed for seeking it, with truth, clearness, firmness, and in tones which, as she went on with her story, revealed more and more to the attentive listener the unchanged rectitude, and the unbroken strength of her who spoke.

Clearsightedness to discern; strength to fulfil:—as we have said, *Madre* Madelina had ventured to believe that these two germs, hidden in the soul, and made fruitful by that dew of Heaven, without which all clearsightedness grows blind, all strength gives way, would be enough to enable this child—despite her youth, her beauty, and all the snares to which a loving and sensitive nature rendered her liable—to walk with firm and steady step in the pathway of life.

Her hope had been realized. She thanked God for this, but she still looked with inexpressible compassion into the girlish face of Fleurange. Life must be so long for her! and from its very beginning, the strife had been so severe! Her courage had gained new temper, it is true, but the end was still so far off! So many storms might yet arise,—so many perils menace her! From the secured haven in which her own life was sheltered, she looked out upon the sea of this world, where this fragile bark was tossing, praying in her heart to Him who commands the winds and the sea, that He would rescue it from the threatening waves, and bring it safe to port.

"My child," said *Madre* Madelina, after she had heard all, " I was not mistaken. Yes; you have indeed seen the path that God has marked out for you, and you have trodden it bravely. I am satisfied with you, my Fleurange —I bless you,—and God's blessing will rest upon you!" And saying these simple words, she laid her hand gently upon the young girl's head.

The frank outpouring of her heart had already been a solace to Fleurange, and these words and the gesture which accompanied them, gave her a feeling of indescribable comfort. Peace seemed to descend upon her like a divine garment, clothing her from head to foot. "Ah!" she cried eagerly, "may I not stay here with you, and never leave this dear home and you again?"

Madre Madelina smiled; at this moment the bell struck four times. "We will speak of this again," she said; "now, the bell calls me. They are wanting me. I must leave you; I shall see you again in the recreation hour, after supper. You have not forgotten the way to your old room? You remember too, I suppose, all our regulations, and how we divide the day? The bell rings at the same hours as it used, and nothing is changed."

XXX.

It is difficult for one who has not experienced it to imagine the effect which such an atmosphere as now surrounded Fleurange produces when one is suddenly transferred thither from out of the midst of the business and the pleasures, the cares and sufferings of the world, and of life; and though it is evident that the course of ordinary life cannot thus be interrupted by every one at will, we may be pardoned for saying that it is hard to understand the scornful surprise with which those who have never made trial of it are wont to speak of these brief withdrawals from the world, in earlier ages so frequent, and coming again into use in our own. Have they found life so easy then, and so free from care? has one joy followed another so surely, in the fortunate current of their days, and have these days themselves so assured a duration, that it were superfluous to regulate their course or to make provision against their close? or indeed, are they to that degree masters of their thoughts that no distraction can disturb their settled serenity, and that they have no need to stop and think, or to stop and rest? We cannot tell. One thing seems clear, that to most persons, some halt like this is fruitful in good—as water and shade and rest are to the thirsty and tired traveller. And true it is that our poor heroine was of this number. For this reason, on leaving *Madre* Madelina, instead of going up to her room, Fleurange returned to the church and there for a long hour, in the profound silence, she rested quietly, feeling how sweet was that sense of divine shelter and protection which depends not alone upon the momentary and external asylum, but upon that inner asylum, real and lasting, against which nothing in the world has any power.

If you consider all that had agitated and troubled this young girl, if you recall to mind that the great tempter, love, had come so near her, leaving her unscathed doubtless, yet not leaving her without producing his accustomed effect—to disenchant with everything that is not himself—will you learn with great surprise that, at this moment, in this place, the idea came to her to stay here always, and never going further in search of happiness henceforth impossible, or a destiny forever incomplete, to devote herself to the noblest life—that of which God only, and those whom He most loves here below, children and the poor, are the object?

While yet in Florence, and in her days of suffering, the cloister of Santa Maria had seemed to her a refuge, and repeatedly the idea had recurred to her of never leaving it again, as at the moment when she was talking with *Madre* Madelina. But now alone in the church it came with new intensity, and fastened upon her imagination with tenfold earnestness.

It was welcome to her, she yielded to it, and already seemed to taste the bitter joy of the sacrifice. She accepted with a real delight the prospect of renouncing all the pleasures of life, and when she at last arose from her long meditation to leave the church, she almost felt that she had received supernatural guidance.

She would have been glad to speak at once with *Madre* Madelina, but she knew that at this hour it was impossible. The children were again in their classes, and after this, a whole hour was devoted to the poor who came, from near and far, to tell her their sorrows and to consult her about their affairs. In the morning there was distribution of food and medicines, and help of all kinds for physical woes; the evening was consecrated to the exercise of charity under another form; and those who came for this were often more in number than the others. All this Fleurange knew well, and she decided to remain in her room, without seeking to rejoin *Madre* Madelina till after supper.

Only when the school-hour was over and she saw the children on their way to the orange-grove, she came down and joined them, to go and say the evening-prayer in the little chapel under the trees.

The vine was in blossom, and its fine sweet fragrance joined that from the orange-flowers, and when the little perfumed grove rang with the children's singing, you would have said that Nature, in all her forms, sent up her incense to the skies. The prayer ended, the young girl went about among the teachers and scholars, and it was for a few minutes like a return to the peaceful days of her childhood; then came the silent hour in the refectory. At last, supper was at an end, and Fleurange hastened to rejoin *Madre* Madelina. She knew that at this hour of the day she would not find her in the parlor, but upon the terrace which, from the summit of the cloister, looked off upon the surrounding country; there, in fine weather, she loved to pass the last hour of daylight.

What Fleurange came intent to say, we know already. To think aloud in the presence of *Madre* Madelina was habitual to her, and cost her little effort. It was but to resume the interrupted conversation of the morning, and to add the recital of what she had thought and felt and believed herself to have resolved, during the hour that she had passed in the church.

Madre Madelina, standing, with folded arms, listened in silence. To see her thus motionless, here, and at this hour of the evening, the noble outlines of her face and the long folds of her garments relieved against the bluish-gray of the mountains and the violet azure of the sky, you would have taken her for one of those visions which have appeared in other days, in that land, to those who have known how to make them live again upon the canvas, and remain immortal for us and for all men. Nor would the illusion have been destroyed by the aspect of her, who, sitting on the low parapet of the terrace, was looking up and speaking, and whose expression and attitude would have suited perfectly one of those youthful saints, placed often by some inspired painter near the divine and majestic figure of the mother of God.

Fleurange had ceased speaking, and looked up, waiting for her answer. *Madre* Madelina was still silent, but she slowly shook her head. "Before I reply to you," she said at last, "answer me one thing: do you think it is permitted to give yourself without vocation, to the Lord in the religious life?"

"Certainly not."

"And do you know what a vocation is?"

Fleurange hesitated.

"I thought I knew, but the way in which you ask me makes me feel I do not."

"I will tell you; a vocation," pursued *Madre* Madelina, while her eyes shone with a light that Fleurange had never seen in them before; "it is to love God more than one loves the dearest in this world; it is to love Him as one could never have loved any person or anything on earth; it is to have felt every faculty and every power turn towards Him and Him only; it is this," she continued, while her glance seemed to pass through and beyond the visible heavens upon which her eyes were fixed, "it is to have learned to know in this life that he is all, all for us in the past, in the present, in the future; in this world, out of this world, forever, and to the exclusion of all save Himself!"

"Fleurange, accustomed to the habitual simplicity of *Madre* Madelina, looked at her with surprise, amazed at this change in tone and expression, no less than at the words which she had just heard her speak. She colored to her very temples.

"My dear mother," she said at last, looking down as she spoke, "without doubt it is not given to all to feel such a love for God, especially to love Him only, here below. "But," she continued with deep feeling, "the willing sacrifice of all affections and joys of earth—is not that an offering worthy also of being made to Him?"

The eyes of *Madre* Madelina had resumed the calm sweetness of their wonted look.

"Yes, my poor child, and I do not seek to throw any doubt upon this. How could I, in this house open to all who have suffered, and where among our sisters, and not the least saintly among them are those who have brought hither hearts broken by the sorrows of life? Yet this is not that irresistible call of God which we name a true vocation; and what I have to say to you, my Gabrielle, is this—being what you are (and who knows you better than I?) you are one of those whom God would have thus called, if He had wished that your life should be consecrated to Him in a cloister, but *you* have no right to devote yourself to Him through discouragement, through disenchantment with the happiness of this world. The strife has been hard, I know, but for that reason, would you give it up? No, Gabrielle, on the contrary gather strength and go on with it!"

Tears came into the eyes of Fleurange, and she bent her head sadly.

"Oh, my poor child," resumed *Madre* Madelina, "it would have been easier to say: remain, do not leave us ever again! It would be sweeter far for me to guard you from all the sorrows that must yet await you! But believe me, the day will come when you will rejoice that these sorrows were not spared you, and you will recognize it as true that she who tells you this, knew you better than you knew yourself."

The stars were beginning to appear in the quiet blue of the sky whence the hues of sunset were fast fading. It was the hour for the *Ave Maria*. The bell struck, and together they said their wonted prayer, before going down into the cloister.

XXXI.

From this moment, Fleurange resolved never again to return to the subject of their conversation and to relinquish utterly the thought that, for the time, she had so eagerly welcomed.

This submission, which was one of the results of her simplicity and of her energy, did not save her from feeling that there would be a great effort to make in commencing upon a new life, and life would have seemed new to her, even in the old house, for she was no longer herself the same. An abyss parted her from the sweet and peaceful days which she had spent there. But the old house was no more than a vanished dream; towards some new spot she must direct her steps. Those who awaited her there were dear to her, no doubt, and at times the thought of seeing them again made her heart beat with joy. More frequently, however, even this thought was powerless against memories too keen and too recent for control, and, notwithstanding all her efforts, regret, constant and poignant, made her indifferent to everything save to the great sacrifice which had been its sublime consolation, and upon which, henceforth, it was forbidden her to think.

But as the days glided by, the benefits of her quiet resting-place made themselves felt, and ere long it seemed to her that past and future had alike ceased to be of any moment. Memory and anticipation occupied her no longer and, as in a little skiff, equally removed from either shore, and hearing no sound from either, she suffered herself to be lulled by the calm and silent present, feeling only the infinite peace which surrounded her — seeing only the unchanging smile of the sky above her! Days like these cannot last, but they do not pass without leaving a trace behind them, were it but a memory filled, not with regrets, but with promises,—were it but that momentary taste of blessedness, whose exquisite sweetness vanishes indeed, but whose inspiration remains and grows, in the soul which has known it, though but once and for a single instant!

And now, she must think of her departure, and of the

excuse which she might seem to offer to the princess without the latter's apparent expectation of it. For this she awaited the return of the Steinbergs, and much as it would cost her to reveal to them the true motive for her resolution, she was ready to do this, rather than give to them also a fictitious reason. But an unforeseen circumstance came sadly to spare her either the frank confession or the deceit.

She had been in the convent now about ten days, when, one morning, some one came to tell her that the travellers had arrived an hour earlier at the village inn, and that, at this moment, Clara awaited her in the parlor.

To see her cousin's lovely face was always a pleasure for Fleurange. To this was now added the delight of presenting to *Madre* Madelina one of the daughters of that Ludwig Dornthal whose opportune appearance in the life of the orphan child was regarded by her earliest friend as an evident token of the intervention of the glorious archangel to whom she had given her in charge. The arrival of Clara Steinberg was marked therefore in advance as a *fête* in the convent. But this day of enjoyment was destined to be marred, and Fleurange was to hear from her cousin the sad news which the latter had learned from letters she had found awaiting her on her arrival at Santa Maria.

Her faithful and helpful friend, the excellent Dr. Leblanc, was no longer living. He had died in consequence of an accident received while driving with Professor Dornthal in the neighborhood of Heidelberg.

When *Madre* Madelina appeared, she found the two cousins in tears, and her smile of welcome was changed into anxious questioning. It was a few minutes before she could obtain the explanation for which she sought, and it was only after her gentle words, and the peace which breathed from her presence, had in a degree calmed the distress of Fleurange, that the latter had the courage to open the letter which Clement had addressed to her, there to learn the details of the cruel accident which had deprived her of her old friend: that friend towards whom her thoughts had turned so often in her recent perplexities, and who was now taken from her at an hour in her life when his support and his advice seemed to be more than ever needful to her!

"Returning from an excursion to Stift-Neuburg," wrote Clement, "the carriage was overturned, and they were thrown out with violence. At first, my father seemed to have been the principal sufferer. He was entirely without consciousness, and only came to himself some hours later. But to-day we regard him as out of danger, while his friend, whose head was not at all affected, at once declared that he had himself suffered a serious internal injury from which he should not recover. He ordered the necessary treatment, however, but at the same time made his arrangements with admirable firmness, wrote to his sister, and prepared in every way for death, while we could not believe him in danger. On the third day his anticipations were realized. His condition grew rapidly worse. Day before yesterday his poor sister arrived, and he expired in her arms.* * *"

"Dear cousin," pursued Clement, "I have a request to make in closing. I do not ask it in my own name, but in that of my mother: return; if it be possible, return at once, but at least, return very soon. The sacrifices that you were so willing to make are no longer needful, but your presence among us is indispensable. My poor father asks for you, and we cannot make him understand your absence. Dear cousin, no desire to convince you would make me willing to deceive you, I assure you; and you may believe me, the assistance which your generosity has enabled you to offer us is now no longer needed. You can without hesitation now return to the roof which is yours, unless (which God forbid!) your own choice leads you to prefer another. Poor Mlle. Josephine has but a single wish,—to see you again. It is the only consolation to which she looks forward; Hilda is near us, do I need to tell you how she desires your return? Do I need to tell you how *your brothers* implore it and await it?"

Fleurange henceforth had not to seek a pretext. She had no longer a confession to make, nor a secret to guard, all was decided for her and without her, by the rigorous and imperious force of events, and her letter to the princess Catherine suddenly became easy to write. It was written before the close of the day, and, two days later, at the hour when the sun was gilding with its earliest rays the summits of the mountains, *Madre* Madelina saw for the second time, the child whom she loved pass out from the convent shelter to go and meet the perils lying beyond. Would she again return as she had done? would she come, like the dove beaten by the tempest, finding nowhere to rest, and seek shelter and peace once more? or, indeed, had she gone this time never to return,—would she find the earth smiling and verdant, the road made easy and bordered with flowers?—She did not seek to know, and, as we have seen, these matters were not of great importance to *Madre* Madelina: that the road should be lighted with the sunshine of heaven, and that courage to walk in it should not be lacking, was everything to her. Beyond this, prosperity, as well as adversity, has its dangers, and the soul's sunlight may be obscured in bright days, as well as in cloudy. "Let us leave to God the choice of all that is accidental in our lives, and without noticing too carefully where we are walking, let us think only of walking well. * * * *"

"And then, the road is short, however long it may be, and leads us to the true life when we shall live together always, my Gabrielle,—where all that this poor heart has wished, sought, hoped in vain, here below, shall be given it in measure, full, pressed down, running over,—where all that it has suffered will become some little portion of its radiant joy! God is faithful! Let us wait: Oh, what is it, thus to wait, when it is He whom one waits for, upon the faith of His promise!"

These were the last words of *Madre* Madelina, and when she had given her blessing to the young girl who knelt at her feet to receive it, and had seen the convent gate close behind her, she went up to the terrace, as long as possible to follow her with her eyes; then she went down into the church and prayed for her, with tears of tenderest affection. With affection, for there is not in this lower world anything which equals the tenderness of those grand hearts which God's love fills and expands! To be sure of this, one needs only to think of the intensity of devotion which they (and they only) have mani fested through love for the most unknown of their fellow-creatures. You may understand then what, towards those whom they love, are these hearts, kindled by a flame where all that is noble and worthy to endure, is fed and purified, while nothing is chilled, nothing extinguished, save what is fragile, frivolous, impure, and destined one day to perish utterly!

XXXII.

The princess Catherine, in elegant morning costume, was ensconced in her little *salon*, alone with the Marquis Adelardi, when some one brought in a letter upon a silver salver.

She glanced at the address.

"Ah! from Gabrielle!" she cried. "The very letter I was just expecting!"

She opened it and read it eagerly.

"Good," she said, "excellent, nothing could be more natural! She has found the very best thing in the world to say. It would be impossible without actual cruelty for me to refuse my consent. George himself will agree to it. Here, Adelardi," she continued, throwing the letter towards him, "read it. I must confess she is faithful, and one can trust her word, and, besides, she has a deal of good sense."

Adelardi, meantime, read the letter attentively.

"All that you say, princess, is perfectly accurate," he said; "but this time, circumstances have come to your aid. This letter is not written to suit the occasion; it is true, from one end to the other. That young girl well knows how to be silent, but she does not know how to tell a lie. This is not the letter that she would have written, if its contents had not been the simple truth."

"You think so?" said the princess; "it makes very little difference to me, except perhaps it simplifies the matter. However in that case—ah, Heavens! give me that letter!"

She took it, and read it carefully from beginning to end.

"Ah, Heavens!" she repeated. "But do you see,—have lost my physician. I have indeed,—the only one who understood my case. Indeed! what a misfortune! If, at least, he had answered my last letter, in which I asked him to decide to which springs I should go for the summer! What shall I do now!—It is now the last of May, and next month I must go somewhere. I have certainly bad luck!"

"But what do you expect, princess," said the marquis, with a tone of almost imperceptible irony. "No one has good luck all the time; on the other hand, you have been so well attended recently!"

"I know it, and—to return to Gabrielle—under the circumstances, I have nothing to say of her but praise. We came out well, Adelardi,—but I can hardly forgive her yet for the fright I had, and the anxiety that I still feel. What news of George, since yesterday?—in what mood will he be to receive the tidings I have to give him?— What are you thinking about, Adelardi? You worry me, you look so anxious; I hope you do not apprehend his doing some foolish thing?"

"Foolish in what way?"

"Oh, but you know what I mean; the only foolish thing he could do at this moment. Will he make one of his scenes that we know so well? Will he escape from us, and follow her?—Or indeed—what shall I say?—Will he be likely to do worse, in order to distract his mind,— and hurl us from Charybdis into Scylla? You never know what to expect with him!"

"Well then, princess, I acknowledge that I wish I were sure that this charming girl, in sacrificing herself—for you do not imagine, I suppose, that she was indifferent towards George?"

"It is not very likely," said the princess, "but you do not expect, I hope, that I should take into consideration the impression which George must naturally produce, when he gives himself the trouble of turning the head of a girl of twenty, especially a girl in Gabrielle's position!"

Adelardi said nothing, and his face, already serious, grew darker still.

"But I ask you again, what is the matter, Adelardi? One would think you were in love with her yourself."

"By no means, although it is easy for me to imagir

that she also—and not less easily than George—might turn anybody's head. However, I have striven with all my strength against him, to keep him out of the danger which, before yourself, I saw and recognized, and I return to what I said before: I should be glad to be sure that we shall never regret the time when the influence of this noble girl over him seemed to us so much to be dreaded."

"What do you mean to say?"

"Princess, I declare to you that I wish to-day that she were here, and that the charm of her presence could now keep him every evening in this *salon*, from which—though not speaking to her, and scarcely looking at her—he could not tear himself away while she was here. You observe that since her departure he is never at home, and why?— It is because a passion quite as dangerous to him as that of play or that of love, has re-awakened since he finds the days long, and the evenings dull and vacant. Pardon me, princess; you know that he loves you, and that he is my friend; but you know as well as I do that he cannot endure *ennui*, and we cannot wonder that the absence of Gabrielle has left in his life one of those vacant spaces whose effect is to produce the most enormous, the most intolerable *ennui* that there is in the world. I feel it myself; and you will not deny that—without this supreme interest which dominates you—you, even, would have supported with a very ill grace the sudden disappearance of this charming creature whose mere presence—"

"Come, come, Adelardi! Be calm, or I shall say again—"

"No, princess; I am not in love with her; do me the honor to believe my word; but as regards George, I have come to the point where I ask myself if it would not be better that he were and should remain so, whatever came of it, rather than—"

"Finish your sentence; I am dying of fear!"

"Rather than that he should be again the victim of that mania, that passion for politics, whose attraction is so great, as you know, and which may lead him to commit acts of the last degree of imprudence."

The princess became thoughtful.

"Yes, it is true, Adelardi; I know it, I know it only

too well, but since his return I had found him so much more tranquil in that regard that I never thought even of troubling myself about it."

"It is because he was then occupied by another idea; but, thanks to an accidental meeting which occurred just at the time of Gabrielle's departure, and which interested him at the very moment when he had an imperative need of being occupied by something, he is now so absorbed and drawn away that, in fact, what I regret at this moment is, that—instead of an absence indefinitely prolonged—we have not this evening to announce to him the immediate return of her who, better than any one (and the only person in the world, perhaps) could save him from this new danger."

"A thousand thanks, my dear friend! But this is a regret which I cannot share!" exclaimed the princess, ironically.

"For the rest," resumed Adelardi, "I will venture to say that, sure of the future, as, thanks to your admirable diplomacy, he deems himself, we shall find him much more resigned to this information than we might have expected."

"Very likely," said the princess, smiling; "especially since another whim has seized upon him, and I confess, I cannot to-day be very much in earnest about this latter. *Un 'alla volta, per carità!*—Let us take the most pressing first,—the enemy was in the place, and this enemy was Love! It was indeed needful to try all means to dislodge him! Now it is politics that will seize upon him!—later we will attend to that! for the moment, the one important thing in my eyes is to efface, as far as possible, the memory of this beautiful Fleurange (for among other discoveries I have learned that this is the true name of Gabrielle.) As an ally against her, I accept even politics, with the provision of treating my ally as an enemy when I have no longer need of its services."

At this moment a servant appeared, and asked orders in relation to a picture which had just been brought in.

The princess left the room for an instant, and returned, laughing.

"What picture do you suppose it is?" she said.

discovery like that picture of Cigoli which you obtained the other day by buying the frame which held it?"

"Oh, not at all! It is a modern picture, which has for subject 'Cordelia at the feet of her father,' and had for model—"

"Come now, princess, are you in earnest? Has George really given you that picture?"

"*Given!*" said the princess, her eyes twinkling with laughter, playing with her necklace of pearls as she spoke: "at least that was not his intention; but could he refuse to lend it to me during the absence of Cordelia? This picture which pleased me so? It was the whim of a convalescent suddenly deprived of her nurse,—could I fail to obtain its gratification with a little urgency, especially having been so gracious towards him, so indulgent to her."

"Ah princess! what a finished diplomatist you are?"

"Seriously," said the princess, "do you know that I never had noticed this resemblance, having seen the picture but once and carelessly, at a time when I did not as yet know Gabrielle. You know that George's own room is a sanctuary whither I rarely penetrate, and besides, this picture has been for the whole of this year hidden from sight."

"What suggested to you then to go and look at it?"

"He himself, by the romantic story of it which he related to me the other evening here in this very room.

"And where have you placed it now?"

"In my dressing-room where he never sets foot," replied the princess with a new burst of laughter.

The Marquis Adelardi had deplored, as much as did the princess, the passion of Count George for Fleurange. Nevertheless at this moment he felt dissatisfied with her and with himself, and he soon left her to go and look after his friend. He was ill at ease, for he knew the latter was tempted by a dangerous curiosity, and he would gladly never have lost sight of him. They were to meet at a kind of Casino, then in fashion, to dine together, and he hoped to retain him in his own company for the rest of the evening. But, arriving at the place designated, he did not find his friend; George had gone, and there was handed,

Adelardi a note left for him, which wrung from the latter a sharp exclamation of annoyance.

The note was thus worded:

" Once does not make a habit. I have accepted for this evening the proposal of Lasko. Dini accompanies me, but be easy about it. I do not appear under my own name, and shall be identified by no one."

" Lasko ! " murmured the marquis, stamping with rage ; " that is his name to-day then ! The heavens confound h'm ! Why is he not still in the depths of the Spielberg, which is the only fitting place for him ! "

III.—ON THE BANKS OF THE NECKAR.

Brama assai—poco spera—nulla chiede.
TASSO.

XXXIII.

"RETURN, Gabrielle; if it be possible, return at once; at least, return very soon."

In reading these simple words addressed by Clement to his cousin, it would have been difficult to imagine with what a beating heart they had been written. No such thought surely would have ever come to Fleurange herself, less than ever at the moment when this letter at once so afflicting and so helpful reached her. She had indeed paid but slight attention to the assurances contained in her cousin's letter concerning the needlessness of any further sacrifice on her part to the welfare of the family. Clement had, however, told her the exact truth. The situation of the professor and his family had changed greatly, no doubt, but was far from being such as in the first excitement and alarm there had been reason to suppose.

To leave the house that has been one's home for twenty-five years, to see so much that has made it beautiful offered for sale, to forsake the place where one has dwelt so long,—all this at first excluded the possibility of finding anything but privations and sadness in this event.

Madame Dornthal herself expected nothing else from it, and the courage with which she relinquished her old home, was the same which she would have manifested for her husband's sake, had it been a literal exile which she was to be allowed to share with him; she wished to comfort him as far as possible, without really anticipating for herself or him the slightest possibility of pleasure in this changed existence.

Yet there had been much pleasure in it, for not infrequently to reverses, endured without a murmur, are accorded unexpected compensations.

In the first place, the new house, though simple and even rustic compared to the other, was neither gloomy nor inconvenient. Two spacious rooms upon the ground-floor allowed the family to assemble with ample space either for meals, or for those evening re-unions in which, on the return of the absent ones they hoped to find real delight once more. A little garden surrounded the house, and an emerald lawn sloped down to the river, edged, to right and left, by a shaded alley. The place, called *Rosenhain* justified its name by the abundance of flowers, roses especially which, on every side, brightened the scene, and made the air fragrant. So, from the first day, the impression had been extremely different from that which they had feared. Clement had saved from the sale, too, several engravings and a few pictures,—his father's favorites,—as well as some other objects of value; these the family met again on their arrival, like old friends come to bid them welcome to the new home.

Then again, it had happened that the collections of the professor, both curiosities and pictures, gathered by him with faultless taste and profound science, possessed a value far superior to that which had been estimated, so that out of their lost opulence, a more than comfortable competence was soon assured to them. To this was added all that the future promised to Clement, whose uncommon talent, once recognized, was soon in a fair way to justify the anticipations expressed in regard to it by Wilhelm Müller. To tell the truth, fortune is neither so blind nor so capricious as they say, and if she sometimes grants her favors to those who are unworthy of them, she reserves always some for persevering labor, for loyal uprightness, for intelligent and skillful calculations, for severe economy, for rigid exactitude. These virtues, and not chance, preside at the foundation of durable and honestly-earned fortunes, and the most consummate ability, where these virtues are wanting, often cannot save a fortune from vanishing in a single day.

Of such legitimate success Clement was worthy, and such appeared to be his destiny. At all events, his efforts were sufficient for the support of the family, and he would gladly have spared his father the task that the latter had undertaken; but he could not deter him from it, and soon it became evident that it was better so. His father had transmitted to Clement the poetic side of his nature, but from his mother he derived that strength and energy of which the professor, despite his rare and exquisite gifts, was completely destitute. A deep dejection mingled with the apparent resignation with which the father had accepted this misfortune, and this dejection arose from the conviction, late and humiliating, that he had brought it on by his lack of foresight, and that he was responsible for his children's ruin. From this fixed idea it was needful to distract him, and, on this account, the forced occupation which the post that he had accepted imposed upon him, and the necessity of busying himself with his favorite studies, were too useful for his family to advise him to relinquish them. By degrees this new life, on which weighed no longer any worldly anxiety, became both active and serene, and the hours when the family were together would have assumed almost the same aspect as heretofore, had it not been for the many vacant places at the fireside. But after the arrival of Hilda and her husband, and of Dr. Leblanc, the evenings at Rosenhain were animated, and almost gay. Ludwig renewed with Hansfelt his delightful conversations of other days; Hilda rejoiced the heart of her father by her beauty and her happiness; the voices and laughter of children again resounded, and from Clement's violin was heard, as of old, an occasional strain of dancing-music. More frequently, however, by his father's request, he played graver melodies, with an expression so pathetic, and with such perfection that Hilda, in surprise, one day asked how he could find time in his busy life to cultivate this talent of his with such success.

Clement at first had not heard his sister, he was so absorbed by a strain from Beethoven which wailed with heart-breaking pathos from under his bow. When she repeated her question: "I play in the evening," he said, "with Müller and his wife. It is a rest to me after my detestable days, and it saves me from losing what you are 'eased to call my talent."

Such was the scene which Fleurange would have found at her uncle's new home, a month earlier, and perhaps, in that case, her involuntary sadness would have been more apparent. But the peace, so lately dawning again upon this household, had been once more rudely disturbed, and no one could be surprised that tears should mingle with her joy upon returning to those whom she loved, since among them, in deepest black, was the sister of Dr. Leblanc, and since, on her arrival, it was necessary at once to explain to her a new calamity which Clement, in his letter, had hardly made clear.

The life of Professor Dornthal was no longer in danger, but Fleurange learned that his memory had become strangely enfeebled, and that the light of this noble mind, if not extinguished in utter darkness, had at least become fitful and uncertain. It was hoped this might be temporary; time, perfect rest, and abstinence from all labor, would bring, it was believed, his restoration to health. But it was a very severe trial, and Clement saw, for the first time, his mother's courage give way. Madame Dornthal's smile was sad enough as she saw her husband recognize Fleurange and embrace her, without testifying the least surprise at her presence, or having any idea of the time and distance which had separated her from them. It was the same with Clara, but when the latter placed her child in his arms, with a sudden effort the slumbering memory of the invalid seemed for an instant to awaken; tears came into his eyes, he kissed the child, murmuring, "God bless him!" and returned it to the mother with an expression which gave them one flash of hope, then the light vanished, and he fell back into his former condition.

So it came about that when that evening the family gathered in their great parlor, every brow was thoughtful, young and laughing faces were serious, and a common sadness weighed upon the hearts of all. It was well, perhaps, for Fleurange, for, prompt to forget herself, she seemed no longer to feel, and in truth felt no longer aught save the general grief.

Ah! how dear was this sadness—which seemed to be all sympathy—to him who, with silent transport, beheld her sitting there with his sisters, while the light from the hanging lamp fell on her lovely head, and her voice, so dear and so long absent, was heard for the first time in this place where all things seemed transformed by her presence.

The evening, sad to every one else, was not sad to Clement;—even his anxiety about his father was lulled to rest. Hope seemed to have touched all things, since his cousin was at home again. With what gentle and confiding affection she had clasped his hand; with what tones she had said, "Clement, my friend, how glad I am to see you again!" Was the future really to be so sombre as he had believed? So far as fortune was concerned, he had now no further anxiety; he felt well able to conquer and to attain it. He had once believed himself powerless to do this, but he had been mistaken. Had he deceived himself also in thinking that he could never be loved? In answer to this question, he heard only the quick beating of his heart and the sound of the rushing water near which he had seated himself under the trees.

Meantime, Fleurange and her cousins had gone up stairs. Soon he saw them together upon the gallery which surrounded the house, and on which the windows of the second story opened. Then they went in-doors, but the lamp, lighted this evening for the first time, long remained visible, and not till he had seen it extinguished, did Clement leave his place.

XXXIV.

It was when Fleurange had, by insensible degrees, resumed the customary routine of this family life, which had been formerly the realization of all her dreams,—and it was only then—that she understood the extent and the depth of the change which had taken place in herself, between the time which had removed her from her friends and that which had brought her back to them again.

She was no longer the same; by no effort of the will could she conceal this from herself; her heart, her thoughts, regrets, desires, hopes, were all elsewhere. Italy with all its splendors was not more different from the quiet landscape now before her eyes than was her Italian life from that which she must pass under these misty skies, amid these ruins and these great sombre forests that bounded her view. While she was in Florence, struggle, and effort and action had stimulated her courage, and the tranquillity of Santa Maria had still further fortified it. But there, as we have said, past and future seemed alike to have ceased to exist. Now, the battle was ended, and so was the halt which had followed it; she must begin anew to live and act in the present, and to resume, with good courage, life as she might find it, with its duties and its fresh conflicts. Never had Fleurange felt more difficulty and reluctance in an attempt at self-conquest.

After the long restraint which she had undergone, she would have wished to be released from all necessity for effort, especially from all dissimulation; to yield to profound melancholy, to remain for hours in a state of dreamy inaction, to weep, when her heart was full of tears, and if not to speak to all of her grief, at least to take no pains to conceal it from any.

This was her natural inclination, and she had great difficulty in resisting it. But in so doing she would have proved that her courage was at last unequal to the task laid upon her, and we have not to record this act of weakness in our heroine's character. Whoever had seen her, on the contrary, rising at day break, to spare her aunt the fatigue of domestic duties,—busy in the store-room and in the kitchen,—going out to market with a basket on her arm, and returning, fresh and glowing with the rapid walk and the splendor which youth and health gave to her cheek,—whoever had seen her thus, could scarcely have believed that more than once the night had passed without an hour's sleep, and that in listening to morning service at the break of day, she had shed torrents of burning tears.

Other cares, dearer and more absorbing, next employed her day. Her special gift of attending upon the sick, and the salutary influence that she exerted over them, was manifested anew in the case of her uncle; and Madame Dornthal blessed the return of Fleurange as she noticed an evident gain in this slow and sad convalescence, and felt renewed hope of the gradual and complete restoration of the mental powers of the Professor, even though he might never be able to apply them again to assiduous or difficult labor. These cares were sweet to the young girl, and the new duty which she had to perform toward her dear old friend, Mlle. Josephine, was not less so.

Josephine Leblanc had loved in all the world no one but her brother. She had lived for him exclusively, and she had never once dreamed that she could survive him. A man left the only survivor, in a house visited by war or by fire, would not feel himself more strangely and suddenly alone, than was this poor solitary woman after the fatal blow which had torn from her a brother so loved, admired, venerated by her,—younger than herself, and as she had believed, so sure to survive her.

Still, she remained calm and collected. But the mute despair expressed in her face as she went about the house, making no claim for sympathy, striving to weary no one with her sorrows, touched the hearts of all. She asked only to remain among them, that she might not return to live alone in that place where she had dwelt with him. Madame Dornthal had at once invited her to remain with them, and the return of Fleurange had decided her old friend to take this important step, finding in it, however, so great a consolation that God, she said, had marked it out for her. The doctor's fortune was considerable, and belonged entirely to his sister. All his other relations were rich, and lived in the country, and nothing recalled Mlle. Josephine to Paris. She therefore resolved to make her home among these new friends, and with her whom she had long since adopted in her heart. It was a formidable undertaking for one who, during forty years, had made no change in her manner of living, who had dwelt in one house all her life, and whose ignorance of the world was as great at sixty as it had been at sixteen. But all became possible, so soon as she found one creature in the world for whom to live. As to Fleurange, it was good for her to devote herself in return, and, in the fulfilment of this new debt of gratitude, her heart found strength for that inner struggle which was now become the daily duty of her life.

For the rest, notwithstanding the marriage of her two cousins, all was now almost the same as formerly. Clara and Julian, living close by, came daily to Rosenhain. Hansfelt had no thought of leaving his old friend, and with her husband and her father whose recovery now seemed almost certain, nothing more was wanting for the calm and radiant happiness of Hilda.

Clement only was no longer at home; he came every week on Saturday, in the evening, and returned to Frankfort early Monday morning.

In general, *ennui* does not accompany the fulfilment of duties for which one has great natural aptitude. But the ability of Clement was manifold, and of all which he was capable of doing, that which occupied him, in the office to which he had riveted his existence, was certainly that for which he had the least taste and inclination, and nothing retained him in it save the conviction that there, better than anywhere else, could he promote the interests of his family. Working for them he felt that he must make his work lucrative, and having once regarded it from this point of view, henceforth nothing could weary that courage of endurance which was eminently his, a courage to which the desire of attracting attention, or producing effect added nothing, but which nothing under any circumstances could subdue, and which was as able to brave *ennui* as it was to brave danger. Yet this weary disgust which he could conquer at times by his intensity of application, at other times became overwhelming, and he would have had violent attacks of discouragement, had it not been for the repose which he enjoyed every evening in the modest home circle where he was a constant and welcome visitor.

Wilhelm Müller perceived that the varied acquirements of Clement were a great assistance to himself in many ways, and his affection for him was mingled with an almost enthusiastic admiration. He gladly offered to Clement the opportunity to talk of other things than their commercial affairs, and, by aid of music, the evenings passed agreeably. But Bertha, good and simple, and with that instinct that aids a woman to lay her finger upon the wound which the most discerning man could never discover, had found a surer means of affording him relaxation. The children had never forgotten the great event of their life, the journey, and the beautiful young lady, their fellow-traveller. And this story, of which Clement seemed never to weary, and to which Bertha added her comments, had been the first step toward a sort of confidential intimacy, which she used discreetly, but which solaced him more than he was himself aware. In short, here was the one luminous point; and more than ever would he need it now, when at the end of the leave of absence obtained at the time of his father's accident, and prolonged from day to day, he saw the moment approach for him to resume his chain, and resume it this time with an effort which added one degree more of heroism to the task which he had laid upon himself.

It was the evening before his departure; Fleurange and Hilda sitting in the twilight, on a little bench by the river, were talking together, and Clement, leaning against a tree, watched the water and listened attentively without taking part in the conversation which went on between his sister and his cousin.

They were speaking of what had occurred during their separation, and Hilda was questioning Fleurange upon her journey, Italy, and the life that she had led in Florence, so far away from them all. Fleurange replied, but briefly, and with that kind of apprehension that one feels when a conversation seems to be drifting towards some point we desire to avoid. She felt in advance that she should not be able to avoid it, and she sought, but in vain, to control her embarrassment when the name of Count George was mentioned by her cousin. After a few questions to which Fleurange replied only with monosyllables, Hilda went on:

"Count George!—one of Karl's friends who has seen him, assured me the other day that no one could know him without loving him. What do you think of it yourself, now that you have seen him so often?"

The question was direct, and, as we know, Fleurange could not tell a falsehood.

She blushed and was silent; she was silent so long at Clement turned suddenly and looked at her.

Had she grown pale now, or, indeed, had the moonlight, falling through the foliage, made some change in her, and was it this silvery ray which gave an expression to her face which he had never before seen in it?

He regarded her with attention, intense even to anguish, while, in a voice which she tried in vain to render unconstrained, she replied:

"I think, Hilda, that Karl's friend judged rightly.

After all, it was but a few simple words, and yet the darkest hours of the future never effaced from Clement's memory the place, the hour, and the moment when they were spoken, the silence by which they were preceded, and the tone and the look which accompanied them."

XXXV.

Love is blind, they say, but the proverb would rather be, Love is clear-sighted, were it not that a voluntary self-deception aids the heart in escaping from revelations which it dreads. The very flash of light leads one to shut one's eyes, and when the truth threatens either happiness or pride, the number is not great of those who know how to look it boldly in the face.

Clement, however, was of this small number. Nothing in his nature was adapted to create illusions which might obstruct his clearsightedness. Thus the truth was revealed to him suddenly and without mercy, and his young hope, just springing to life, was crushed never to revive.

This moment of silence was as tragic to him as if all his heart's blood, then and there poured out, had left him lifeless at the feet of her who all unconsciously had just given him that mortal blow.

Since a year ago—since that day when he had believed himself separated from her forever, not merely by his own inferiority, but by the sad necessity of his new position—two unexpected changes had taken place. The first, in his outward life, when all had seemed annihilated, and when he had felt himself capable of reconstructing all; the second, in the opinion which he, not long before, had had of

Does this imply that a sudden self-conceit had seized upon our modest Clement? By no means; but it is true that the great reverses of his family had enfranchised him, in a single day, from his boyish timidity, and a kind of barrier seemed to be suddenly removed from before him. Until that time his real worth had never been understood outside the circle of his immediate family, and even there they loved him without fully knowing him. Now, necessity was bringing him in contact with the world and with men; all his faculties had been forced to come in play, and by exertion they had already grown and strengthened themselves. His face, his bearing, his manners, all had shared in this transformation, and the shy silence which had formerly made him pass unnoticed, had given way before the necessity of making himself understood, and before that confidence in himself which follows the consciousness of exerting influence over others. This influence, at which he was himself surprised, was not due merely to his superior ability as manifested in the dull and prosaic career which he had embraced; but here, as everywhere else, he brought to bear nobler faculties, and, while he had the eye and hand of a master for the material details with which he was charged, through loyalty, self-sacrifice and generosity, he gave them soul, and lifted them to a higher level.

Moreover, he reserved in his life, large space for the studies which he loved, and with which he was always busy, as well as with a thousand subjects, foreign to his daily occupation, but most useful in his mental development. Hence he acquired the simple and persuasive eloquence which gave him an ascendancy with all, and caused him to be sought in a thousand instances not at all connected with his new position. Once or twice he had been called upon to speak in public meetings whose object was either the interests of the city, or questions relative to arts and letters, and he had acquitted himself with a success that had made him remarked not only by those to whom the name of Dornthal was familiar, but even by strangers. Invitations came to him from every side, and he might easily have passed all his evenings in society. But such was not his desire. The company of Wilhelm and Bretha sufficed him; music was his chief pleasure, and it was their delight also, and, as is often the case in Germany, they were able to perform together pieces which many a professed musician would have heard with gratification.

But over all his life, thus employed and portioned out, one dear image presided constantly. At first seen afar off, like a celestial vision, remote and inaccessible, of late, and under the influences we have named, it seemed to have drawn nearer to him.

This appreciation by others to which, for himself, he attached so little importance, for her sake he now valued. This favor which all seemed to show him, had encouraged him to hope that sooner or later he might win something more from her, and he dared believe that his favorite poet was not wrong in promising to him who loves, the boon of love in return.

Thoughts and dreams like these, when access to the heart is once granted them, end at last by ruling it completely, and, as we have said, that of Clement was wild with hope at the time when Fleurange re-appeared among them. Dreams, thoughts, hopes, which one word of hers had crushed; one word, of which her eyes, seen in pale moonlight, had revealed to Clement the sure and fatal significance!

The grief which possessed his soul revealed to him the extent of his illusions, and he was surprised that he had ever thought himself unhappy before. For a few days after his return to Frankfort, a despondency which he had never before experienced, seized upon him, and he seemed to himself to be henceforth as incapable of all effort as he was indifferent to all success. The work of the day became insupportable, and the evening's study, impossible. Instead of joining the Müllers at his accustomed hour, he resorted to long excursions on foot or on horseback, as if to weary out his grief by physical exhaustion.

Now he saw clearly that during two years he had lived, thought, acted, but for her; he had given her, with his heart, his entire life, and he had given himself but one aim and end,—to gain in return this heart, which could never be his, which was indeed given to another! And while he repeated the name of Count George with jealous anger, he could not forget that he had himself admired the irresistible fascination of his rival. The noble face, the charming manners, the voice, the words of Count George were brought by pitiless memory before the mind of Clement; he remembered the Count, on his visit to the picture gallery in the Old House, and his imagination did not spare him the contrast, between himself, then the unknown young student, and this faultlessly elegant and accomplished man of the world. Could he wonder that such a man should succeed better than himself,—could he wonder that such a man, thrown into the immediate neighborhood of Fleurange, living in the house with her—and with the thought a transport of jealous pain seized him and raised in his heart a storm that neither duty, nor honor, nor strength of will, could control. There are times when passion knows no longer any earthly power equal to itself, and they who know not how to seek strength from above are always vanquished. But this Heavenly power had always been supreme with Clement, and he had found his strength in obedience to it, and so he did not sink under the conflict, but soon was able to lift his eyes and seek the aid of which he had need, in order to recover his self-command.

XXXVI.

The power of self-conquest, energy, and self-forgetfulness, were, as we have seen, qualities common to both Clement and Fleurange. There existed indeed between these two a resemblance, which had been for him one cause for the transformation of his first interest into a warmer sentiment; for her it had given rise to a confidence which remained still the same, in spite of the transformation of another kind which she had undergone as well. Now, they were to find themselves both engaged in a like strife, a strife where they were drawn near each other by suffering of a kindred nature, and at the same time separated from one another by an abyss.

Ah! if Clement had still hoped as before that from his sympathy and this confidence might spring one day a tenderer sentiment, with what delight and pride he would have enjoyed that conformity which, on every occasion, showed itself between them! But the aspect of everything was now changed, it was no longer a question of his own happiness; he had nothing to do now but suffer, and by the light of what was passing in his own heart, to penetrate the one which was at the same time open before him, and irrevocably closed against him.

All Clement's strength would have been insufficient to conceal from his cousin the condition of his soul, had he been with her. But, after the desperate days of which we have spoken, after having given himself up to a despair which was almost madness, Clement at last recovered himself in a degree.

One morning he rose before sunrise, and left the city on foot. He went a long distance, so far that you might call this walk a pilgrimage, for it had for its end, a church; a little church, so modest that it differed from the surrounding dwellings only by a stone cross which was not in sight till one stood at the doorway which it surmounted. This door was opened by him whom Clement came to seek, a young priest, pious and simple, his school-mate formerly, inferior to him in mental ability, but his guide and master in those regions into which the soul goes only. What Clement sought at this moment was not the relief of a frank confidence; nor was it Christian consolation and discreet sympathy. What he needed was to recover strength by a manly avowal of his weakness; then in presence of a friend, who should be a judge too, to call God to witness a resolution which he pledged himself to keep. This resolution he had already taken once, when he was yet a boy; to-day he would repeat it with more of a man's mature feeling, for he had hoped and lost; with a devotion more difficult, for the woman whom only he loved and should love,—she now had given her heart to another. His voice trembled, saying these words, but he continued: "And neither word, nor look nor act shall trouble her, or let her know what she has inspired in the heart of him who will teach himself henceforth to live

destroy hope," which he now solemnly repeated with that devout and serious emotion which accompanies all self-sacrifice.

It may be said that much exaltation mingled with this devotion. I acknowledge it. But it was that exaltation, which true to the significance of the word, elevates the heart, and which, powerless certainly if it assumes to be all-sufficient, can nevertheless do much when Divine help, earnestly sought, assists it in aiding, augmenting, in a word, exalting human strength!

The evening of that day, Clement came tranquilly to his wonted place at the fire-side of the Müllers. To Wilhelm's questions he replied that, during his long stay at Rosenhain, he had neglected some affairs to which he had of late been obliged to give all his time. "Then, I confess," he added, "I have been out of humor, and I thought it wiser to spare you my presence." To Berta, who questioned him less vaguely, he said with more frankness, but without detail, that he had been very unhappy, and that he begged her to say no more about it. Then he took up his violin, and began to play some strains from Bach.

Berta seated herself at the piano, and while she accompanied this *morceau* and several others, her husband who was beating time at her side made the observation that the ill humor of their young friend had a singularly favorable effect upon his musical talent.

"I declare, Dornthal, you have never played so well before in your life."

"Perhaps," said Clement, with a thoughtful air, "Yes, I think you are right."

So it was with him; music was the veiled but eloquent language of his soul; all that he so well knew how to re-

toward Fleurange. No one divined—she, least of all —that between the past and the present there existed for him the difference between life and death. But, without her knowing it, the new and strange sympathy which existed between them, gave to her cousin the clue to all her thoughts and efforts. She, also, in appearance, had become the same as heretofore. Her days were filled and busy; her duties with little Frida, the cares she lavished upon her uncle, household employment, sewing, exercise, and study, all this occupied her time so completely that it was rare to see her idle or pensive.

Hilda, her favorite cousin, had been also for an instant struck by the hesitation with which Fleurange replied to her questions about Count George, but had ceased to attach importance to it, noticing the apparent tranquillity of her busy life. One only saw clearly, and well understood the fleeting expression of suffering and weariness which sometimes overshadowed her face, and gave a vague trouble to her look. One only, when the family were gathered in the evening, noticed her absence, and in thought followed her to the little seat by the river, whither he knew she had gone, for an instant to be alone and unconstrained with her grief. All that she suffered, he suffered also, and he lived thus, united to her, and separated from her, each day more and more.

And so the weeks glided by, bringing back content and happiness to the family circle. The Professor was gradually gaining in mind and body: work was still forbidden him, but reading and conversation had become salutary diversions. Thanks to the presence of Hansfelt, these conversations were at times as interesting as of old, and it would have seemed that Ludwig Dornthal had recovered the full use of his faculties, had not a partial

his intellectual nature revived first, and strengthened itself more and more by contact with the noble mind of his friend. Thus the evenings passed without weariness, even for the youngest of the family, in listening to their conversations.

These evenings usually closed with music which the professor enjoyed, and even required as part of his treatment. Then Clement took up his violin, and he did so the more willingly, when he perceived that his cousin always was glad to listen. Thus he dared to speak to her in a mysterious language which, he only understood, but which made her start sometimes as if she had heard the echo of her own pain.

One evening, when he had played even better than usual, she said with emotion:

"You call this a romance without words; but, Clement, this music must have been composed for a song, and you know the words, surely,—do you not?"

"No;" he said, "but, like yourself, I seem to hear them; and I believe they must exist somewhere."

Hansfelt, for his part, had listened attentively to the music.

"Yes," he said with a smile, "they exist in the heart of all who love, especially of those who love hopelessly. Stop, I will tell you in common words—no, in rhyme, what this composition means which Clement has just been playing."

He took a pencil and wrote hurriedly four stanzas whose idea, as rendered by a French poet, was nearly this:

> Du mal qu' une amour ignorée
> Nous fait souffrir,
> Je porte l'ame dechirée
> Jusqu' á mourir!

Clement made no reply, and abruptly began to play something else; the children rose and clapped their hands on hearing him play their favorite *Tarantelle*, and their gayety soon became noisy.

Fleurange left the room unnoticed, or at least, so she supposed;—but Hilda had been watching her attentively ll the evening, and followed her, resolved to obtain a full avowal of all that was passing in her heart. She softly entered the room of Fleurange. The latter was not expecting to see any one; she had thrown herself into a chair, her head resting on her hands, in an attitude expressive of profound grief and dejection.

Hilda approached and threw both arms around her. Fleurange looked up quickly, her eyes full of tears.

"Do you remember," Hilda said, in a gentle and caressing voice, "do you remember, Gabrielle, that day in the library in our dear old home—that day when I was so unhappy? You asked me the cause of my tears, and I told you all. You have not forgotten, I know. Will you answer me to-day with the same frankness?"

Fleurange shook her head, and did not speak.

"It has always seemed to me," continued her cousin, "that the happiness which since then has crowned my life dates from my confidence in you that day. Why will you not be as frank with me, and take heart as I did?"

"Your happiness was waiting for you," said Fleurange, at last. "Only a fancied obstacle prevented you from grasping it."

"How many obstacles that seem insurmountable disappear in time, or by the exercise of a resolute will! Why should not Count George—" she went on slowly, with lowered voice.

"Stop, Hilda, I entreat you!" cried Fleurange, with agitation.

Her cousin stopped, frightened.

"Listen to me," resumed Fleurange in a calmer voice, "and since you wish, we will speak of it; I am willing to do it once, and once only. Now tell me," she pursued, with a sad smile, "can you render me rich and noble like himself, or can you deprive him of his rank and make him poor like me? In one case or the other—in the latter es-

beings! Help me then, Hilda, I beg you, help me to forget—to live—perhaps even to recover,—by never speaking to me again of myself or of him!"

Hilda clasped her silently in her arms, and long held her thus, without speaking a single word.

"I will obey you, Gabrielle," she said, at last; "I promise you to be silent henceforward; I will never mention his name till I hear it first from you."

XXXVII.

Summer and autumn passed, and brought no new occurrence, save an occasional fluctuation in the slow convalescence of the Professor, and for Clement, a few moments of happiness, lighted by the reflection of his vanished hopes. They were rare, and followed by sad awaking; yet they were sweet and lived long in his memory.

One day remained graven there; a fine October day, when his sister Hilda and his cousin had consented to accompany him in a boat to a point a few miles distant, where a little wooded promontory juts out into the river. They had passed some hours there, conversing with all the unreserved frankness of sisters and brother, and reading aloud by turns favorite passages from books which they had brought with them. As he listened to the silver tones of Fleurange, and met her cordial and sympathetic glance bent on him when he in turn was reading, as he found himself with her in this lonely and beautiful spot without other companionship than that of her whose affection for both seemed to form one bond the more between them, hope again forced its way into his heart, like

now fixed upon the dark and rapid current, now wandering over the shore, that expression which he had so well learned to understand; an expression which filled his heart with pity and with sympathy for her, but which made him thrill and shiver with sudden anguish, as if, each time, fire or the knife had touched the hidden wound and made it bleed afresh!

Two months later, the Christmas holidays brought to him again one of these fugitive moments of happiness. Christmas eve (never-forgotten anniversary of the arrival of Fleurange among them!) the re-united family seemed to find all their former happiness renewed. As of old, the Christmas tree was lighted, Mlle. Josephine, as prompt to share the joy of her friends, as she was careful to avoid causing them to share her sorrow, contributed to its decoration, and for each one there was a present from her, chosen with generous hand. Then, as of old, there were wreaths of holly worn, and Fleurange this time needed no urging; later, with the music and dancing, the happiness of those around her communicated to herself an unwonted gayety to which she yielded naturally and without resistance: that gayety of youth, which, at certain moments, triumphs over everything, and has its revenge for unreasonable restraint. The laughter of Fleurange rang like music; her merry voice mingled with the voices of the children and filled the heart of our listener with surprise and delight. That brilliant light in the eyes, that vivid color, all the splendor which happiness adds to beauty,—had long since been missing in the face of Fleurange, and Clement could not see her thus restored to herself without feeling the intoxication of hope once more. But he was soon and sadly recalled from his brief dream.

Madame Dornthal was seated near the arm chair of her husband, whence, indeed, she was seldom long absent. The old kind smile reappeared again upon her lips, as she watched her children surrounding their father, and

chair. He seemed, in truth, to be suddenly fatigued; he had closed his eyes, and his head was resting against his wife's shoulder. They awaited with anxiety his first word on emerging from this momentary attack of slumber. He did indeed soon open his eyes, and looked about him vaguely and with anxiety; then, turning to his wife, he said sadly, passing his hand over his forehead:

"Tell me, why is not Felix here? I know, but I cannot remember."

This extreme failure of memory, this name which called up so many painful recollections, spoken in a manner not less painful, put an end to all the gayety of the evening, and though this occurrence, caused by a little too much excitement and fatigue, was not in itself serious, yet the impression made by it was of ill omen, specially to Fleurange who had a double and recent motive to dread the sound of that name.

Clement, informed by Steinberg of their meeting with Felix, shared silently in her feeling, and once more the ray of light, which had shot across his path, vanished, leaving the darkness more sombre than before. But there was something he could not forsee, namely: the decisive influence upon his destiny which was to be exerted by an event, serious and public, at that very moment taking place in a far distant land, a sphere completely removed from his own.

XXXVIII.

The Christmas holidays were over, and it was nearly the middle of January, when arriving at the house of his friends a little earlier than usual, Clement found Wilhelm Müller standing at the door.

"Well!" he cried, "you are just in time! There's trouble! A courier came in this morning from St. Petersburg with important news. There will be a great shock to our affairs."

"The death of the Emperor Alexander? Yes; I knew it yesterday. But what more?"

"A good deal more, I can tell you. Constantine is

set aside; the Grand Duke Nicholas will succeed."

"Are you sure?"

"Yes. But that is not all. We had that yesterday; this morning, the courier brings things of much greater importance. A conspiracy has broken out."

"A conspiracy? Where?"

"In St. Petersburg. The courier left on the 24th of December. At that very time they were fighting in the square in front of the palace, and the Emperor was in the midst of the melée."

"Constantine?"

"What? No; his brother."

"The Grand Duke Nicholas? Was he at the head of the conspiracy then?"

"On the contrary. It was more likely to be Constantine; it was not he, however. To tell the truth, we don't understand it at all; everything is confused. But, however, will you come and help me? We must send off despatches in every direction. We shall have news this evening, no doubt; and I imagine that at this very moment Waltheim" the head of the house of which they were the principal agents "must be actually beside himself with excitement."

The two friends left the house together. They had gone but a few steps before they came upon a crowd gathered before the *porte-cochère* of a handsome building which stood near Müller's house.

It was the Russian legation. In answer to their first question they learned that a courier had just arrived on horseback, covered with dust and half dead with fatigue. He had left St. Petersburg on the 26th, and had accomplished the journey in ten days.

"Do you know anything about the news that he brings?" asked Müller of the person who had just replied to him.

"Nothing, of course. Besides, *they* will only know," said he, pointing to the diplomatic mansion, "what it suits them to tell us."

Müller and Clement went on their way.

"The twenty-sixth!" Müller said. "But it would be

"There will be news of the same date soon received at the other legations, without counting on our own private dispatches. Now I think of it, one of the *attachés* of the French legation is a friend of mine. Suppose I go and see what he has heard?"

Müller approved of the idea, and without further delay, Clement left him and hastened to the house of the French legation, while Müller went directly to his office, where Clement was to rejoin him as soon as possible.

The young *attaché* to whom Clement referred was the Viscount de Noisy. He had been present on one occasion when Clement had spoken in public, and had taken a great liking to him from that moment. Since then, they had made excursions together on foot and on horseback, and the Viscount had improved every opportunity to meet his new friend, while Clement had had occasion to reproach himself for not having responded more warmly than he had done to the other's advances. He was, therefore, quite sure of a friendly reception; and, in truth, as soon as his name was announced, he was introduced into a little parlor adjoining the principal office, where M. de Noisy passed the greater part of his days, and where he was now sitting at a table covered with papers. Before Clement had spoken a word, the young *attaché* exclaimed: "Do you come to bring me news, or is it to hear something yourself?"

"What a question! You know that our commercial couriers do not usually have the honor of outstripping the messengers of the diplomatic service!"

"But they do sometimes."

"At least that is unfortunately not the case to-day."

"That is a pity, for we have as yet no news."

"The courier of the Russian legation has just arrived; he left St. Petersburg on the twenty-sixth."

"Yes, we have just heard so. It is a speed absolutely fabulous; I have no idea that ours will be able to accomplish any such thing. However, they don't fall asleep at the French Embassy in St. Petersburg."

At this moment some one rung loudly. An officer opened the door, and beckoned the Viscount, who sprang to his feet.

"The courier!" he cried. "Bravo! Long live the ambassador! To be only one hour behind the Russian courier is marvellous! Here, *mon cher*, here are cigars; take that arm-chair and wait a few minutes; I will bring you news worth waiting for!"

Clement seated himself, lighted a cigar, took a newspaper, and patiently awaited the young diplomate, enjoying meanwhile the blazing wood fire which, without prejudice to the great stove at the end of the room, seemed none too much for the rigorous weather. However, after an hour had passed, he began to think he was wasting his time, when the Viscount de Noisy reappeared, bringing a handful of letters, which he threw upon the table.

"*Ouf!*" he said. "This is not all that I must read, and most of them are in cipher. We shall be obliged to write in cipher also, and I have no idea when I shall get through!"

"Can you tell me a word or two, without indiscretion?"

"Yes. Our news is good. All is ended. The struggle was violent, but short. The new emperor has done well. The regiments in revolt returned at once to obedience; the leaders of the conspiracy are taken. The only serious thing is that among them are many individuals of high family, and that a quantity of society men are compromised. This is particularly serious to me, because, being in the French Embassy at St. Petersburg before I came here, I know nearly all of them personally."

"Do your letters name any of the heads of the conspiracy?"

"Certainly—Troubetzkoi, Rilieff, Mouravieff, Wolkonski, and a host of others. But among all these names there is one that I am amazed to see. Who could have imagined that Walden would mix himself up in such an affair as this?"

Clement's heart beat violently.

"Walden, did you say? What! Count George von Walden?"

"The same. Do you happen to know him?"

"Yes."

distinguished as he is, could have participated in such a conspiracy as that? An atrocious affair—for its object was nothing less than to assassinate the Emperor and declare some crazy republic, for which the name of Constantine should serve as a pretext!"

"And Count George is seriously compromised?" asked Clement.

"He cannot be otherwise; he is classed among those who have no other alternative than Siberia or death. But, excuse me, Dornthal, I shall have to leave you. I'll wager we shall be scribbling all night. Here," he added, feeling in his pockets, "here's a private letter from St. Petersburg that the courier brought to me. You will find interesting details."

The young *attaché* vanished into the main office, and Clement went out of the room, and out of the house, and finally found himself in the street before he had recovered from the stupor into which he had been thrown by this news which he had just learned. He directed his footsteps mechanically towards the office where Müller was awaiting him, gave him an account of what he had just heard—with the exception of the one fact in comparison with which all the other circumstances attending this event were insignificant to him—then remained for some time at his desk, making a superhuman effort to control his thoughts and to bring them back to the work which he had to do. This accomplished, he took leave of Müller, and regained the house first, where, without stopping below as had been his custom, he went up stairs, and shut himself into his room. He had need to be alone, and to reflect at leisure upon what he ought to do, in presence of an event so unforeseen and so momentous.

Gabrielle! He thought but of her,—of her only. How would she endure a blow like this? How could he tell her of it?

For a long time he remained lost in thought, without recalling to mind the letter which he had in his pocket. Finally, it occurred to him, and in the hope of deriving thence some light, he began its perusal.

After some few unimportant remarks, came the following:

"This conspiracy, which has burst upon us like a thunderbolt, and seemed to be the spontaneous result of a certain indecision which characterized the first few days of the reign (leaving it doubtful which of the two brothers was really emperor) dates, on the contrary, from a remote period, as now appears. I am assured that its ramifications are deep and wide, and that its leaders have but taken as a pretext the circumstances which followed the death of Alexander. The plan had been formed, they say, and was to be executed in the spring, if the life of the late emperor had been so far prolonged. But it appears equally certain that a great many of those who to-day find themselves seriously compromised, had but a very imperfect idea of what had really been going on. To this number, I cannot doubt, belongs our unhappy friend, Von Walden. You know that he has always dreamed of reforms, possible and impossible. As ill-luck would have it, during the last year he has met in Italy a certain Lasco, a very intelligent and capable person, but dangerous, and for the last ten years busy in all the plots that have agitated Italy or the German states. Incarcerated; then released—Heaven knows how; passing under a hundred different names; in a word, one of those evil-doers, of whom the true chiefs of the great net-work of conspiracy that surrounds us, make docile instruments. George made his acquaintance accidentally, and allowed himself to be persuaded by him to be present once, out of simple curiosity, at a meeting where, by still worse luck, one of these very chiefs chanced to be present. The latter promptly understood the advantage that might be derived from the name, the position, the enthusiasm of Count George, and from his very ignorance of the whole subject. He persuaded our friend to meet him at a given time at St. Petersburg, and to stand ready to second a combined movement which was to make a demonstration, planned with great secrecy, but so strong in numbers that it could not be stifled. It must, he said, result in realizing many of Count George's cherished dreams. I have these details from the Marquis Adelardi, that delightful Milanese, who was here three winters ago, and who is, as you know, Count George's intimate friend.

The Marquis, uneasy at his sudden departure from Florence, especially anxious when, after three months he had not returned, came to find him. He arrived only three days before this fatal twenty-fourth. It appears to be certain that upon that day George was in the square, in the very foremost rank of the insurgents. Adelardi maintains that he went thither in good faith, convinced by those who urged him on that Constantine's refusal of the empire was a fable, and that it was essential to maintain his rights, for the sake of their own projects, which this prince, it was said, stood ready to promote. However this may be, it is only too true that in the square, and close by Count George, was this Lasko, who was killed at the moment when he was holding a pistol to the breast of the Grand Duke Michael. One witness—and one only, for it requires courage to testify in favor of a man in his position—declares that it was George who turned aside the pistol and saved the life of the Grand Duke, before an *aid-de-camp* could draw upon the assassin. But too much excitement exists against him at court and in the city for this circumstance to be greatly urged in his favor. He himself obstinately refuses to say a word in his own defence, and his haughty demeanor since his arrest does not help matters. What makes the case still worse is the presence of his secretary, also an Italian, and whose relations with Lasko have rendered him more than suspected. This Italian, whom they call Fabiano Dini, was also in the square on the day of the *émeute*, and was severely wounded."

Here Clement ceased reading. These last few lines had brought his emotions to its height. All their terrors were confirmed, and the fatal destiny of their course had followed him to the last. Unhappy himself, and bringing unhappiness to others!—Yes, that was indeed Felix: capable of perceiving his disgrace, incapable of extricating himself from it; seeking action and danger, yet only safe in concealment, he would be sure to fall an easy prey to those agitators, who at that time even more than at the present day, were undermining Europe. He would become their agent, useful by reason of his talents, convenient because of his contempt of danger and death; and thus, quickly reach the goal to which his career tended.

Clement walked up and down his room, unable to collect his thoughts; finally, after long reflection, he came to the conclusion that the prosecution of Count George would, doubtless, drag on for some time; that its result might be less fatal than this letter had seemed to give cause to fear; finally, that it was better, as long as possible, to spare his cousin the distress of uncertainty. At Rosenhain this was easy, for reading the papers had been forbidden to the Professor, and none were even seen in the room where the family assembled. Hansfelt was the only person who received them. Clement hastened to despatch a few lines to Hilda, confiding to her all that he had just learned, and begging her and Hansfeldt to watch carefully that Gabrielle should hear nothing of it: "Next week," he wrote in conclusion, "I shall be at Rosenhain, and we will consult together, dear sister, as to what it is best to do later. In the mean while, I rely upon you, you are prudent, and you love her."

Until now the brother and sister had never exchanged a word upon the subject to which he referred in his letter, but for a long time they had understood each other. Hilda now agreed with him entirely, and Fleurange would have much longer remained ignorant of this which they wished to conceal from her, had not an unforeseen occurrence, some days later, suddenly overthrown the plan which their good sense and affection had dictated.

XXXIX.

"THE poor ye have always with you," is a divine prediction, and human experience adds to this: "and in all places shall ye find them, unless carelessly or wickedly, you turn your eyes away from them."

Mlle. Josephine, as we know, belonged neither to the blind nor the hard-hearted, and she quickly found as much on her hands in Heidelberg as she had had in Paris, with this difference always, which was a great trial to her, that here she could communicate with her poor *protégées* by gestures only, which were rarely, on either side expressive enough to be readily understood; this condition of affairs had obliged her to relinquish what had always been with her the favorite side of charity, that is to say, those kind words and occasionally long conversations with which she had been wont to accompany her almsgiving.

"I only would ask them to understand a little French," she used to say; "it seems to me they could do that so easily, while it is absolutely impossible for me to understand German!" In a word, to know German, and not to know French, seemed to Mlle. Josephine a mystery of nature. However, as the unfortunate natives persisted in speaking only their own tongue, and in so doing were not so much to blame as to cease to be deserving of charity, Mlle. Josephine had gladly accepted the aid of Fleurange as her interpreter in her visits among the poor. Every day, at the same hour, the young girl came, sometimes to accompany her, sometimes to make the daily round in her place.

She usually found Mlle. Josephine in her *laboratory*, that is to say, in a room on the ground-floor, whose chief article of furniture was an enormous wardrobe and chest of drawers, a receptacle of all sorts of objects destined to be distributed among her present or future *protégées*, for she delighted to make provision in advance, and it was rare that any appeal from the poor found her unprepared. "Here, Gabrielle," she said to her, one morning when Fleurange appeared as usual with basket on arm, ready to select the charitable luggage for the day, "here, all is ready."

And she designated certain objects placed on a table which, with a couple of chairs, completed the furnishing of the room. There were ranged in good order the following articles: on one side, two pair of stockings and a flannel petticoat; on the other, a covered tureen containing soup, a little package of sugar, a bottle of wine, a paper of tobacco, and last of all, two or three newspapers. To all this was added a little vial, whose contents could not be guessed.

"The stockings and the petticoat," said Mlle. Josephine, "are for the mother of the little girl to whom you carried some clothing yesterday; the tureen and the sugar go to the poor old woman whom you know, together with this little vial of balm-water, prepared by myself, and none the worse on that account! Lastly, the wine and the tobacco are for the old soldier, the carpenter whom you visited last week. His daughter succeeded yesterday in making me understand that the thing which would give the poor man the greatest pleasure would be to lend him a few papers, from time to time; you are to give him these which I sent for this morning expressly for him. Oh, by the way! your cousin Clement has left me two excellent cigars for him. I forgot them entirely; I will go and get them now. Meanwhile, you can put all those things into your basket."

And the worthy Mlle. Josephine went in search of the cigars. It was necessary to go up stairs, but she was not accustomed to count her steps when she could do a favor, small or great, to any. However, she was much more moderate in all her movements than she had been wont to be, and going and returning, it took her nearly a quarter of an hour.

During this time Fleurange, standing before the table, arranged in her basket the different objects prepared for her, and, last of all, she was about to put in the two newspapers when her eyes rested on a few lines that made her start. She seized the paper, opened it, and began to read with extreme curiosity. Suddenly she uttered a faint scream—the paper fell from her hands—her eyes grew blind—and when her old friend returned, Fleurange lay pale, motionless, senseless upon the floor.

Mlle. Josephine happily lacked neither presence of mind nor experience; she made haste to get down on her knees beside the fainting figure of the young girl, lifted her head and supported it in her arms, then drew a *vinaigrette* from her pocket and made her inhale the strong odor, all the time ransacking her brain to understand what could have caused this strange accident in the case of a person ordinarily so tranquil and in such good health. At this moment she observed the newspaper which had fallen upon the floor.

"Ah!" she said to herself, "she has been reading this queer stuff; she may possibly have found bad news in it,—but, good Heavens! what news could have thrown her into such a state as this? Dear child!" she continued, looking down tenderly upon the pale and beautiful face resting against her breast, "she was telling me yesterday that she had never fainted but once in her life, and that was in Paris, two years ago, when she fainted with weakness and hunger, in *our* house!"

Poor Mlle. Josephine! the remembrance thus awakened caused her a second pang, and her eyes were yet filled with tears when those of Fleurange opened, and fixed themselves upon her with an expression of surprise soon followed by a partial return of memory.

She raised herself slowly; but before Mlle. Josephine was able to assist her, she flung both arms around the neck of her old friend.

"Oh, dear *Mademoiselle!*" murmured she, "did you know it? did you know it?"

The poor old lady had never been more at a loss what to say; to confess that she was totally ignorant of the whole matter, would have been to invite a confidence most completely inopportune at this moment; to say the contrary thing was unsafe. She essayed a small, innocent falsehood.

"Yes, yes,—my poor little girl; but what is the use of speaking about it now? Be composed, don't say anything at present; we will talk about it by and by. Be consoled it will come out right!"

And after aiding Fleurange to rise and placing her in a chair, she went to bring a glass of water, and pouring into it a few drops of some sovereign panacea with which she was always ready, she held it to the young girl's lips. Fleurange drank it all; then drew a long breath and said:

"What happened to me, just now?"

"Nothing; you were faint, that is all."

"How strange! I am never faint."

She passed her hand across her forehead.

"O Heavens! I remember now," she cried suddenly, "but was it true? Perhaps it was a lie, only a false rumor which somebody invented!"

"Who knows? Perhaps it was," replied Mlle. Josephine, vaguely. "It is very likely it was; they do say so many things."

"But tell me all you know about it!"

"No, no; not now, Gabrielle, not yet. You are not in a condition to listen. Do as I ask you; compose yourself. Later we will talk about it."

Fleurange was silent for a few minutes; then she rose: "I am better now," she said, "my strength has returned."

She gathered up her long hair which had fallen about her shoulders, fastened it with her comb, picked up the paper and put it into her pocket, then tied on the little fur-trimmed velvet hat which she wore in winter.

"Dear Mlle. Josephine," she said, "thanks, and pardon me! I am quite recovered now. But for to-day, you will excuse me from these visits, will you not?"

"Yes indeed; I see you cannot go."

"I must go home at once."

"And I shall go with you; you must be put to bed. You are usually so pale, and now your cheeks are the color of *that!*" and she designated a curtain of vivid red which hung at the window.

"Oh no, I am not sick," Fleurange said with animation, "and the air will do me good. Do not be anxious; you see I have quite recovered."

As Mlle. Josephine had not the most remote idea of the cause of this sudden indisposition, and as the young girl was now apparently quite restored to her usual health, she no longer opposed the wish of Fleurange to go alone, and on foot; the distance was not great, she came and went daily alone. The old lady accompanied her as far as the gate and they separated, to meet at evening.

XL.

It was severely cold weather; the little round hat which Fleurange wore covered her forehead and left exposed the masses of hair gathered at the back of her head, and she often drew up the hood of her mantle, the better to protect herself from the cold. But at this moment she did not do it; she only gathered the heavy folds of her mantle more closely about her and walked on rapidly. The keen and icy air cooled her burning cheeks, and aided her to regain her strength, so that except the unwonted brilliancy of her color and of her eyes, there remained no trace of her recent indisposition by the time she reached home. As soon as she entered the house, she went straight up stairs, and, knocking lightly at the door, entered at once a room situated between her own and Hilda's. It was Hansfelt's study, since he had made his home at Rosenhain, and when Fleurange entered she found the young wife and the husband there together. When they saw her they both started involuntarily, and interrupted their conversation with a kind of embarrassment. This did not escape the notice of Fleurange.

"I can imagine what you were talking of," she said; "and it is upon that subject that I want to speak to you."

Hilda looked up, uncertain what she ought to say.

"Hilda," said Fleurange, "you and I agreed that you should never mention Count George again to me, until I should name him first myself. Very well, I do it now, and I desire you both to tell me all that you know in regard to him. There," she continued, throwing down upon the table the paper she had brought; "read that and then tell me whatever else you know about it."

What to say to her? She stood there before them, calm, firm, decided. No further concealment seemed possible.

Hansfelt glanced over the paper. He saw that the article which had fallen into the hands of Fleurange contained no details; only a list of the accused, and some very plain reference to the fate that awaited them. Upon this list, figured among the very foremost, the name of Count George.

"Of what do they accuse him? what is this crime?" she said, in an abrupt voice.

Hansfelt still hesitated, but his wife knew better than he did the person who put the question. "Karl," she said, "you may speak,—you must. There is no longer any concealment towards Gabrielle."

"And why has there been until now?" said Fleurange,

"Ah yes! I understand it—(and a faint blush rose to her face) my secret, which I thought I had kept so well,—you have all guessed it?"

"No, no," Hilda cried, " only myself—and you know I could not keep it from Karl—only Clement and I."

"Clement too?" said Fleurange, with sudden surprise and confusion, while her blush deepened. "But what difference does it make?" she added. "I am willing to tell all now, and I insist that all shall be told to me. Tell me, Karl; be sure of this, I am very strong, there is no need to be very guarded in what you say; only the surprise overpowered me for a moment. Now I am ready for anything. I will listen."

But, for all that, when, after renewed hesitation, Hansfelt decided to satisfy her, when he commenced a detailed account of the circumstances which had placed Count George in this supreme peril, the color vanished from the young girl's face, and she became very pale.

"Siberia or death?" she repeated once or twice in a low tone, as if it were as hard to utter as to understand these frightful words.

"From the most dreadful of these alternatives, there is good reason to hope he may escape," said Hansfelt.

Fleurange shuddered. *He! He!*—Was it indeed Count George of whom they thus spoke.

"But tell me Karl, is there no other alternative than these? There is imprisonment, or some lesser exile,—surely they are great and terrible punishments. Why do you only mention these two, one of which is almost as dreadful as the other?"

Karl shook his head; "His name," he said, "his rank, the favors that have been offered him so many times, all, in the eyes of his judges, aggravate his crime. His life will be spared, I trust, but—"

"But—the mines—the chains—that fearful and cruel Siberia,—you suppose that he can be condemned to undergo these rigors without alleviation?"

Hansfelt was silent. Hilda clasped her cousin's hands in her own, and pressed her lips tenderly to the colorless

brielle, why do you question me like this? Hilda why did you tell me to answer her?"

"Because I must know the whole," Fleurange said, lifting her head which she had rested for an instant upon her cousin's shoulder, and resuming all her former composure.

Then, after a moment's silence she went on : "And so nothing can possibly save him?"

"You wished for the undisguised truth, Gabrielle, and I have concealed nothing from you. According to all human probabilities, nothing can rescue Count George from his fate, that is past a doubt. But it happens sometimes in Russia, that a sudden and capricious exercise of sovereign power arrests the hand of justice, yet I should mislead you if I did not add that nothing justifies the hope that he will be the object of such an act of clemency. All agree in saying, on the contrary, that the irritation against him is extreme, and surpasses that felt against any other of the conspirators."

Fleurange remained silent for a long time: "Thank you, Karl," she said at last, "you will tell me all you hear further, will you not?"

After having received the desired promise, she was about to leave the room, when she stopped suddenly. "One question more," she said; "my head must be confused not to have asked you before. Does any one know how his unhappy mother heard the news, and how she supports it?"

"Clement has heard that at the very moment when she received the tidings at Florence, she was preparing to set out for St. Petersburg."

"St. Petersburg, at this season of the year? The poor woman! she would die on the road."

"Further, I can tell you nothing; Clement will be here to-night. He will perhaps have more recent news."

But in the evening, when Clement came, Fleurange, overcome by the fatigue and emotions of the day, was unable to leave her room. Her aunt had said that she must see no one, and the wished for interview with Clement was postponed until the morrow; and Clement, meanwhile, was preparing himself for the new phase of trial which awaited him, by hearing in detail all that had passed. Mlle. Josephine related to them what had happened to Fleurange at her house, and learned, in return, with an interest mixed with the most extreme surprise what had been the real cause of the fainting fit. Of all the sufferings in this world those caused by love were to her the most utterly incomprehensible. Had they told her that her dear Gabrielle was suddenly attacked by consumption or by insanity, her anxiety and surprise would not have been greater. They might even have been less, for, in that case, there would not have mingled with her sadness that terror which is inspired by the unknown, and that complete ignorance of the remedy which accompanied her ignorance of the evil, and thus added powerlessness to her anxiety. She who had so many remedies, small and great, to suggest in every other supposable case, could imagine absolutely nothing suited to this.

How this unknown personage, whose name till to-day she had never even heard, could have become suddenly so important to the happiness of this dear child, surrounded by a world of other affection, in which she had always seemed content and happy, was a problem beyond solution.

It was in her eyes a greater mystery than to understand the German language; but great though it was, she resolved to study it out; "for," she thought to herself "the day may come when there may be something to do for her, something which I can understand and which will come within the scope of my ability. I will try to understand this matter, so that I may not lose the opportunity when it arises."

This vague hope for the future consoled Mlle. Josephine for her present uselessness, and served for the moment, as a satisfaction to her kindly soul, deprived of its wonted power to help.

XLI.

The next morning, Fleurange had so far rallied from the shock of the preceeding day that she rose, as usual, at daylight. She wrapped herself warmly from the cold, put on her fur-trimmed hat, and was soon on her way to the church, where every day, during this season, she attended early service.

Having arrived, she threw back her hood, and knelt, as near the altar as possible. The church was so dark that each one brought a lantern, a bit of wax candle, or some other portable light by which to see to read, and these various lights, increasing with the number of worshippers, finally spread throughout the church rays sufficient to reveal to view persons and objects.

Fleurange had brought no light, she had need of none, for she had no book, but she was not the less profoundly absorbed in devotion. Her hands clasped, her head a little thrown back, her eyes fixed upon the altar, her pure and regular profile thrown into strong light by the candle of some one kneeling near her, she resembled—so white and still was she—a statue of marble covered with sombre drapery. She prayed fervently, but without agitation, without tears, not even moving her lips; all her soul was in her eyes, and her eyes expressed at the same time, the faith which implores and hopes, the submission which accepts, and the courage which acts. It was a prayer from which one rises, accepted, or else strengthened and submissive.

Service ended, one by one the lamps were put out, and the gray daylight stole faintly into the church, growing stronger ere long, so that when Fleurange, who had lingered behind the others, turned to go out, she recognized Clement who stood near her, and who at once joined her.

Together they left the church; out doors, it was now broad day, but the sky was overcast, a furious wind was blowing the light snow into the air, and as they emerged from the shelter of the great wall of the church they encountered a perfect hurricane which made Fleurange lose 'r footing. Clement supported her for an instant, then drew her arm through his and they walked on silently for a few steps.

In spite of himself, Clement dreaded this interview, and he gathered all his strength to bear tranquilly what she might be going to say. But, at last, as she still remained silent, he spoke first:

"You were ill last evening, Gabrielle; I was far from expecting to find you in the church this morning, so early and in such severe weather."

"Ill?" Fleurange replied; "No, I was not ill, but I had received a great shock; you know it, Clement, do you not?"

"Yes, Gabrielle, I do know it."

These simple words exchanged, the barrier was removed; the phantom that had haunted Clement's dreams stood between them; but an energetic nature prefers realities however painful to vague apprehensions, and even to vague hopes, and Clement felt his courage increase as a more perfect self-abnegation struck its roots deep into his heart.

"Why," he said to her, after a moment of silence, "why, Gabrielle, have you so long withheld from me the confidence you had given me a right to expect?"

She replied unhesitatingly: "Because I had laid upon myself the duty never to speak of *him*. I laid this upon myself," she continued, without noticing the faint shudder which her cousin had not been able to repress, "because I wished to forget him. It was best for me to be silent, even with Hilda, even with you, Clement. But now," she went on, with a sort of exaltation, in which grief and joy were mingled, "now that is no longer my endeavor. It seems to me a new life begins for him and me. We are separated, I know, as if by death itself. But death removes barriers and re-unites, sometimes. What can I say, Clement? It seems to me I am nearer him to-day than yesterday, and in spite of myself (I know it is all imagination), the idea is constantly present to me that, in some way, I may be able to serve him. In any event, I have no longer any motive to conceal my real self, and the absence of this constraint is already a great solace to

Clement listened patiently. A keen pang shot through him at each word, but he nerved himself, as a soldier going into battle, that not even the tremor of an eye-lid should betray the fear of death or the expectation of a wound.

And this imaginary hope of which she had just spoken,—it was the last dream of love and grief! He did not seek to destroy it.

"Cousin," he said, "let us not despair. Many an unforeseen change may occur during the continuance of a prosecution such as that which is now about to begin. Nothing is as yet to be despaired of. At all events," he added, as they drew near the house, "from this day forward, promise me, Gabrielle, to give me your fullest confidence as before; be willing to tell me everything, and to expect everything from me! You have made me this promise once; have you forgotten it?"

"No Clement, and I renew it willingly. You are the best friend I have; I told you so long since; I think to-day just as I did then."

Yes, she had said it; he had forgotten neither the day nor the place, and his heart throbbed at the recollection. Although he was but just past twenty, and the spray of honeysuckle gathered on that day was still green, it seemed to him that a long life had flowed between that moment and this in which now they were exchanging almost the same words.

Yet when at the close of this interview, they clasped hands for an instant, and separated, there remained to Clement from that gloomy winter's morning, a less painful impression than the one which had filled his heart, that lovely night on the banks of the Neckar, when by the soft moonlight he had received, in one accent of her voice, one look from her eyes, the sudden and fatal revelation of her love for Count George.

To-day, she had told him nothing that he did not already know. Happiness having failed him, a vague future of self-devotion opened itself before his mind. That made it worth while for him to endure the pain of living.

This day and several which followed passed without any new incident. The necessity of concealing from the

Professor the pre-occupation of all, obliged them to make an effort which all found useful, Fleurange especially, who remained faithful to her daily duties and passed the same time as before at her uncle's side or with Mlle. Josephine and her *protégées*. A feverish anxiety betrayed itself, however, in all the movements of the young girl, and in the troubled expression in her eyes when, daily at the same hour, she came to ask Hansfelt the news in the papers. But for more than a week, nothing came to alleviate or to increase her distress.

Clement had returned to Frankfort, and the days dragged on heavily and painfully, when one morning on a day and at an hour when they did not expect him, he appeared suddenly, bringing unexpected news; the princess Catherine was in Frankfort, and would be in Heidelberg on the morrow!

Fleurange was greatly agitated. The princess Catherine!—All the recollections attached to this name awoke with such intensity that for a few moments she was almost stifled by her emotion; voice and language both at once failed her.

"She is coming here?" she said, at last, "here to Heidelberg! why,—what can bring her? How do you know it? Who has told you? Tell me all—oh! speak quickly, Clement!"

Clement implored her to be calm, and she became so by degrees, while he informed her that he had learned it from the princess herself. Yes, the princess Catherine, who, immediately upon her arrival hearing from her banker, M. Waldheim, of the presence of young Dornthal in Frankfort, had sent to beg him to come to her at once. Clement had complied, not without emotion, with this request from Count George's mother, and had found her in a fearful condition of suffering and weakness. He had, however, had a long conversation with her, of which this was the sum : on the receipt of the fatal news, she had left Florence, travelling day and night, and had fallen ill in Paris; after four days, however, she had resumed her journey; reaching Frankfort, the physician had assured her it was absolutely impossible for her to go further, and especially impossible for her to bear the rigor of the season increasing as she drew nearer towards St. Petersburg. Being unable to proceed further she had resolved to come at least as far as Heidelberg where she hoped that the advice of a young doctor, since,—and even at that time—famous, would enable her at the earliest moment to resume her sad journey.

"I shall make this effort," said the princess Catherine, "for I wish to live, I wish to be near him, to see him, if it is possible. I hope much from the advice of Dr. Ch—— and from your cousin Gabrielle's nursing; I depend upon her. Tell her so. Tell her," she added, with tears in her eyes, "tell her that I am eager to see her again, and that I implore her to come to me as soon as I reach Heidelberg."

"And to-morrow she will be here," cried Fleurange.

"Yes, towards evening. I am going to see the physician, and to have prepared for her the best apartments in the city. But without her saying it, Gabrielle, I feel sure she depends upon finding you there on her arrival."

Fleurange contented herself with saying that she should be there, but her heart throbbed with a delight that she had never expected again to feel. To see once more the mother of Count George! Was it not to be brought very near to him,—did it not involve the certainty of hearing his name, and having the most speedy and direct news from him,—was it not, in a word, the realization of a secret wish which she had not dared to put in words?

The next day, long before the appointed hour, she was at the house where rooms had been prepared for the princess, arranging the furniture in the manner which she knew would best please, striving in every way to prevent the sadness of the surroundings from increasing that of the unhappy traveller who, towards the close of the long day of expectation, arrived, worn-out with fatigue, and fell sobbing into the arms of the young girl.

The time when she feared no other danger for her son than from the presence of Gabrielle, was long since past. The feeling of the moment, in her case, had always had the pre-eminence, and her present grief was well-suited to drive all others from her mind. And so in meeting her young *protégée* again, she only thought of the comfort of once more enjoying her presence and her services, at this hour when she most needed them, and everything, save her first affection for Fleurange, seemed to have vanished from her mind.

XLII.

A shaded lamp burned on the table. A brilliant wood fire sparkled and crackled upon the hearth, lighted for ornament only, since the room was well warmed by the stove built into the wall, and fed from the outside. The princess as of old lay on a sofa, sheltered by a tall screen; beside her a little table, loaded with all those luxurious trifles without which she never travelled; not far off, Fleurange, in her accustomed attitude.

All was changed, nevertheless; it was no longer a question of reading aloud to her, or following the routine, more or less frivolous, of her ordinary occupations. One subject only possessed all her thoughts, and to the one who listened it was even more engrossing than for her who spoke. And so the poor mother returned to it incessantly, now with extreme agitation, now, with the dejection of utter despair, but always with the most heart-felt and agonizing sorrow, to which responded a sorrow equal to her own.

It was the first time that the princess Catherine had been conquered by misfortune. Conquered, but not transformed, for, just as she preserved instinctively all her elegance and all her refinement, so her ungovernable temper remained unchanged, and broke forth in violent recriminations against those whom she accused of being the cause of her son's misfortune, that she might be able in regard to himself, to pity only, and not to blame. And so Fleurange heard her exclaim that Fabiano Dini was his evil genius, and she shuddered, recalling her own presentiment, too quickly and fatally justified.

"Yes," said the princess, during one of their earliest conversations, "it is he, it is Fabiano Dini, who brought

And she related to the young girl the whole story of the acquaintance of Count George with Lasko, the influence the latter had acquired over him, the skill with which he had known how to avail himself of Count George's weak points:—she herself had been unwilling to believe it at first; despite the warnings of Adelardi, she had been too long, too foolishly unsuspicious,—but, her fears once aroused, what had she not suffered, what not essayed!— alas, in vain!

"He was always so,—this dear, unhappy child!" she exclaimed; "no prudence, no fear of danger ever arrested him when his inclination allured. O the wretches! they knew how to take advantage of his imprudence, his generosity, his courage! and now," she cried, raising herself upon her elbow, while her hair, thick still but turning gray, fell over her shoulders in unwonted disorder, "can it be possible that they confuse *him* with *them!* Oh, if I were well once more,—if I could have the strength to go, to reach St. Petersburg, to see, if but for once, the young empress! I should obtain his pardon, I know it—I am certain of it!"

She fell back exhausted, wringing her hands, and murmuring, "and Vera!—Vera! absent from court at this moment! She was expected, but who knows whether she will arrive before it is too late? Who knows if she may not be his worst enemy, and if he has not poisoned the very fountain whence his safety might come!"

These words, which might have caused a new pang, were not heard by the person to whom they were addressed. Fleurange, at this moment, had gently withdrawn to the remote end of the room, where was preparing a sedative, which from hour to hour the poor invalid took mechanically when it was offered her, without having as yet obtained the relief of a moment's sleep. This devouring anxiety, which no remedy could control, was a little tranquilized on the arrival of the letters which Adelardi wrote from St. Petersburg, which kept her well informed of all that went on, and by turns, revived her hopes, or confirmed her fears. But up to the present moment, he had no positive and definite information, in regard to the ͏te awaiting his friend. And so, after having read these letters with avidity, she often threw them into the fire with despair.

All this excitement finally brought on a high fever, and the princess had been obliged to keep her bed for several days, when, one morning, came a new letter from St. Petersburg. Fleurange approached the bed-side softly and perceived that the invalid was asleep. It was important not to disturb this brief moment of repose; moreover, for several days the physician had ordered that no letter should be given her till it had first been read, so that, in the supposable case that one should contain decisively bad news, it might not fall into her hands until she had been in a degree prepared for it. Fleurange had been the person to read these letters, and she had done it with the less scruple, in that the princess had herself desired her, for more than a week to read all letters aloud, being too feeble herself to open them.

At this moment then, leaving the invalid to the faithful care of Barbe, she re-entered the parlor, and broke the seal of this letter, which like the rest, was addressed to the princess by the Marquis Adelardi:

"At last," he wrote, " I believe that I have attained the certainty that we no longer need dread the most terrible result. The extreme rigor of the law will be executed only towards the recognized chiefs of the conspiracy, four or five in number. All the rest, including George, will undergo a terrible punishment alas! but we are obliged to consider ourselves happy that we have not to apprehend one yet more fearful. I say *we*, dear and unhappy friend, but as to him, I dread, on the contrary, the effect this sentence will produce, and I am persuaded that he will regard it as tenfold more to be dreaded than the other.

"Since my last letter, thanks to the intervention of one of the ambassadors, I have obtained permission to visit George in the fortress where he is confined, and to see him for a few moments alone. His pardon has been offered him, if he will name some of his accomplices. He has refused; this, of course, does not surprise you. But the countless proofs of their criminal intentions which have been brought before him, in the hope of wringing some confessions from him, have revealed to him the true nature of the enterprise in which he has madly suffered his honor and his life to be compromised. The effect of this discovery has been to throw him into a condition of the deepest dejection, and his sole fear seems to be that he will not be condemned to death.

"'I have deserved it by my folly, Adelardi,' he said to me, 'and you were right in predicting in an extremity such as this in which I now find myself, that fact would afford me no comfort. Still, I shall know how to endure my fate without weakness; you do me the honor, I trust, to have no doubt of that. And yet, I will not represent myself as any more courageous than I am; I tell you frankly, if, instead of death I am sentenced to drag out an existence in Siberia, I do not know to what lengths my despair would carry me.' It will be needful, therefore, to use as much circumspection in telling him of the mitigation of his sentence, as with others, of the rigor of theirs. To this end I hope to succeed in visiting him again.

"Meantime I have heard with equal surprise and admiration, that many of those condemned to the same penalty with him, are to have an unexpected and unheard of consolation. Their wives, their admirable heroic wives, have begged to share their fate, and at this moment, while I am writing to you, many of them whom you personally know,—beautiful, young, elegant,—are preparing to accompany their husbands, by undergoing a sort of a noviciate of the rigors of Siberia. These unhappy men are deprived of rank and fortune, made destitute of all things, but there is left them a devoted affection whose fidelity fears nothing. I acknowledge to you that I am ashamed and abashed, for, I see it clearly, never have I understood or even suspected, what heroism and generosity can lie hidden in a woman's heart."

The heart of Fleurange throbbed so violently that she could read no further. Her eyes bathed in tears, she read and re-read the page, when suddenly some one came to say that the princess was awake, and had asked if there were a letter for her. For some days an agonizing dread of the worst had seized upon her imagination, and had caused her at times a paroxysm of delirium. So when the letter just received was imparted to her, she felt a sudden and unexpected relief.

His life was spared! time was before her in which to work! She began once more to hope, and experienced a degree of tranquillity long unknown to her.

In the evening she was able to sit up: she talked, she spoke of her plans, her hopes, of all that she would do to soften the exile of her son, of all that she would attempt even, in regard to shortening its duration; but, strange to say, Fleurange scarcely listened and made no replies.

Toward nine o'clock, some one came, as usual, to walk home with her. Sometimes it was Julian, sometimes Clement, who came to accompany her in the half-hour's walk which separated Rosenhain from the abode of the princess.

This time she was so lost in thought that she did not notice which of the two young men it was. The sky was starry, but it was very cold, and under her hat, her hair was floating in the night wind.

"Raise your hood, Gabrielle; it has not been so cold this winter."

It was the voice of Clement. She roused herself abruptly from her reverie. "It is you, Clement! Pardon me, I had not noticed whether I was under your escort, or that of Julian."

And, as he gently touched her hood to lift it: "no, no," she cried eagerly, "let me breathe the air! Although it is scarcely two years since I saw the snow for the first time in my life, I am not afraid of the cold, and I could, if necessary endure a much severer climate than this. See!" and she uncovered her head completely, and walked a few steps exposing her face and her forehead to the icy night air. "Don't you know," she continued, with an animation which contrasted strangely with the silence that had preceded it, "don't you know, in the campaign in Russia, those who felt the cold least were the Neapolitan soldiers? Well, that is the way with me. I have brought from Italy a supply of sunshine that many frosts like these will not exhaust."

ing, and they walked on rapidly, scarcely leaving a footprint upon the hardened snow.

Her gayety this evening was so strange! Clement observed it, but could not understand the cause. And her joyous voice and charming smile, instead of rejoicing him as usual, caused him an inexpressible anxiety, and rendered him sadder than ever!

XLIII.

As it often happens in the case of persons of violent and excitable temperament, the princess Catherine rarely saw anything long under the same aspect, and although a settled sadness had been thrown over her thoughts by the tragic circumstances which suddenly surrounded her, and veiled in gloom a life till now so prosperous, she found means to give a thousand differing aspects to her misfortune, and it was not always easy to follow the capricious phases of her grief. What consoled her to-day, irritated her to-morrow; what she had affirmed in the morning, in the evening she denied with vehemence. At times she expressed fears, only that they might be combated; at other moments she burst into tears at the slightest contradiction, and no one was allowed to seek to re-assure her, except on penalty of being accused of cruelty and indifference to her distress.

In consequence of one of these fluctuations, on the day following that when the letter of the marquis Adelardi had seemed to her so consoling, Fleurange found the princess in a condition of the most extreme dejection.

All things had changed their aspect, or perhaps it would be more reasonable to say, all things had resumed their terrible reality in her eyes. Was it in truth enough that life would be spared to her adored son; was the vision which now offered itself to her eyes, anything less than the cruelest torture?—He, George,—her son! that finished type, in her eyes, of beauty, elegance, and rank, —clothed in the frightful garments of the convict!—and in that wretched crowd, making his lonely way towards those desolate regions, where the rudest and most degrading toil awaited him, without even the consolation of a friendly voice to encourage him, a hand to clasp his own, a heart to love him, and to tell him so!

"Oh!" she cried, with that tone which is like no other, as a mother's grief is like no other grief, "oh! feeble, ill, exhausted as I am, if they would but grant me permission to go with him! Do you know, Gabrielle, it seems to me I should find strength, I should find courage,—I would set out, I would reach Siberia, I would share his miserable life, and by my love, I would render it endurable!"

The more rare it was to see any such disinterestedness on the part of the princess, the more touching was this outcry, whose sincerity could not be doubted. Pale, mute, motionless, Fleurange listened with an emotion that seemed to arrest the words which her trembling lips desired to speak.

The poor princess was sobbing, exhausted by her own vehemence, when, kneeling down suddenly beside her, Fleurange said softly:

"Do you remember, princess, the promise which you once required from your son?"

The princess raised her head with surprise and a faint shade of resentment.

"What of it? Do you wish to reproach me with it now? The time is scarcely well selected, and this surprises me in you, Gabrielle!"

"To reproach?" cried Fleurange. "No, I had no such thought; it was a request, a petition,—or rather, no, it was a question which I wished to ask you!"

"A question?"

The princess looked at Fleurange. The expression of the latter's face struck her, and an interest, mingled with surprise, drew her out of her dejection. What so extraordinary could Fleurange be about to say? and why was her voice so imploring, and yet her face so resolute?

"Say,—speak,—tell me what you want, Gabrielle?"

"Well then, first let me say this. The evening before I left Florence, while I was coming down the San Miniato with him,—with Count George,—he asked me if I would

"Why, Gabrielle, do you recall all this?—I believed you generous, and I find you cruel!"

Fleurange continued, as if she had not heard: "I said to him that I should never listen to words like those, unless, which I deemed impossible, a day should come, when you, princess, you, his mother, should say to me, 'Gabrielle, be my daughter, I gladly consent.'"

She stopped a moment, as if her heart were beating too strongly for her to go on.

"To what are you coming?" said the princess.

"Princess, now listen carefully. This is my question: when the dreadful sentence shall be pronounced; when Count George von Walden shall have been degraded from his rank, despoiled of his wealth, deprived of his very name even (you shudder, alas! and so do I, as I speak;) but, in a word, when that day shall have come, if he then should ask for that consent which he once promised you to await,—would you grant it then?"

The princess looked at her in amazement, and scarcely seemed to understand what she had been saying.

"Will you give me permission myself to say to him, 'yes!'—will you say to me, at last, on that day, 'Gabrielle, be my daughter, I am willing?'"

The princess began to apprehend the meaning of what she heard, but she was too stupefied at first to make any reply.

"Princess," continued Fleurange,—her radiant face expressing all the love and the courage which animated her heart, "you have only to say those words to me now, and I go! I will be at St. Petersburg when this sentence is pronounced, when he comes forth from his prison I will be there, and before his departure into exile, a tie shall unite us which will give me the right to accompany him, and to share with him all that he is to suffer! And if ever," she continued, speaking in a voice of deepest feeling, "the tenderness of a mother, a sister's cares, a wife's love, were able to alleviate misery, my heart shall have the strength of all these varied forms of affection, united in one!"

We have seen that when certain chords in the heart of

in any circumstance of her life, had she felt an emotion to be compared to that with which she now listened to the words and tone of Fleurange.

For an instant, she looked at the young girl silently; then clasped her passionately in her arms, and covered her forehead and eyes with kisses, exclaiming over and over again, in a voice broken by sobs: "Yes,—oh, yes! Gabrielle, become my daughter,—I consent gladly, gratefully. I give, with all my heart, a mother's consent and a mother's blessing!"

XLIV.

Fleurange, as we have said, usually returned to Rosenhain in the evening, but this day she left the princess several hours earlier than usual, and it was not yet noon when Clement, who sat alone in the parlor absorbed in a great book which lay open before him, suddenly saw her appear, at an hour when he least expected her.

Perhaps, instead of reading, he was at this exact moment thinking about that unusual gayety on his cousin's part, which had rendered him, the evening before, so sad. At least this is certain, that when she appeared thus suddenly before him, at this unusual hour of the day, the same sensation tightened about his heart once more. Yet nothing in her appearance seemed to justify a foreboding of ill. He had feared to see traces of long-continued weeping, which would, it was likely enough, follow such feverish and unreasonable gayety. But at this moment, if she was no longer smiling and gay, as yesterday,—if, on the contrary, she seemed serious and grave, still her brow was radiant, and in her brilliant eyes it was easy to read an expression of almost triumphant joy. In short, her appearance bore no trace of that dejection which habitually follows a paroxysm of factitious gayety.

"You are alone;" she said at once. "So much the better, Clement, I have to speak to you—to you first and before all others. You shall see," she continued, throwing off her mantle, "you shall see that I am faithful to our engagement, and that I come to you at this moment as to my brother and my best friend!"

While Clement looked at her, and listened to these preliminary words, the instinct of his heart warned him more and more that a great trial was coming upon him, and that he must be ready to suffer. But when, without delay, she came at once to the point, when, with a simplicity, terrifying by the strength of tenderness and devotion which it revealed, she unfolded the plan of this self-immolation, offered, accepted, Clement was literally overpowered with horror, and it seemed to him that reason itself wavered under the shock.

What! this being so dear, so precious, so adored,—to lose her!—to lose her forever, and how! To know that she was condemned of her own will to all the horrors of a destiny so shocking that the imagination refused to face it. And why?—why?—Ah! that cry of Othello was at this moment the cry of Clement's heart: "The cause! The cause!"—yes, the cause of this self-immolation, this it was which added a sting to his grief, so keen, so cruel, so intolerable, that, beaten down by this unexpected revelation, conquered by uncontrollable emotion, Clement, for an instant, lost all self-command. A smothered cry escaped his lips, and letting his head fall upon his clasped hands, the tears which he could not repress forced their way through his fingers and fell, one by one, in great drops, to the floor.

The habit of self-control was so strong with her cousin, that Fleurange had not imagined it could ever fail him, and it is possible that, at that instant, the deep and hidden cause of this passionate despair was made clear to her, as by a flash of lightning! But this was not the hour when such a thought could find lodging in her heart, nor did Clement leave her time for this.

He had risen and walked for a few times silently up and down the room. This strong and brave heart struggled hard to recover itself, and lifted an earnest appeal to Him who alone could save it from utter despair, and renew all its failing energies.

Soon he approached her; he had triumphed over his emotion, and his first words gave her an explanation which was natural enough.

"Forgive me, Gabrielle." he said. "I have been in

conceivably weak. But indeed, I must be utterly destitute of regard for you if I could look calmly upon the frightful prospect which you have thus abruptly placed before me. You will understand this, I am sure."

"Yes, I had expected to see all the others greatly shocked. But you, Clement, I believed capable of hearing it calmly."

"Well then, dear cousin, you see you had too high an opinion of my courage. But be sure I will conduct myself better in the future. Do not deprive me of your confidence,—this is all I ask."

"Oh no, indeed I shall not; for it is upon you that I depend to make known my resolution to the others, and especially, and first of all, to your mother. You may well suppose that I desire her consent and her blessing, too! and you must plead my cause with her."

Clement was silent for a few minutes. He was trying to steady his voice, but it trembled still as he said:

"And when do you propose to set out?"

"Next week, if it is possible."

"Next week! That is to say before the close of January! And have you thought how to make such a journey at this time of year?"

Fleurange hesitated.

"I know," she said at last, "that it will be difficult for me to go alone."

Clement interrupted her with alarm mingled with impatience.

"Alone!" he cried. "I swear to you, Gabrielle, that it is utterly impossible to listen to you with composure, when one knows perfectly well that your rash words are not to be taken seriously."

"They must be taken seriously," she said, with the same expression of energy and tenderness which had so struck the princess Catherine: "you must be reconciled to seeing me go alone, if there proves to be no other way for me to go to him!"

Oh! how gladly at this moment would Clement have exchanged his fate for that of the condemned man! He regarded Fleurange with sad admiration, and she continued:

"But I have thought that it might not be impossible to find some travellers going into Russia, with whom I could make the journey!"

"Strangers, with whom to make this long and difficult journey! It is impossible, Gabrielle; this is the most impossible thing of all!"

"Ah!" cried Fleurange, "with what confidence I should have turned to that good friend whom Heaven gave me, and how greatly at this moment,—how more than ever before, I feel his loss!"

"You refer to Dr. Leblanc?—Yes, I do justice to his memory, and I am convinced that his devotion to you would not have proved wanting under the present circumstances. But indeed, Gabrielle, patience fails me,—and you are too cruel!"

"Clement!"

"What! you need a friend who has only the humble merit of being faithful, devoted, capable of watching over you during a distressing journey, resolved to remain with you until—until he can do so no longer! And at such a moment, you do not deign to remember that you have a brother? And do you not see that, in thinking of others, you forget that it is at once his duty, and his right?"

"Clement! my dear Clement!" said Fleurange, with surprise and emotion, "what do you mean to tell me? what can I say to you in reply? Assuredly, I had counted and do count upon you as upon a brother, and yet I confess, I should not have dared to ask you to make such a journey as that for me!"

Clement smiled bitterly. He was comparing at the moment what she was ready to do for another, with what she had judged him incapable of doing for her.

"Well, cousin, you were wrong," he said coldly; "it seems to me this was the time to remind you of your promise to me. As for myself, I am only faithful to the engagement I made with you at the same time. That is all."

"May heaven bless you, Clement! bless and reward you!" she said earnestly, "yes, I do recognize my error. I should have known that there is not upon earth kindness like yours!"

She held out her hand. He clasped it in both his own, saying nothing, and without looking at her. Then they parted. Fleurange needed to be alone again. Clement went to obey her, and fulfil her wish in relation to his mother.

XLV.

It was the prescribed hour for the professor's daily repose,—toward the close of the forenoon. All was very still around him. In the adjoining room his wife sat at her wheel, for Madame Dornthal knew how to hold the distaff, and, according to a usage kept up in Germany much longer than elsewhere, it was her hands which had spun the two most beautiful pieces of linen for the *trousseau* of each of her daughters. She raised her head, on seeing her son enter, and remarked instantly that he had been undergoing some great excitement. Her eyes questioned him.

"I want to speak to you, mother," he said, "let us go where we can talk."

Madame Dornthal laid aside her distaff, and having called a young servant-maid to take her place, with directions to call her, if she should be needed, she followed her son out of the room, gently closing the door behind her.

Another door, across the corridor, was that of Clement's room; thither they went together.

Clement began the recital of the conversation he had just had. An exclamation of surprise responded to his first words, then Madame Dornthal listened in silence. Interest, pity, admiration, showed themselves in her face, while her son was speaking; and she had tears in her eyes, and a voice broken by emotion, as she replied at last:

"My consent and blessing, do you say? You ask them of me in her name? Poor child! How could I refuse my blessing to such devotion! But my consent," she continued gravely, "I cannot give it unconditionally."

"What, mother," exclaimed Clement with surprise, "could you think of refusing her permission?"

"No, Clement, but I refuse to you permission to accompany her."

Clement started.

"Mother?" he said.

Madame Dornthal pushed back her son's hair, and looked in his face, as we know she loved to do, under the influence of unwonted tenderness for him. Then she said slowly:

"Alone with Gabrielle from here to St. Petersburg? Have you considered well, my son?"

Clement colored slightly, but his beautiful look met that of his mother, loyal and pure.

"Mother," he said, "to Gabrielle, I am a brother; to me—"

He hesitated a moment, and grew pale. Then he resumed firmly:

"To me she is now the wife of another; you do not think me capable, I am sure, of forgetting this at any time?"

Madame Dornthal's eyes filled with tears. For an instant she looked at her son in silence, never had she so loved him! never so well understood how worthy of her love he was! But the hour had come, the only hour perhaps in life when the most impassioned maternal love has become powerless, and can do nothing, absolutely nothing, to console the suffering child.

She understood this; she knew that she must respect the secret grief of her son, and suppress the impulse of her own tenderness. Neither compassion nor sympathy at that moment, could be of use to him. And so she abstained from them with that sure instinct of the heart to which the heart responds, and the painful throbbing of Clement's calmed itself. He resumed directly with a composed voice:

"If, however, you judge, for her sake, and especially for the sake of others, it is indispensable that a third person should join us for the journey, well, mother, we will seek to find her."

"Ah!" exclaimed Madame Dornthal, "were it not for the dear and imperative duty which keeps me here, you would not need to go far to seek one."

Clement raised his mother's hand to his lips : " I was thinking so," he said with a smile.

Then he continued: " But this person we shall find, I am sure ; for to-day, no matter; we have other things to do."

And by degrees, by the aid of Clement and of his mother, the startling news was made known, first to the professor, then to all the other members of the family. We will not enter into the details of each one's sentiments, nor tell of the tears that were shed, nor of the emotions which poor Fleurange was called to undergo in the course of that day; suffice it to say that the expression of sympathy far surpassed that of surprise. There reigned about this simple household an atmosphere so pure that all things beautiful and grand were perceived at once, and readily understood. To lose this sister, so charming and so beloved, was a grief that no one strove to conceal ; but the daughters of Madame Dornthal, like herself, had deep in the heart the germ whence springs all self-sacrifice. So the young girl felt herself understood and regretted without being blamed, and this sympathy, while it added to her love for those whom she was leaving, was a great support to her courage.

The only person who, at this moment, felt no share in the general heroism, was Mlle. Josephine. Since the resolution of Fleurange had been made known to her, she had remained in a state of stupefaction which, under other circumstances, would have been comic. Her eyes wandered from one to another, with an expression of distressed perplexity, as if she implored some explanation which could make her understand a fact so extraordinary. When she joined the family in the evening she was still dumb ; and she took her place among them, knitting-work in hand, without saying a word or looking at anybody.

The professor, gently prepared for this new separation, accepted it with the same resignation as he did his wearisome illness. Fleurange was sitting beside him, and Madame Dornthal and her daughters, with Mlle. Josephine, were at work by the table.

Clement sat removed, talking with his little sister whom he held upon his knees. The child in her turn was asking the explanations which no one had thought to give her. While her brother talked with her in a low voice, Frida's great eyes opened wider and wider, her little mouth quivered, and a flood of tears deluged her face; then she threw both arms around Clement's neck, sobbing:

"Oh Clement, what shall I do without her?—I love her so!—I love her so!"

Clement hid his face in the child's long curls, clasping her in his arms and kissing her tenderly, but he could not comfort her till he had promised perhaps Gabrielle would return,—perhaps he would bring her back himself! Frida's tears upon this ceased to flow. She was silent, and sat grave and thoughtful in her brother's lap.

Suddenly Mlle. Josephine broke the long silence:

"It is very far—Siberia, is it not?"

A general smile accompanied the reply to this question which was the first fruit of the good lady's long meditations.

"And Clement is going to Siberia, too?"

"No. He goes to St. Petersburg."

"And from here to St. Petersburg, it is how far?"

She was answered by a complete sketch of the route which was to bring Fleurange to the first limit of her journey. After this enlightenment, Mlle. Josephine fell back into silence again, but for only a brief period. A new and sudden idea dawned upon her. She pulled off her glasses in a hurry.

"But these two children cannot travel alone!" she exclaimed.

Madame Dornthal and Fleurange looked up. Clement moved slightly, and disturbed the sleep into which his little sister had fallen.

"No, assuredly not," continued the old lady with animation. "How would that appear, I ask you?—I ask your pardon, Clement, you know how I esteem and love you; but how old are you? tell me that. Then, as regards Gabrielle, besides her age (which is no better than yours) she has, I have a thousand times told her—she has an unfortunate face!—a face, which forbids her from doing things which might be quite right for others, no older than herself. This is true, all of it, and I defy anybody to say that I am mistaken, this time!"

No one attempted to do so, for the thought which she had expressed in her own peculiar way, was shared by all.

"Now then," resumed Mlle. Josephine, "it is necessary that Gabrielle should be accompanied by a respectable person. I beg your pardon Clement a second time; I do not mean to say that she could do without you (you are a protector who could not easily be replaced), but, my dear friend, propriety requires that, besides you, she should have a safe and elderly companion, like myself!"

At these unexpected words there was a general exclamation. Everybody was speaking at the same instant, and for awhile nothing could be heard. The excellent old lady understood, however, quickly enough, that her proposal was universally approved. But before any one else, before Clement even could grasp her hand to thank her, Fleurange had sprung forward and, throwing herself into the arms of her old friend, exclaimed:

"Thanks, thanks! oh may God repay you for all that it is His will I should owe you in this world!"

And so, without more ceremony, the generous offer of Mlle. Josephine was accepted. An hour ago, Madame Dornthal had made the condition of which we are aware, and at that very moment, she had been occupying herself with a solution of this very problem.

As to Mlle. Josephine, from that time, all seemed to become clear before her. The occasion she had so much desired had not kept her long waiting. In this extraordinary phase of Gabrielle's life, there was an act of most useful self-sacrifice which she could perform, an act, too, which would retard by just so much the hour when she must needs separate from her *protégée*. She felt herself greatly comforted, and brought back to almost her former placidity.

The situation was, however, so foreign to all her preconceived ideas, that many of its details still remained shrouded in mystery.

"But why," she said, an hour later, when escorted by her own servant carrying a lantern, she took Clement's arm to walk home, "but why not go to Siberia with her,—if this gentleman, whose name I can never pronounce, would not have any objection?"

Clement could not help smiling at her question, but there was too much bitter sadness in his heart, for him to be willing to reply. She did not notice it. At that moment she was thinking aloud, quite regardless of her companion, and, following the course of her meditations she soon gave utterance to another remark, which, far from causing a smile, made her auditor shudder from head to foot.

"Provided," she said, after having remained silent for some minutes, "provided this Monsieur George is worthy of the sacrifice that she is going to make for him!—provided that after having left us who love her so much, she does not some day make the discovery that he loves her less than we did!"

XLVI.

Clement left Mlle. Josephine at her gate, and returned with rapid steps, struggling against the new storm which had been raised in his heart by these words which he had just heard.

Until that moment, thanks to his recollections of Count George, and still more to the *prestige* with which the latter was endowed in Clement's eyes by his cousin's preference, Clement had regarded his rival as unquestionably his superior. With simple and genuine modesty, he deemed it but natural and almost right that his humble love should be sacrificed. To doubt if Count George were worthy of Fleurange, to fear that, beloved by her, he might cease to love in return,—these were ideas which had never occurred to him, and without knowing it, the excellent old lady had applied the last torture to his already bleeding heart. To admit this fear was indeed to make his devotion tremble to its foundation, it was to add despair to self-abnegation. He repelled it then with a sort of terror, and to re-assure himself, had recourse to the reflections which had but lately been most intolerable to him, taking pleasure now in thinking of the devotion of which his rival was the object, the better to persuade himself that it was absolutely contrary to the nature of things that any one should be ungrateful for it.

The reflections of Fleurange at this very hour were of a different nature; freeing herself by degrees from all the violent and successive emotions of the day, she gave way without restraint to the secret joy with which her heart was overflowed:—free, at last!—free to think of him, to love him, and to tell him so!—This thought, so long repressed, beaten back, hidden, was now no longer denied her. Yet a few weeks and she should be with him!—she should be his!—The horrors of the fate which she was about to share disappeared before the thought that she should bring him, in this hour of desolation and wretchedness, all the wealth of her love and devotion, and it seemed to her that this was a more beautiful realization of her dreams than if they had been fulfilled amid all the splendor of rank and fortune!

Ah! Madre Madelina was right. This was not a heart called to the supreme honor of loving God only,—of feeling for Him that ineffable love which suffers the contact of no other love,—that one love which, if it has not always reigned, annihilates from the instant that it dawns upon the heart whatever love may have preceded it, as light destroys darkness, and so long as it is present, renders the other's return impossible! "Those who love hear that voice.

"'This voice it was which had spoken directly to the heart of *Madre* Madelina.

But Fleurange had not heard it thus distinctly, even when she listened for it in the momentary lull of all earthly sounds. And yet we know that she was not deaf to the Divine voice; she was pure, she was devout and strong, she had a brave and fervent heart, a heart closed against evil, and which would have chosen God above all earhlty happiness; but it was ardently alive to human affection where she felt that this was not forbidden to her. Doubtless this is the law for almost all, even among the noblest, and it is the wonted path of well-doing. Only it may be said, it is not that of the exquisite and inexpressible happiness of which we have spoken heretofore; this also is true, that when a soul is in danger of making an idol of the object of its love, and of placing it on an insecure foundation, not infrequently does suffering, and that the more acute as the soul becomes purer and more beautiful, come to bring it back, sooner or later, to the point whence may be perceived that true centre towards which, ignorantly, we all aspire, and which every human passion, the most noble even, and the most legitimate, hides from our view.

Fleurange had perhaps some confused intuition of this, and it made her regard as a sort of expiation for her happiness the frightful conditions upon which it was granted her, and believe, in accepting these conditions joyfully, that she could thus ensure the permanence of that one impassioned feeling which ruled all the rest.

Since the conversation of Gabrielle with the Princess Catherine, the health of the latter had greatly changed for the better; her physical sufferings and even her sorrow seemed to have been tranquilized. A new activity awakened in her, since she perceived a way to busy herself for her son, and to come into almost direct communication with him. Add to this the natural liking of the princess for all things extraordinary, and we shall readily understand how the heroic resolution of Fleurange was most interesting to her, and added a motive for activity which was useful and beneficial to her in the extreme.

She arranged everything, and it was necessary to let her decide upon even the least details of the long journey which the young girl was about to make. As far as St. Petersburg, she and her elderly companion were to travel in one of the best carriages which the princess possessed, and all that could soften the rigors of the cold for Gabrielle was prepared with the utmost solicitude. Arrived in St. Petersburg she would be lodged in the princess's own house, and remain there from the day of her arrival till that of her departure on that other fearful journey.

All this was transmitted to the Marquis Adelardi, who was charged with the care of Gabrielle during her stay. He must furthermore find a way to communicate to Count George the unforeseen solace that Heaven had prepared for him in his misfortune. As to the steps to be taken to obtain the necessary permissions for this strange and sad marriage, and for the newly-made wife to accompany her husband into exile, the princess judged that the best means for success would be, to obtain for Gabrielle an audience with the empress.

"Either I am greatly deceived," said the princess, "or her heart must be touched by this heroic devotion, by the sight of Gabrielle, lovely as she is, and, perhaps even by a faint trace of pity for my poor George."

"This pity," she continued,—"something tells me that it yet survives the favor of which he showed himself, alas! unworthy, and a day perhaps will come, when I can myself appeal in his behalf with success! To obtain pardon for my son!—to see him again!—

"Yes, in spite of everything, I hope—I believe—I may say, I am sure this happiness will be granted me, if only all these miseries do not too quickly terminate my life. Yet the traces of this frightful sentence, did he undergo it but for a single day only, will never be effaced! That I know well: my dreams for him are shattered forever. How then could I hesitate in accepting the generous sacrifice of Gabrielle, at first, with a transport of enthusiasm, which I confess overpowered me when, with a voice and look that I cannot describe, she knelt before me, asking my consent,—and afterwards, upon reflection, and seeing the circumstances of distress in which we found ourselves, with real and lasting gratitude for her devotion to my unhappy George."

"Doubtless," she continued,—with a return of that ruling passion, which, they say, is never driven off very far, or for a very long time,—" doubtless when this hour for which I hope, this hour which will restore him to me, shall strike, other regrets may indeed awake! But after all, as I have said, the execution of this sentence, which is but too certain, puts an end to all hope in that direction. The conspirator acquitted, or even pardoned, might touch a heart where perhaps love still plead for him ; but the haughty Vera will never cast one look upon the exile who shall return from Siberia, having undergone his punishment. I resign myself, therefore, thinking that, after all, Gabrielle is charming, and, to my knowledge, he has loved no woman so well. You will tell me perhaps that the most ardent flame goes out readily in the heart of

George; I know it very well, but there can be no doubt that the devotion of this young girl to himself must insure the continuance of the affection with which she has inspired him, or its renewal, if the revolutionary storm through which he has passed may for the moment have seemed to extinguish it utterly. For myself, I know that if any thing can make me endure this fearful separation, it is the knowledge that in his exile, my son has with him this noble and lovely creature who will be better able than any one else in the world to save him from despair."

In the eyes of the princess, Gabrielle, in spite of the pure generosity of her love was but a last resort, or rather she was nothing at all, except relatively. She overwhelmed her now with care and caresses, as once she had rudely separated herself from her; as to-morrow she would have been equally ready to banish her, if a sudden return of fortune had brought about possibilities more in conformity with her own wish. . But all these thoughts, even though they had been penetrated by her who was their object, could not have changed her resolution, or impaired her courage; her fate seemed to her already united with that of George. All, outside of this thought, and the joys and sacrifices that gathered around it, had become a matter of indifference to her. Calm and serene, she made her preparations for departure, without anxiety or undue haste, and superintended those of her companion, for whose use she reserved the costly furs, and all other defences and aids against the cold, which the princess Catharine had been zealously providing for herself.

The days, however, passed rapidly, and as the time of departure drew very near, more courage was needed by those who remained behind, than by her who was about to leave them. At last, when the very day was come, and kneeling in the church, she and Clement said a last prayer together, the eye of God alone could see to which of the two at this moment the palm of devotion and self-surrender rightly belonged.

IV.—THE IMMOLATION.

"L'amour vrai, c'est l'oubli de soi."

XLVII.

OUR travellers were now far on their way; for more than twelve days they had kept on without interruption, and, notwithstanding the constantly increasing intensity of the cold, as far as Berlin, and even further, Fleurange and her companion had scarcely noticed the change in temperature, thanks to the numberless precautions the princess had taken for their comfort.

But having reached Königsberg they were obliged to leave the carriage that had brought them thus far, for it was of the highest importance that they should travel rapidly, and they were now obliged to traverse the *Strand* (the only route to St. Petersburg, at that time), the Strand, that is to say, that narrow strip of sand which extends along the Baltic as far as that arm of the sea which separates Prussia from Courland, as by a broad canal, and forms at last the basin or sheltered lake of the Kunsche-Haff. This lake bounds the Strand on the right, while at the left its gloomy beach is bordered by the sea, and the few scattered habitations in this desolate region are built facing the lake and turning their backs to the ocean, and are separated from the road by high mounds of shifting sand, thrown up by the fierce winds which sweep down from the Baltic Sea.

The carriage of the princess was left at Königsberg to await the return of Clement and Mlle. Josephine. Fleurange retained and took with them, for the defence of her old friend, all the rich furs, at once light and warm, with which the princess had provided her. For herself she took only a coarse and heavy cloak, which sufficed for her against the cold, for she intentionally avoided accustoming herself to luxury which would later be forbidden her

A change of vehicles was promptly made, and the little *calèche* in which Fleurange and her companions found themselves closely crowded together, was soon on the road along the Strand, by which they expected to reach Memel on the evening of the same day. Clement sat silently with folded arms, and, with secret horror, examined the desolation around him. All that he saw seemed to him a fitting prelude of that icy Inferno, towards which was going, under his charge, she whom he would have desired to shelter from the rudeness of a summer breeze.

The cold was less keen than it had been the evening before. The clouds, gray and heavy with rain, seemed to presage an unseasonable thaw, and through the clouds, the sun, shorn of its rays, shed a pallid light upon the gloomy waves and the sandy beach. The postilion, to make it easier for the horses, drove them so near the sea that the waves broke over the track which the wheels left behind them. On the right, rose the melancholy sand-heaps, and on that side as well as in front, nothing was visible but sand as far as the eye could reach; at the left, nothing but the stormy, threatening sea. Far or near, not a roof nor a tree, not a bit of grass, not a living being save a few sea-birds swooping down upon the waves with bewildered flight, and adding one sad feature more to this landscape whose wan melancholy, mingled with storm, served well to represent the mental condition of him who contemplated it.

Meanwhile Fleurange, instead of taking any notice of the scene that surrounded her, had closed her eyes, the better to summon up in imagination all that was dearest to her in the past and in the future. She saw once more the blue waves of the Mediterranean, and the radiant sky whose azure they reflect, and wreathed in pearly vapor the graceful outline of the distant mountains; then Florence, brilliant and poetic, appeared in the warm and golden light of sunset, and close beside her she heard a voice murmuring words, once dangerous to hear, to-day, sweet and charming to recall and to repeat over to herself.

What had she not suffered then in the struggle against

herself? how could she, in comparison with that past suffering, dread any of the discomforts that might await her?
—Discomforts—whose compensation was to be the endless bliss of loving—of loving fearlessly, and without self-reproach!—Besides, they were both young,—his mother's hopes might one day be fulfilled.—Yes, perhaps some day they might revisit together that beautiful land, and with her then at his side, in the recovered splendor of his most prosperous days, he would indeed know—he would know, past all doubt, that this was not the charm that had won her, that it was indeed himself, himself only whom she had loved!

Yes, at this moment she was happy; no fear disturbed her; and she hoped all things, and as is said of the great, the only, the true love, that *it believes all things possible and all permitted*,—so this, its shadow, faint only, yet faithful, made all the happiness in the world seem to Fleurange possible and certain, since the greatest happiness of all was now permitted, now promised her.

Clement was still absorbed in his mute contemplation, and Fleurange in her sweet dreaming, when Mlle. Josephine emerged from a state of somnolence favored by the ample furs in which she was buried, and which preserved her not only from the air but from the sight of external objects. She raised herself, and, looking about her for the first time in several hours, made a sudden motion of surprise, crying out in alarm:

"Oh Heavens!—Gabrielle, what is all this?"

Fleurange, recalled abruptly from her land of dreams, came to herself, and replied:

"It is the sea. Have you not observed it till now?"

"The sea! the sea!" cried Mlle. Josephine, stupefied; "no, I have not seen it before, and I never supposed that we were to go through the sea in a carriage!—What a country! What a journey!" she murmured in a low tone, seeking to conceal the mortal terror which had increased daily with her, as the distance grew greater, the aspect of everything more and more strange and frightful. In her way, she exercised heroic self-control in conquering, so far as she could, the fear and surprise which all these new sights and sounds caused her. Of all things she desired not to be wearisome or annoying to her fellow travellers. "Besides," she thought to herself, "if these two children are not afraid, I ought at least to seem as brave as they."

But she could not help repeating with astonishment: "To go through the sea in a carriage,—there is certainly something very strange in that!"

Fleurange began to laugh. "Look here, dear Mlle. Josephine," she said, "look out on my side and you will see that we are not really on the water,—only very near it, that is all."

"Very near it, certainly, then; for our carriage goes along through the water."

"That is only a wave, which breaks over the road, and retires again. See, we are on dry ground now!"

Mlle. Josephine was slightly reassured; she looked to the right, she looked to the left, she looked forward into the distance; then she turned her gaze upon the immense and gloomy sea so close to whose verge they made their way.

"Ah! how dismal and horrid that is!" she exclaimed, finally.

Fleurange, in her turn, was now examining the road with attention.

"The landscape is certainly most dismal," she said. "This gray sky,—this sun, which does not seem to shine,—this sad, dark sea,—this interminable sand,—yes, this is certainly frightful!"

She shuddered faintly.

"They have always told me," said Mlle. Josephine, "that the sea was something so beautiful to behold! I suppose it was one of those travellers' lies they tell, for good honest folks who never stir from their own firesides to be cheated by!"

"No, no," cried Fleurange, "do not say that. The sea is beautiful—yes, indeed, it is,—most beautiful, where it is as blue as the sky; and flowers and trees grow down to its very edge;—but not here, I admit!"

And, in spite of herself, the sweet vision of her recent dreams, for one instant again recalled by the contrast, vanished quite away. Her heart grew heavy; she was silent, and for a long time, not a word was said by any one of the three.

The length of the Strand (about twelve or fourteen leagues) was at that time divided by many relays of post-horses, who awaited the traveller beyond the sand-hills; but as no carriage could go across these shifting mounds the travellers, in stopping to change horses, still had no consciousness of being near any human habitation. Only the sound of a horn in the distance answered to that of the postilion announcing their approach, and the horses made their appearance over the sand-hills, led by a single peasant.

They had reached the last relay, and were changing horses on the beach. Clement stood apart, looking anxiously at the sea, and the threatening sky. The wind was rising and the waves ran higher and higher. It was evident that a fearful storm was coming on.

Fleurange had noticed Clement's anxiety, and she now made a little gesture which brought him quietly to her side, unremarked by their companion. "The weather is going to be very bad, don't you think so?"

"Yes," he said, in the same low tone. "We have not more than an hour of daylight before us, and I fear we shall find the road exceedingly bad. It is not on your account that I say this," he added, with an attempt to smile. "I am aware that it is forbidden me to be anxious about you, whatever may be the danger. But I fear that later you may find it hard to reassure your poor friend."

He resumed his seat, and ordered the postilion to make all haste. The light carriage was off as quickly as possible, drawing a little further inland, as the waves had once nearly swept it away. But with all the speed which they could make, the night was black and the full fury of the storm was upon them when they reached the point where they must cross that arm of the sea which unites the Kunsche-Haff with the Baltic. The passage was short but not easy; it would not do to delay an instant, for the sea, although somewhat sheltered just at this point, grew more and more rough, and the boat in which the little carriage was to be taken across was managed with great difficulty on account of the storm. They descended as rapidly as possible the slope which led down to the boat, and Mlle. Josephine was awakened from the half-slumbering condition into which the motion of the carriage had again thrown her, by a sudden and violent shock, accompanied with shouts and outcries, mingled with the roaring of the sea and the terrific howling of the storm.

"Oh, Father in Heaven!" cried the old lady in mortal terror: "is it thus that we are to die!"

The rain fell in torrents. The waves were breaking over the boat, darkness gave additional horror to what seemed, to her inexperienced eyes, the extreme of danger, and the sweet voice of her young companion strove vainly to tranquilize her. Soon, by the glare of lanterns, carried from side to side, to give light to the boatmen, she perceived Clement, standing outside the carriage, holding a sail firmly, which had been arranged to shelter them on the side most exposed to the invasion of the waves.

"My poor Clement!" she exclaimed, "it is all over, then?"

"No, not all, unfortunately," replied Clement, "it will be half an hour yet, before we are again on solid ground."

"On solid ground!" exclaimed Mlle. Josephine, hiding her head upon the shoulder of Fleurange. "On solid ground! Does he think we shall ever live to reach the shore?"

"Yes, indeed," replied the young girl, clasping her in her arms. "There is no danger, I assure you; believe me all that troubles me is to see you so alarmed."

"Forgive me, my child; I had vowed you should not know it,—but—but—this time, surely Gabrielle, you cannot say that we are not crossing the sea in a carriage," she continued, with new terror as she felt the increasing shock of the waves.

Fleurange kissed her, and repeated words of encouragement, and the poor old lady was silent, and in a degree conquered her terror by an effort which was truly a grand and courageous action on her part.

"Danger or not, it is just as I have always imagined great storms in which people perish. But, after all," she murmured in a low voice, "God rules the storm, as He rules other things, and nothing can happen except as He wills it."

Her nature was weak, but she was strong in soul, and her religious faith, always ready, now seemed to tranquilize her. She began to pray, mentally, and said not another word till they reached the shore.

XLVIII.

But a danger more real awaited our travellers the other side of Memel, whence on the morrow they pursued their journey in sledges. The foremost of these sledges contained the baggage, and preceded them by some hours, announcing them to the relays who were kept ready. The second was in shape like a heavy boat placed upon runners, surmounted by a chaise-top, and having an immense apron of furs. In this sledge Fleurange and Mlle. Josephine were seated, almost lying down to avoid the rush of the wind. The third sledge, quite uncovered, was extremely light, and so small that there was only room for Clement, and a young lad, strong and vigorous, but whose slender figure, wrapped closely in his *caftan*, was quite in proportion with the seat which he occupied, and the little vehicle which he drove. Clement, in this light equipage, went like the wind, now preceding the other sledges to see that the way was open,—now gliding along beside them to watch over their safety.

The cold had set in with intensity, but only within a few hours, and the torrents of rain of the night before, succeeding the unusual and alarming thaw, had done great damage to the roads, and had made it especially dangerous to cross the rivers, all of which, at this time of year, were to be passed upon the ice.

Although it was scarcely four o'clock, daylight was rapidly fading when the travellers came to a river which they must cross to reach the little city of Y.; a deep and rapid river, which, every year, at the coming on of winter, was for a long time full of floating ice before it congealed smoothly and solidly, and which, on the approach of spring, was first always in breaking up, and freeing itself from its icy chains. Hence, this river was almost always difficult, and often dangerous to cross, and it was in view of this special point in their journey that the late thaw had caused them so much anxiety.

As soon as Clement had cast a glance over the surface of the river he felt sure that he perceived alarming indications. There was not a moment to lose, and his sledge was upon the ice as quickly as possible. Then he stopped, and put a rapid question to his young guide: "We must get the heaviest sledge over at once, and follow ourselves, if we can?"

"If we can," rejoined the other.

The order was given, and the sledge containing Fleurange and her companion came rapidly in front of his own. But scarcely was it off from the shore more than ten or twelve feet, when an ominous cracking was heard. The driver stopped in alarm.

Clement repeated the order, to advance without an instant's delay. But, instead of obeying, the driver, seized with terror, threw down the reins, sprang out upon the ice, and with one bound, crossed the space which separated them from the shore, and placed himself on solid ground.

This shock accelerated the breaking up of the ice; it parted, and on the side nearest the bank, it broke off in great fragments, and began to float down with the current. The rapid water was visible between the shore and the part of the river which yet remained solid and where the travellers now were.

In this sudden and extreme danger, thought must be rapid as lightning, and the word as quick as the thought.

"Get out of the sledge, Gabrielle," said Clement, imperatively.

The young girl sprang out upon the ice.

Clement lifted Mlle. Josephine out in his arms, and placed her beside Fleurange.

"Now take your seat in my sledge, Gabrielle," said he, speaking calmly, though very quickly. "Go forward! The instant you are in safety, the sledge will return for your companion. We have time, but you must not hesitate an instant."

"I do not hesitate," said Fleurange. "Only, I shall remain. You must save her first."

Clement shuddered. But this was not a time to argue the case. He knew from the tone in which Fleurange spoke that her decision was irrevocable, and he yielded at once. He placed Mlle. Josephine who was unable to understand what was going on about her, in the light sledge, gave an order, which was obeyed on the instant, and the sledge was off. The sound of the bells hung at the horse's head was heard for a few seconds,—then lost; and the young girl and Clement remained alone.

Night was closing in about them. Not far behind them the gradual breaking of the ice went on, under the weight of the heavy sledge left standing where it had been at the moment of the first alarm. Soon, the same ominous sound was heard once more, and a second great fragment of ice broke off, remained stationary a moment, then began slowly to float down the river, carrying on it the sledge. The space which the water had invaded enlarged, and became appalling.

Clement looked forward to see if it were possible, carrying Fleurange in his arms, to cross on foot the wide space that separated them from the other shore. But the darkness had made it impossible to discern the single track; once missing that, death was inevitable, they would have lost their sole chance of safety; they must await the return of the sledge. On the other hand, to remain where they were would soon become impossible. Everything seemed giving way around them. But a few minutes had passed when the ice cracked again, and, this time, in front of them, and they found themselves upon an island.

At a single glance, Clement perceived his only chance; he hesitated not an instant; lifting Fleurange in his arms, in the vague light reflected by the snow, he crossed with a desperate leap the black chasm which had just opened in front of them.

They were thus once more on that part of the river whose surface was as yet solid, but who could say how long they would be safe there? Who could tell if the little sledge would be able to return so far, or whether indeed it had not been engulfed somewhere in that impenetrable darkness where possibly the ice might already have broken up as it was now giving way all around them; otherwise, would it not have already returned?

These thoughts crowded all at once upon Clement's mind, and Fleurange who stood beside him, silent and intrepid, measured like himself the full extent of the danger. Bending her head, she prayed silently.

Leaning thus against him, her hair brushing against his face, she might have heard the beating of his heart and felt the arm which supported her tremble, and the hand which held her own. But he said not a word, and what was passing in his mind was strange: a resolve to save her, which doubled his strength, his faculties, his courage; yet, at the same time, a rapture which he could not control that she was there alone with him, that they were to die together, and that she would never—*never* attain the detested end of her journey!

But this moment of passionate and desperate selfishness was short. His thoughts came back to her, to her only. To save her? To save her at all risks! But how? It seemed to him as if an hour had passed. It was useless longer to expect the return of the sledge. He thought he felt the ice again tremble under their feet. He looked back at the dark current. Should he plunge in with her, and try to regain the shore which they had left? For a moment he hesitated. But no! It would be to expose her to a certain destruction,—certain, and more speedy than that which now threatened her. It was better to remain where they were, and endure this mortal anxiety even to the end.

They stood motionless, and the mute agony lasted yet for many long minutes.

Notwithstanding all her courage, the young girl's strength began to give way. The sight grew confused, and a strange humming made itself heard in her ears. At last her head sunk upon her cousin's shoulder.

"I am dying," she murmured,—" Clement, may God restore you to your mother!"

At this moment of supreme anguish, Clement looked up to Heaven, and the prayer which affection and despair caused to spring from his heart was pure and ardent as the faith of his childhood. It seemed to him that it was heard. And yes; almost at that instant,—did he deceive himself? Afar,—so far that it could be scarcely caught,—he seemed to hear the sound of bells! He listened, breathless. Oh Divine goodness, is it true?—Yes, yes,—there is no doubt of it now! The sound becomes distinct. It comes nearer. It is indeed the sledge!—It is coming rapidly, it draws near, it stops,—here it is!

"Ah! God be thanked, she is saved!"

But even as Clement spoke, Fleurange, overcome by terror and distress, fainted in his arms.

He lifted her from the ice and placed her in the little sledge, and, while she half recovered her consciousness, he clasped her once again in his arms, with an affection which he no longer sought to conceal.

"Adieu, Gabrielle," he said, "do not pity me that I die here. God is good.—He spares me the pain of living without you?"

And he added, in a lower voice: "Gabrielle, I have loved you more than all the world. I tell you now, because I am to die."

Then he stepped back, and in a firm voice gave the order to drive on.

His other words had been heard confusedly and as in a dream by Fleurange; but this order,—clear and definite,—this she heard, and understood, and it brought her to herself in an instant.

"Go?" she cried, "go?—and without you?" What are you saying?"

"It must be so," Clement said. "The sledge can hold but one person beside its driver. A heavier load, too, would be dangerous. Go forward, without an instant's delay!"

"Never!" said Fleurange resolutely, "Clement, we will perish all three of us on this spot, sooner than leave you here!"

"It must be so!" repeated Clement, with decision. "Go forward I say to you! The sledge can return and I will follow you."

"It will be impossible, a third time," said the young driver.

Clement knew it well. He made no reply, save to repeat the order to drive on. But, no less decided than himself, Fleurange rose, and laid her hand upon that of the driver.

Suddenly the boy sprang from his seat.

"You can drive?" he said to Clement.

"Yes."

"Very well,—you cannot miss the track. As for me, I can swim. Keep this for me, and I will come across to-morrow for it," he added, throwing off his *caftan*. "Do not be anxious; I know my way and the river knows me."

And, without hesitation he plunged into the black water, while Clement sprang to his seat on the sledge.

With that rashness which in a case like this, gives safety, Clement struck the horses sharply with the whip, and they sprang forward at the top of their speed. They thus crossed at a headlong pace the considerable space which lay between them and the shore. The ice cracked more than once under their flying feet. To slacken their course for an instant would have been sure destruction, but the sledge seemed scarcely to touch the ice, and a steady hand was on the reins.

In less than a half-hour the shore was reached, and Fleurange, pale, exhausted, overcome, fell into the arms of Mlle. Josephine.

The old lady had been awaiting them peacefully in a warm and lighted room in the post-house, where she had ordered supper to be gotten ready; but Fleurange could neither talk nor eat. Her companion was forced to admit that rest was the most needful thing. She insisted however that before going to sleep, Fleurange should receive from her hands a preparation of heated and sugared wine, and then she went to find Clement who was yet in the waiting-room where they had left him. Then, and only then, did she learn the dangers from which they had escaped, and which she had herself in a measure shared.

Since their crossing in the boat, on the preceding evening, Mlle. Josephine had formed the resolution never again to show herself surprised at the incidents of this strange journey, whatever they might be, and she would have taken her seat in a balloon, just as in the sledge, without a word, at the slightest order from Clement, who seemed to her more and more worthy of boundless confidence.

Possibly, at the close of this terrible day, Clement could not have said the same for himself. He recalled those words which under the stress of danger he had dared to speak, and asked himself anxiously if she had heard and understood them,—those words which had come straight from his heart at the moment when death seemed close at his side. Had she already recovered her consciousness when he bade her that last farewell? He could not decide, and in this state of uncertainty, he anxiously awaited the morrow.

He was re-assured by finding his cousin calm and ingenuous as ever. It was evident that she had not understood—probably had not even heard—his words, or possibly that their common danger had seemed to her a sufficient explanation of that violent emotion which he had not been able to control.

XLIX.

While our travellers are finishing the last few stages of their journey, we will precede them to St. Petersburg, and will conduct our reader into regions widely different from those into which hitherto the incidents of our story have led them.

Sentence had been pronounced upon the accused; for some days the names of the five condemned to death had been known and circulated quietly,—quietly, for the prosecution which occupied the thoughts of all, was rarely mentioned in the high society of the capital. At that epoch (widely differing from our own, when liberty of speech has made its way into Russia, in advance of any other form of liberty,) whether through prudence, servility, or possibly, fear—a legacy from the reign of the emperor Paul, rather than from the one just ended—they forbade themselves by common accord all public expression of opinion concerning the acts of the ruler. Flattery itself learned to be discreet, that it might not be accused of giving rise to discussions in process of which, blame might be expressed. The government did not care for approval; it cared only to be obeyed, and not discussed. This being well understood on all sides, there resulted general silence in regard to everything appertaining to the forbidden subject, while, as if in revenge, upon all other subjects, Russian intellect gave itself free scope, and with such results that the nation which chooses to call itself the wittiest in the world, unable to dispute the palm with Russia, contented itself with saying that Russian intellect after all was truly French. It cannot be denied that at this epoch, when the last survivors of the reign of Catherine I. had not yet all disappeared, the French language was in use in good society in St. Petersburg to this degree, that men, as well as women, of the highest rank spoke it to the exclusion of their own, and wrote it with such rare perfection that French literature owes additional wealth to them,—while they would have been greatly embarrassed to know how to write correctly in Russian the most ordinary note, or the simplest business letter.

It is not worth while to seek here to explain what causes had brought about that sort of inoculation with a foreign spirit, nor to examine whether the Russians of that day, in imitating the French, were always mindful that in copying others, "it is in their best characteristics that we ought to seek to resemble them."

Still less would it be opportune to consider whether a people endowed with that faculty, and capable of that degree of assimilation, are the most noble, the most energetic, the most sincere of all. All this would lead us far beyond our modest limits, and we return to add, that, notwithstanding a splendor and a magnificence of which those who live in other lands can scarcely form an idea, notwithstanding an aroma of good taste and courtesy almost vanished from France at the present day, notwithstanding a superb hospitality, a trait of the Slavic nations, completely foreign to our habits,—a constraint, indefinable, yet felt by all, weighed upon this brilliant and fascinating exterior, glided everywhere like an invisible spectre, modifying and directing the course of conversations apparently the most frivolous, disturbing not only the social intercourse of the ball room but also the freedom of the smaller circle, and even the confidential *tête-à-tête* of the most faithful friends.

The Marquis Adelardi had often frequented the society of the Russian capital; it suited him well, and he was specially fitted to shine in it, having passed his life, as we know, in the school of forced silence, and if at one time he was to be counted among those to whom this servitude is revolting, now that he had given up all attempt to shake it off, he had learned how to ignore it. Better than any one else he knew how to navigate among the reefs and shoals of conversation, to be amusing, amiable, interesting, even rash, apparently, without ever embarrassing his listeners by an unsafe remark, and if sometimes he seemed to have approached limits dangerous to cross, the promptness with which he knew how to read and interpret the mute expression of a thought, sufficed to make him change with graceful carelessness the entire direction of a conversation, in which the moment before he had seemed to be most eagerly interested.

He was, however, in humor to talk with no one, on the day or rather the evening, when we meet him again at the house of the Countess G., a woman of brilliant intellect, at this period already advanced in years, and whose *salon* was one of the most admired and frequented in St. Petersburg, everything was disposed in such a way as to most facilitate conversation in all its forms, and if there was a place where the limitations of which we have spoken, though always present, were invisible, certainly it was here. That which one could no more say aloud here than elsewhere, one had a thousand facilities for saying softly. On the other hand, for the accommodation of prudent people who prefer to say nothing at all, there were not wanting tables where they could have their game of whist, or of chess. Add to this that a piano, placed at one end of the extremities of this great drawing-room, always stood open, and at the disposal of amateurs,—more numerous than at the present day, when it is agreed that even in the domestic circle, one must not risk musical performance without possessing very superior talent!

But in this friendly *salon*, our marquis, usually so social, was now absent-minded and disposed to silence

Sitting in a corner, alone upon a sofa, he had not shared in the general conversation, notwithstanding that, as the room grew full, and different groups formed here and there, a few of the foreign *attachés* who were the habitual guests of the house, had ventured upon the important subject, and by degrees, might be heard in low tones, here and there, the names of Mouravieff, Ryleief, Pestel, and the two others condemned to death, as well as those of the exiles who awaited a fate nearly as dreadful as theirs.

Soon a young *attaché* belonging to one of the German legations, perceiving Adelardi, came and sat down beside him. "And Walden," he said in a half-whisper, "you have had permission twice to visit him, I understand?"

"Yes."

"And since he knows his sentence have you seen him again?"

"No; but they have given me reason to hope that I shall obtain that favor."

"He will not be sorry, I imagine, to have escaped the gallows!"

"The gallows,—yes; but as to death, I am certain he would greatly prefer that to the fate which awaits him."

"Poor fellow; but what business had he—"

"To be in such company?" said the marquis, interrupting him in a tone of vexation. "The question is extremely appropriate, and I should ask it myself, if the answer would now be of any use."

"By the way," said his companion, "you know, I suppose, who has just arrived in St. Petersburg?"

The marquis questioned him by a look of uncertainty; he was expecting the arrival that day of more than one person.

"Eh! *parbleu!* the fair Vera, who has at last returned to her post."

"Indeed!" exclaimed Adelardi, "but in that case we shall see her here this evening; I am told that when she is in the city she comes to these receptions without fail."

"Yes, but only after her duties are ended at the palace. It is nearly ten o'clock now; she will be here soon no doubt. Our amiable hostess is a relative of hers."

"I was not aware of that. I know the countess Vera

but slightly. When I was here three years ago, she was not yet at court; I saw her two or three times at the house of the princess Catherine Lamianoff who was living here at that time, but I have never been presented to her."

" At the princess Catherine's? I believe you; it was the talk that she wished to make a match between the young countess and her son, and he really did, for a minute, pay her the most devoted attention. The young lady was not indifferent to him then; I wonder if she cares for him still?"

" I do not know."

"The poor girl! I pity her if she does, but it is not likely she would long remain in love with a galley-slave! She will find men enough ready to console her, if she will condescend to look at them."

At this moment the piano was heard. They came for the young diplomate to take part in a trio about to be performed. This unpremeditated music put a stop to conversations, which were beginning to become a little too animated on all sides, under stress of the interest awakened not by the crime, but by the sad fate of the guilty ones. All present knew them, they had once been members of this very coterie where to-day it was scarcely safe to speak their names aloud.

Adelardi remained in the same place, his head resting on his hand, more lost in thought than ever. He feigned to be listening to the music, and beat time mechanically, but he was thinking of something far different, and emerged from his reverie only when the sound of the bell announced the arrival of some new visitor; then he looked up and scanned the doorway eagerly; but after each arrival, he resumed his former attitude, and it was evident that the person who had entered was not the one whom he desired to see.

L.

Early this same evening, another scene was passing at no great distance in a drawing-room yet more elegant and stately than the one of which we have just spoken. This apartment, however, was not, like the other, arranged to receive visitors, but solely for the pleasure and comfort of the person who occupied it,—a woman, evidently, although there was no profusion of useless trifles or superfluous ornament; but it seemed that her hand could touch nothing which was not rare and costly. Gold, silver, gems, sparkled from all the objects destined for her daily use, from the open work box which contained a bit of dainty sewing, to the sumptuous covers of the books scattered over the embroidered table cloth or placed near a great arm-chair upon a little *étagère* of malachite. This great arm-chair, destined for reading, was also arranged for repose by a soft cushion, covered with the finest lace, where the head could recline in an attitude at once graceful and comfortable. Everywhere were flowers, in as great abundance as if they had grown in the open air and in their season, and their exquisite fragrance,—joined with perfumes, more artificial but not less delicate—filled the air of the room.

If, as they say, and as we have already observed, places resemble those who live in them, one would be eager to know the mistress of this apartment. We are about to present her to the reader, and we shall strive to portray her as she appeared to the eyes of those who saw her at the date of our story: a woman at the age when beauty is in its flower, and of whom it was said with truth that she had the mien of a goddess and the figure of a nymph; a face sweet and pale, with noble, delicate features, pure complexion, made attractive by the charm of look and smile, and framed in floating hair which fell in long soft curls over the white and graceful shoulders.

Such was she, who, at the sound of a man's voice came forward into the apartment we have described and threw herself into the arms of him who had pronounced her name.

Their first words were of joy at the meeting again (after a lengthy separation of some hours!) and, for a long while, they seemed to have no thought but of each other. Smiles and looks were interchanged, and one might have supposed they had nothing else to do but to love one another and to express this love.

But by degrees the character of their conversation changed. She grew serious; he seemed to be full of care and anxiety; and in replying reluctantly to the questions addressed to him, and which she sometimes repeated with persistence, he seemed to yield against his will to his consideration for her, and to resist with difficulty the desire to bid her be silent. One time he rose and walked away from her; but she followed him, gently passed her arm through his, and rising upon tiptoe (for though she was very tall, he towered above her by a full head) she whispered a few words in his ear.

While she was speaking, a change came over the face of him who had bent his head to listen,—a change sudden and alarming. She remarked it, and looked at him surprised and with a new and strange uneasiness while he, without answering her, crossed the room, and leaned against the chimney piece, standing with folded arms, grave and silent.

He was twenty-nine years of age and as yet in all the splendor of that beauty which the suffering, the anxiety, the stormy passions of a later day, the years themselves, would scarcely be able to change; but at that time, to his grand and commanding figure, to a regularity of feature that no sculptor could have rendered more ideal, was added a something winning in the face and in the sound of the voice which inspired not admiration alone, but a far warmer sentiment. Up to this time, it had been rare to perceive either resentment or anger gleam in the look, or tremble in the voice, and this may have been the first time that, in her presence, that gloomy and threatening flash shot from those blue eyes. She dared not question him, and stood waiting till he should break the silence. By degrees this expression which had disturbed her gave way to one of deep and bitter sadness.

"Ah!" he said, at last, "this is a sad beginning!"

After a silence he added, looking about him: "This dear home of ours! We shall perhaps often regret the happy days that we have spent here!"

"We will never give it up," she replied, with an animation which betrayed a person utterly unused to contradiction. "We will keep it just as it is, and we will return here always. Our grand days we will pass, if we must, in that dismal Winter Palace; but our happy days—we will come back and spend them here, and they will be just the same in the future as they have been in the past."

He shook his head. "The past was ours; the future no longer belongs to us. To our great country we must give ourselves henceforth,—to her we must sacrifice all things. God requires this at our hands."

"All," repeated she with a kind of alarm. "What? even happiness? even trust? Oh no, that portion of the past shall surely go with us. Something else, too, I will never relinquish. It is the right to implore a favor, to obtain a pardon."

She hesitated, and then clasping her hands and fixing her eyes upon his, exclaimed entreatingly:

"Shall I never more be listened to?"

"For the unhappy always; for the ungrateful, never!"

His brow darkened as he spoke, and he was about to leave the room, but she detained him.

She knew however she must be silent upon this point, and with that tact which is the allowed diplomacy of love, she suddenly changed the subject, and obliged him to listen to her while she made plans conformable to wishes of his which she well knew. She spoke of herself, of him, of the happy past, of the dazzling future, of everything save the one thing which had been the subject of her whispered words, and which, at this moment, she cared most to make him forget.

It has long since been guessed that we are in the presence of the imperial pair whose unexpected reign had just begun in the midst of storm and tempest. They still lingered in the palace which had been their abode in the first days of their happy union, when no vision of royalty mingled with their youth and love. Both were long reluctant to leave this charming palace, and go to live in the

Imperial residence, and when they were constrained to it by the necessities of their position they retained unchanged all those places which had been witnesses of the days which, notwithstanding the splendors of the Imperial purple, they ever remembered as the best days of their life.

When the empress was left alone, she remained thoughtful for an instant; then, approaching the malachite *étagère*, she took up a little golden bell, and rang it quickly.

At the same moment, a door, concealed behind the tapestry opened, and a young girl appeared.

She stood still, without speaking, awaiting some word or order.

Nothing in her attitude however indicated the timid submission that one might have expected from a maid of honor, answering her sovereign's bell. She who had just appeared united to her stately loveliness, an expression which would have seemed too haughty, had it not been modified as soon as she spoke. Her eyes became now caressing, now animated to a degree that seemed to betray more passion than tenderness; but her exquisite figure, her black eyes and heavy blonde hair, and the soft paleness of her complexion, made her beauty at once striking and imposing.

She waited in silence a few minutes,—then finding that her mistress said nothing, she came forward and was the first to speak.

" Your Majesty has dared and deigned to plead his cause ? " she said.

The empress came out of her reverie, and shook her head sadly.

" My poor Vera," she said, " you must think no more of it."

The young girl grew pale. " Think no more of it ! " she cried. " Ah, madame, is it possible that can be your advice ?—Can it be that there is nothing to hope for ?"

The empress, without making any reply, seated herself in her arm-chair, and, taking up a book, began to turn the leaves idly, as if to put an end to the conversation.

The eyes of Vera flashed for a moment, and with difficulty she suppressed a sudden outcry of pain or of

She kept silence, however, and remained standing near the table, picking to pieces one of the flowers in the bouquet which stood near her.

The empress all the time, kept her eyes fixed upon her book.

After a moment she looked up, and glanced at the clock.

"I have no further need for you, Vera. It is ten o'clock; you were going, I believe, to the Countess G.'s this evening, were you not?"

"Yes, madame, if your majesty has no further orders to give me."

"No, I have nothing further to say to you. Ah! I forgot—open that drawer," pointing to a writing-table at the other side of the room: "you will find a letter there."

Vera obeyed, and brought the letter to her mistress.

"Take it and see that it is sent," said the empress. "It is a permission for the princess —— to follow her husband to Siberia. I am happy to have been able to render that sad service to this heroic woman; nor is she the only one."

"What a fate these women are preparing for themselves," said Vera, with a shudder.

"Yes, it is truly frightful," replied the empress; "yet I admire them, and would serve them to the utmost of my ability."

Vera was silent, then seeing that her sovereign had apparently nothing more to say to her, she approached gravely to take her leave.

As she bent to kiss the imperial hand, the empress kissed her on the forehead.

"Come, Vera," she said, "be a little less serious, I entreat you! I would gladly, to satisfy you, make you the promise that I will try again; but do you know, my dear friend, it is very generous in you to interest yourself so much about him, for it is not the emperor alone who has the right to call him ungrateful!"

Vera's face became scarlet.

"Your majesty has the right to say anything to me," she said, and her voice trembled, "but usually that right 's kindly exercised."

"Whilst now you think me cruel! Well, so be it, let us say no more; good night, and we part friends, *ma chère?*"

She made a gesture of dismissal; Vera bent her head, and without another word, went out.

LI.

"The Countess Vera von Leiningen!"—

At the sound Adelardi again raised his head, and this time he was not disappointed. She whom he so impatiently expected, had at last appeared.

The cause of that impatience on his part was this, he had resolved to make an attempt to induce Countess Vera to lend her influence to the cause of his friend; but first, he must be certain what were her inclinations upon this point. Would he find yet some remnant of that passion she had so ill known how to conceal upon her first acquaintance with Count George? Or, indeed, had time and vexation done their work—the influence at court aiding—and had his fickleness at last inspired an indifference which his misfortune could not now disarm? All this Adelardi flattered himself that he should be able in a single conversation to discover, if only she would consent to talk with him.

From the moment that she entered, he watched her with the keenest interest, and with an utterly unscrupulous attention; having seen her but twice, some years earlier, without having spoken to her, he did not suppose that she would recognize him until the formality of an introduction had taken place.

Vera crossed the room without embarrassment, with the ease and grace of a person accustomed to society, and to the effect which she produced. She was dressed entirely in black,—the court, and even the city, still wearing with unexampled rigor, the customary mourning for the Emperor Alexander. This costume rendered yet more striking the dazzling fairness of her complexion, and the golden tint of her hair, and suited her figure, which was of faultless symmetry, but noble rather than slender. For her only ornament she wore, attached to the left shoulder, the knot of blue ribbon from which hung the diamond monogram (insignia of her rank as maid of honor) where were interlaced the initials of the three empresses: Alexandrine, the empress-consort; Marie, the empress-mother; and Elizabeth, the broken-hearted widow of Alexander, herself destined shortly to follow him to the tomb.

Her recent emotion still colored the young girl's cheek, and those tears of wounded pride brushed hastily away, had given to her expression a blended melancholy and disdain, which inspired at the same moment the impulse to sympathize with her, and a fear to accost her.

She began by approaching the whist-table, where the mistress of the house was seated. The latter raised her eyes and contented herself with bestowing a friendly nod. Vera, without taking her hand, bent and made a gesture at once graceful and respectful, in use in those countries between women when the age of one greatly exceeds that of the other: she lifted the edge of the black lace shawl which the old lady wore, and touched it with her lips; then she remained a moment standing near the whist-table, and looking about the room.

There was in this look neither eagerness, nor curiosity, nor coquetry: it was only that she was taking notice of the room, and of those present, and it was easy to see that she sought no one, and was waiting for no one; she replied only by a slight motion of the head, or by a smile, to the salutations addressed to her.

Soon, remarking a vacant seat, she went to sit down, and in so doing came nearer to the sofa where Adelardi was.

She had scarcely seated herself, when the young *attaché*, who had just now been speaking of her, came up with an air of eager devotion, to which she replied by a glance of indifference, giving him two fingers of her gloved hand.

This was the moment selected by the marquis to approach the young German and beg to be presented to the Countess Vera.

Scarcely had the name of Adelardi been mentioned, when some recollection, vague at first, then distinct enough to cause a blush, awoke in her mind, and seemed to give her a moment's almost painful embarrassment: she bowed in silence to the person who had just been introduced to her, and, turning her head away, continued her conversation for some minutes with the *attaché;* but it was only to give herself time to recover from her embarrassment. She had soon ended this unimportant affair, and then turning at once to Adelardi, she said to him frankly:

"I remember very well your visit in St. Petersburg, three years since; but I was then so young that you have probably forgotten me."

Adelardi replied, as he would have done in any case (but—as it chanced in this case—truly), that no such doubt could be permitted her!

"As for me," he continued, "never having had the honor to address you before, I naturally must have supposed myself entirely unknown to you."

"You had friends who often spoke of you," she said, "and for this reason your name has been familiar to me; though, I confess, I had, in a degree, forgotten your face."

"Naturally, I had not forgotten yours; besides, in my turn, I have heard of you constantly."

There was a moment's silence.

"Have you seen the Princess Catherine lately?" she said.

"No; I left Florence early in December."

"To come to St. Petersburg?"

"Yes."

"And you have been here ever since?"

"Yes; you were away when I came, otherwise I should not have waited until to-day to solicit the favor I have just obtained."

Again, a moment's silence, and then the young girl looked about her, and said in a low voice:

"You were here then on the twenty-fourth of December?"

"Yes."

She hesitated an instant, then, lowering her voice still more, resumed:

"And since that fatal day, have you seen your friend

"Yes, and I hope to see him once more,—for the last time, alas!"

Vera bit her lips, which trembled nervously; but soon, with a directness that surprised and, for an instant, disconcerted her companion, she replied:

"I knew Count George von Walden formerly, but for a long time I have seen nothing of him. Still, this sentence is most shocking to me, and I would do anything in the world to have him released,—him and all of them."

"Him *with* the rest? neither more nor less?"

"Neither more nor less; I pity them all, and I would that the emperor might pardon them all."

The tone of her voice was not in accordance with the indifference of her words, but her companion went on, as if he had not noticed this:

"Pardon them all? That would be a dream! But there are some for whom, perhaps, one might implore his clemency."

"The emperor is more indulgent towards the obscure offenders than towards those who, having been loaded with favors, have despised his kindness."

"And yet," pursued the marquis, persistently, "even for some of those, there might be extenuating circumstances which one could plead."

"Do you know any which might be useful in the case of Count George?" she said eagerly.

"Do not speak so loud! we might be overheard."

"Yes, you are right;" she said, resuming her former tone, "and besides, let us change our seats; we have the air of conspirators here, we are attracting attention. Let us go and look over the pictures on the table. There we can continue our conversation more at our ease."

"Well then," she resumed, when they had made the change which she had recommended, and were looking over a port-folio with an appearance of great attention.

"Well," continued Adelardi, "what I mean to say is this, that there are many things useless to plead before the law, which might however not be without effect upon him who is the master of the law."

And while she listened, with an interest that her eyes, now animated, now tender,—her burning cheeks,—her parted lips, showed, far beyond her intention, Adelardi pleaded the cause of his friend, explaining that his complicity was more apparent than real, that he was ignorant of the actual designs of the conspirators, and what were really the circumstances that, on the 24th of December, had caused his presence among the insurgents. He gave her all the details, which she had not as yet heard, knowing only of the crime of which Count George had been accused, and of the sentence which had been passed upon him.

" And the emperor," she said eagerly, " does he know that upon that dreadful day, it was Count George who saved his brother's life ?"

" I doubt if he does. Two witnesses only could attest it. One of these feared to compromise himself, and would not come foward; the other's testimony was rejected."

" Who was this other ?"

" A person named Fabiano Dini, seeretary to Count George, a great criminal, certainly, and declared unworthy to be believed. But he spoke the truth, for all that, and he desired earnestly that his testimony might avail to save his master."

" He is condemned with him, I suppose ?"

" Yes, and more severely than he. For he is condemned for life, and George for twenty-five years only."

" Twenty-five years *only !*" she exclaimed with a shudder.

" Yes,—it is indeed fearful,—more fearful than death. And George I know will envy the wretched man who was the cause of his misfortunes; for Dini, fatally wounded on the twenty-fourth of December, will probably be dead before the day fixed for their departure."

At this moment they were interrupted by an incident not foreign to the subject of their conversation. A person modestly dressed who, till this moment, had stood apart by herself, approached the young maid of honor, and in a faltering and respectful voice, asked if the petition addressed to her Imperial Majesty had been received.

" Yes," said Vera eagerly. " The permission is granted, and at this moment the princess has received it. I left it myself at her door on my way here."

She held out her hand to her who had just spoken. The latter bent to kiss it, but the young girl prevented her, cordially embracing her.

"There is a true and faithful friend in misfortune," she said, as the other went away. "She would be capable herself of accompanying to Siberia the princess whose lady-in-waiting she has been. The princess —— certainly has the happiness, in her misfortune, of feeling herself loved and respected by every one."

"Assuredly," said Adelardi. "What an admirable woman, indeed!"

"So admirable," said Vera, "that I cannot at all understand it!"

"What!"

"No. What she is about to do, she and others, passes my comprehension."

"What!" said Adelardi, with a little surprise, "you do not understand how a woman can thus devote herself utterly for a man,—for a husband whom she loves!"

Vera shook her head.

"No," she said, "I will not make myself out better than I am. If I were in that position, if I had misfortune to love one of these condemned persons, he might rely upon me to strive to obtain his pardon, and to use, for this end, all means in my power. But, to share his fate and accompany him to Siberia,—no, my dear marquis, I declare to you frankly, that is a proof of love and devotion of which I feel myself perfectly incapable."

A vision suggested itself in that moment to Adelardi's thoughts, before which the beauty of the Countess Vera slightly paled, and the earnest admiration with which he had until now regarded her, diminished perceptibly.

"Well," he said to her, after a moment of reflection, "I know one of these men for whom a woman, a young girl of your own age, is ready to perform an act of devotion even greater than that of the princess,—for she is not his wife. She is only his betrothed, and she will marry him expressly in order to share his fate."

"That is something entirely original!" said Vera.

"To accomplish this she has a double favor to obtain, and she is coming to St. Petersburg for the purpose. She will arrive very soon—to-morrow, possibly. I have promised to solicit an audience for her with the empress. Might I fulfil this promise, at the present moment by soliciting your interposition with Her Majesty?"

"Certainly. These requests all pass through my hands, and not one has ever been refused. But this is certainly the most singular of all."

She took out her tablets and a pencil.

"The name of your protégée?" she asked.

Adelardi hesitated, then watching with some slight anxiety to see the effect of his words:

"Her name is Fleurange d' Yves."

He was re-assured on seeing the maid of honor tranquilly inscribe the name, saying as she did so:

"Fleurange! that is an odd name,—I never heard it before in my life! To-morrow," she continued, rising and putting the tablets in her pocket,—"to-morrow morning you shall receive a reply. Good evening!"

As she gave him her hand, she said in a low tone:

"I thank you for what you have told me, and I will try to make it useful. If you see Count George, say to him—but no, say nothing. If, by a miracle, I should succeed, it will be time then to tell him what he owes to my efforts. Otherwise,—it is better he should never know that I failed."

The Marquis Adelardi returned home, lost in thought, and took up, scarcely noticing that he did so, two letters which lay upon the table. But on opening them, he read them both with equal interest.

He noticed the signature of the first: 'Clement Dornthal!' This is the cousin who was to accompany our fair traveller. They have arrived then!—Well, the *dénoûment* of the drama approaches: we must all try to play our parts wisely. Mine, certainly, is not the easiest among them all!"

He glanced over the other communication.

"Tuesday! I am to see him on Tuesday, at two. Poor George! It will be a melancholy visit, notwithstaning the news of which I shall be the bearer; and the unlooked-for consolation which awaits him."

He finished the note, and saw with satisfaction that, thanks to the powerful intervention which was at work for him, it would be permitted him to be with the prisoner one hour every day during the week which was to elapse before the departure of the sad train of exiles.

"Poor George!" he repeated again. "Can it be that we have come to this? Yet who knows? If, as they say, what woman wills, God wills, all hope may not be lost; for, if I do not deceive myself, here are two resolute feminine wills, bent to serve him, and energetic enough to vanquish the most adverse fate. *Two*,—that is one too many without doubt, and I have run the risk—somewhat too boldly, perhaps,—of a dangerous collision. But, in fact, at the point where we now are, things could scarcely grow worse. If the fair Vera succeeds, it will be George's affair to extricate himself from the complicated position in which gratitude will place him, between her who has saved him, and her who would have gone into exile for his sake. If, as is but too probable, she fails, then the case is simple, and this is certain, that our charming heroine will have no occasion to dread the rivalry of Countess Vera."

LII.

After all the unpleasant surprises which had succeeded one another for Mlle. Josephine during their painful journey, she had experienced one of a different nature, but greater than all the others, on arriving at her place of destination. Her imagination, as we have observed, was not lavish in providing for any thing but the strictly necessary. It had not been easy for her to understand that her dear Gabrielle was quite decided to take this long journey for the purpose of marrying an unknown man, condemned to the mines; but this inconceivable idea having once made its way into her mind, it seemed to have driven out every other. She had set forth on a journey to go to join a prisoner, and, from the time of leaving Heidelberg, she had felt that she was on her way to a dungeon. So, when she heard these words: "We have arrived!" and their sledge drove in under a great *porte cochère,* she could not but shudder.

It was therefore with a sort of stupefaction, that she found herself in a brilliantly-lighted vestibule, leading by a broad staircase to a long and beautiful gallery, then to a suite of elegant drawing-rooms, at the end of which the travellers were introduced into a dining-room where awaited them a supper whose luxuries were as unknown to Mlle. Josephine, as was the splendor with which it was served. She looked on with silent wonder, scarcely daring to eat, and, in mute perplexity, gazing from one to the other of her two companions. But both seemed incapable of observing what was going on about them. Faithful to her resolve, Mlle. Josephine abstained from asking a single question.

The repast was finished in silence. Then Clement wrote a note, and gave it, in her presence, to a *valet de chambre* with orders to take it to the Marquis Adelardi; then the two ladies were conducted to the apartments which had been prepared for them. Fleurange kissed her old friend, and bade her good night, and Mlle. Josephine was left alone in an apartment such as she had never before seen, in the presence of great mirrors where, for the first time in her life, she could see her whole figure from head to foot, and a canopied bed, which she could hardly believe destined for her modest self, and of which she eventually took possession with a degree of awe that quite troubled her repose. Never had the worthy lady found herself so much out of her element. She queried with amazement whether it was really herself, there under those silken curtains, and, when at last she fell asleep, she dreamed that Gabrielle, splendidly attired, sat upon a throne, and that she, Mlle. Josephine, likewise arrayed, sat beside her. This restless slumber was of brief duration. Before day she had risen and dressed, and waited impatiently till it would be a seasonable hour to go forth from her magnificent sleeping apartment on a tour of discovery in this unknown dwelling which, the evening before, had seemed to her like a fairy palace.

That impression was not lessened by the effect of daylight. Every thing was superb, in accordance with the tastes of Princess Catherine, and not less elegant and costly in this abode, where she spent but three months in the year, than in her palace in Florence, where she made it her home.

Mlle. Josephine went from one room to another, in a state of ever-increasing admiration; and, wherever she went, she found the same temperature, soft and warm: this seemed to her nothing less than a miracle, for the doors stood open, and not only did she see no fire in any direction, but she saw no glass in the windows nor even the slightest window-frame. Nothing, apparently, separated her from the icy out-door air; icy, indeed, for on arriving at St. Petersburg, they had found the thermometer far below zero, and yet—what could it mean? she was not cold, though the sight of those great windows made her shudder, and she dared, only from a distance, contemplate the view which was to be seen through them.

This prospect consisted of a great plain, covered with snow, cut by roads which were edged with fir-boughs. Sledges were flying in all directions. At wide intervals were enormous structures, and beyond, the sombre walls of a fortress flanked by a church, whose gilded spire shone in the winter sun,—the brilliant, cold sun, which shed upon the snow a light almost too dazzling, and whose deceitful splendor, far from announcing any mitigation of the severity of the weather, was, on the contrary, the most certain sign of its pitiless rigor.

Thus gazing, admiring, wondering, Mlle. Josephine came to the last room in the *suite*, and there, before one of the great windows stood Fleurange, motionless, and absorbed in so profound a reverie, that she did not turn her head at the approach of her companion.

"Ah, Gabrielle! here you are. I am glad to find you; I thought I was lost. But what are you doing there, near that open window?"

Fleurange turned, smiling.

"Open! my dear Mlle. Josephine, we should not remain alive long, if it were, clothed as you and I are!"

"Indeed, I cannot understand why I am not frozen already, and still—"

Fleurange beckoned to her to approach (for the good lady remained standing as far off as possible from these threatening apertures) and made her touch with her hand the thick glass, which, in a single piece, formed the window, a luxury unknown at this date, except in St. Petersburg, and which often has deceived eyes much less inexperienced than those of the simple Josephine.

Re-assured, and more and more astonished, the latter remained standing at the window with Fleurange, and profited by the opportunity to put to her all the questions which until now she had repressed. By degrees all was explained to her, and she understood that this splendid house belonged to the mother of Count George.

"And he," she ventured to say when Fleurange had replied to all her questions, "he,—Gabrielle, where is Count George himself?"

The color came in the face of Fleurange, and her eyes filled with tears: "He is there," she said, "there, dear Mlle. Josephine, behind the walls of that fortress which you see."

The poor lady was much distressed. "Forgive me," she cried, "if I had known that, I should have said nothing."

"But why, my dear friend? Oh! the sight of those walls does not frighten me. I am eager to be within them, to leave all this splendor which now, as formerly, separates me from him! Oh, you will have no cause to pity me, on the day when you shall know that I am with him again!"

This passionate language always produced a strange effect upon Mlle. Josephine; and so she now contented herself with replying in a docile manner:

"Well then, dear child, we will not pity you!—It is poor Clement and myself who are to be pitied when that day comes, and no one ought to blame us, if—"

And, in spite of herself, great tears, which she brushed

for the sake of her dear Fleurange, she was most anxious to restrain.

"What is this great plain here in front of us, between the quay and the fortress?"

"This plain," said Fleurange smiling, "is the Neva."

"The Neva?"

"Yes, the river that divides the city."

"The river?" repeated Mlle. Josephine. "Come, now, Gabrielle, I know that I am very ignorant in regard to foreign countries, but not to the degree of believing what you are telling me now. A river!—upon which I see with my own eyes more than a hundred carriages, sledges, vehicles of every description, which are crossing one another in all directions,—and houses!—and sheds!—and what are those two great mounds that I see down there?"

"Those are the ice-hills, the true Russian ice-hills, that they imitated in Paris, three years ago; you remember them? These, I am told, are only here during the carnival."

"Very well, but all this proves that it is not the river, and that you are mistaken."

"It appears incredible, I know, but it is really so. All that we see there will disappear in the spring, and there will remain only the beautiful blue water, flowing between this magnificent granite quay, and the fortress! Still I confess that, never having seen it, I can hardly persuade myself to believe it."

At this moment Clement appeared. He was pale and silent and in truth showed plainly that he, not less than Mlle. Josephine, although for quite different reasons, had passed an agitated night. After a few words exchanged with his companions, his glance swept across the wide river and fixed itself, like that of Fleurange, upon the sombre walls of the fortress.

It was a strange chance which had brought them there, precisely opposite that spot which he regarded with jealousy, with despair, with horror, and yet, from which, he could not turn his eyes away.

This, then, he thought, was the limit! for her, the desired goal—for him, the tomb in which his youth must lie buried! Yes, once she should cross those walls, all would be ended forever, were he to live beyond the wonted term of humanity. His life,—his own, real life, was going to end at twenty years!

These reflections, and others like them, were not of a character to render Clement social, this morning. And he was, indeed, not only serious, which was often the case with him, but, contrary to his habit, gloomy and taciturn. Their breakfast went on silently, and it was only with a great effort that when it was ended, he resumed nearly his ordinary manner.

" Cousin," he said, " I have a sulky air this morning, I know, and I beg your pardon for it. But, believe me, I am only sad—sad on account of the hour which draws near. This must at least be allowed us," he continued, turning towards Mlle. Josephine and taking her hand, " and I suppose you will not require of us, Gabrielle, that we should part with you without regret!"

" That is what I was just now saying to her," observed Mlle. Josephine, wiping her eyes: " she says that she is happy, that she is impatient to be there," casting a glance across the river as she spoke; " we desire only her happiness, that is certain; but after all, for us— "

" Yes," said Clement, with a smile of bitter sadness, " for us, the coming days will not be happy ones, and we have unquestionably the right to be sad. As for me, Gabrielle, I have still further cause to regret the days which have ended, for from this moment, my part is done; henceforward, I shall never have the power again to be in any way useful to you."

He was yet speaking when the Marquis Adelardi was announced.

Clement rose to leave the room.

" Remain, Clement," Fleurange said eagerly, " remain; I wish to have this good friend know you."

" I desire it also, but not at this moment. Say to him that to-morrow, in the morning,—or even this evening, if he will see me, I will call upon him; do not detain me now."

of indifference. Once more to meet the friend, the confidential friend of Count George, to meet him, who, at this supreme moment, was to be the messenger between them, authorized by his mother!—there was good cause for emotion in the case of Fleurange. Adelardi, moreover, had always inspired sympathy and confidence, and, in this new world wherein she found herself, she perceived how useful and beneficial his experience would be to her, for Clement had spoken truly in saying that here he could no longer serve here. He, like herself, was altogether ignorant of the rules and customs of the court. And yet, to obey the instructions of the princess Catherine, her first duty must be to obtain an audience with the empress. A formidable prospect, at which she was a thousand times more frightened than at all which awaited her beyond. She welcomed the marquis therefore with child-like confidence, and he felt himself tenfold more charmed with her than ever before. There was the same beauty, the same simplicity, above all, the charm,—to his world-wearied eyes, so unique,—of resembling no one else! The new species of courage of which she had shown herself capable, made him appreciate the more that which she had manifested in separating herself from Count George, and revealed to him the full extent of the sacrifice so bravely then performed.

The mission which had been confided to Adelardi suddenly assumed new importance in his eyes, and he was for an instant tempted to reproach himself with having, on the preceding evening, called to Count George's aid a rival and, possibly, an enemy to the charming girl before him.

Looking at it from all sides, however, he could not regret this last attempt in favor of his friend. If it failed, and if Vera was then tempted to be displeased on seeing another fulfil the act of devotion of which she had declared herself incapable, he had taken certain precautions to mislead her, and he flattered himself that the permission would be granted before she could know by whom it had been implored.

Meanwhile, the maid of honor had been punctual. The marquis brought his reply with him, and he now put in the hands of his young friend.

"Your request is granted," he said. "'Mlle. Fleurange d'Yves will be received by Her Majesty on Thursday, at two o'clock. V. L.'"

"Day after to-morrow!" said Fleurange, with faltering voice. Then she continued, blushing: "But how does it happen that this name which I have not borne for so long, is used in this note?"

"It is yours, however, is it not?" said the marquis, evasively.

"Yes, it is mine, but—"

She stopped. One special idea was now attached to the name of Fleurange, in her mind. Within the last three years, no one but George had spoken it. And one day, forever graven in her memory, he had said that she must keep the name for him, and for him only.

She regretted to find it in this note, written by the hand of a stranger, and it gave her an involuntary pang.

"I should have preferred to have had the request made in my usual name" she said.

"Pardon me; I am the person in fault," replied Adelardi; "I supposed it a matter of indifference, and it seemed to me that the name of Fleurange would better fix the attention, and more surely remain in the memory, of her to whom you must offer your petition."

It was but a pretext which came into his mind as a reply to an unexpected question. His true motive had been to conceal from the maid of honor another name, which might possibly have been less unknown to her, and to which some prepossession might attach itself in her mind unfavorable to the success of the petition of which she was the bearer.

LIII.

The clock had just struck two. Vera, according to custom, was in waiting in the antechamber. The door was opened by an officer, and the person to be that day presented to the empress stood face to face with her who should introduce her.

There was a first and involuntary motion of surprise on the part of each.

Fleurange stood still, in uncertainty; the appearance of Vera coincided in no respect with the idea which had presented itself to her mind when she had been informed that at Her Majesty's door she would find the maid of honor on duty; and she queried for the moment whether she were not in the presence of the empress herself.

Vera, on her part still less expected such a suppliant as she who had just appeared.

The princess Catherine, who thought of everything, had planned with care for this momentous day the toilet of her whom she now regarded as the future wife of her son; and the hour having arrived, the young girl opened a trunk kept separate from her other luggage, and obeyed with docility the instructions from the princess's own hand which, together with the attire in which she was to array herself, she found within.

It was, it is true, a black dress, as etiquette then required, but it was a court-dress, and the princess had taken pleasure in making it as magnificent as possible. Fleurange, thus attired, was dazzling. For ornaments she wore only a gold chain, from which hung a cross, concealed in her bosom, (the precious gift of her father, which she never laid aside,) and on her right arm a bracelet which the princess Catherine had taken from her own to give to the young girl, on the evening of her departure, with the assurance that it would bring her happiness. Upon her head, no ornament,—but her beautiful hair, braided high around her head, in a manner unusual at that day, yet graceful as well as striking, and which added yet one charm more, that of originality, to this charming whole,—so noble that the young girl seemed to have been born at court,—so simple, that it was evident she now appeared there for the first time.

The two looked at each other, and, as we have said, the surprise was mutual. But this lasted but a second, and Vera came forward, saying:

"Mlle. Fleurange d' Yves, is it not?"

Fleurange bent her head.

"The empress expects you; follow me."

She walked before her to the door, then stopping a moment, said:

"Remove the right-hand glove,—this is etiquette,—and present your petition with that hand."

Fleurange obeyed, and mechanically ungloved the beautiful hand in which trembled the paper that she held. For an instant, she stopped, pale and agitated.

"Do not fear, *Mademoiselle*, said the maid of honor, in an encouraging tone. "Her Majesty is goodness itself; you have nothing to fear. She is besides already most favorably disposed towards you."

There was no time for a word more.

The door had opened. Vera entered first, bowed, and made Fleurange pass before her. Then, after a second profound bow, she withdrew, and the young girl was left alone with the empress.

The audience lasted beyond a half-hour, and Vera although well used to wait, began to find the time long, when the door again opened, and Fleurange re-appeared. Her face betokened emotion, her eyes were brilliant yet wet with tears. Seeing Vera, she stopped, and took her by both hands.

"Oh, you were right," she said. "Her Majesty has been inexpressibly good to me! But I know also how much I owe to you! I know that, thanks to you, my petition was granted, even before it was heard. May God reward you, *Mademoiselle*, and recompense you for what you have done for me!"

Vera replied with a cordiality not always habitual with her. Then she went as far as the door with Fleurange. Then, in saying adieu, their eyes met, and the same impulse occasioned each to make a slight motion. But a little timidity on one side, a little *hauteur* on the other, arrested each, and the two young girls parted without having kissed each other.

Vera returned slowly, and entered the drawing-room of the empress. As soon as the latter perceived her:

"Well, Vera," she said, "what say you to her? Have you ever seen anything more lovely?"

"That young girl is certainly very beautiful," Vera said, with a thoughtful air. "I have never seen eyes like hers before."

"Yes, truly;—eyes that look you in the face so frankly!

an expression so simple, so straight-forward, so confident one might say,—if it were not so gentle! I had no difficulty, I assure you, in promising to offer and to recommend her petition to the emperor. See there it is. I would not even read it. I have decided that this lovely girl shall have whatever she desires. It is enough for me to know that she loves one of those who have been condemned, and wishes to marry him, in order to go with him. There will be no need of refusing this immense favor, I am quite sure!"

The empress seated herself in her great arm-chair.

"But what fools men are," she resumed. "To throw away in their mad attempts, not only their own happiness, but that of others! I do really admire these women, whom nothing disheartens and who cannot be prevented from sacrificing themselves to these selfish creatures."

"Yes," Vera said, "their devotion is admirable, no doubt; but the women who beg and implore, and at last succeed in arresting the punishment from these guilty men, also perform a good action, and give these unhappy beings cause to bless their names!"

"I understand you, Vera! Your great beseeching eyes have no need to remind or to reproach me. I have already repeated to the emperor all that you said to me yesterday. We must now leave him to be guided by his own magnanimity, and importune him no further."

These words were spoken with a slight shade of authority, and some moments of silence followed them.

Vera, with mingled sadness and ill-humor, stood motionless, her eyes cast down, waiting till her sovereign should speak to her again.

In this attitude, she noticed on the carpet at her feet, a bracelet, which she picked up, to restore it to her mistress when the latter recognized it.

"Ah!" she exclaimed, "this is the talisman that lovely girl wore on her arm just now. Keep it, Vera, you shall send it to her to-morrow with the answer which she expects from the emperor."

Vera examined the bracelet curiously; it consisted of heavy links of gold, closed by a cornelian of the deepest color, on which was engraved a talisman. This bracelet was not quite unknown to Vera; somewhere she had seen one like it. Of this she was absolutely certain, but where? She could not at the moment remember.

While she was investigating this matter, the empress resumed:

"Now, without delay, sit down at the table and write from me to Prince W——, *from me,* you understand!— Put your letter and that petition in the same envelope, and say that I desire the request should be granted, and that I beg him to send me the reply (the favorable reply), to-morrow morning at latest. As soon as it comes, you will send it without delay in my name to this beautiful girl. She lives in the house of the princess Catherine Lamianoff, on the Grand Quay."

Vera started slightly.

"The princess Catherine's house?"

"Yes,—but make haste about this."

Vera again examined the bracelet; this name had fixed the vague recollection. It was a bracelet which she had seen the princess Catherine wear.

"Come, Vera, of what are you thinking?"

"Nothing, madam. Pardon!"

"Write then as quickly as possible what I have told you, and send the letter and the enclosure without delay."

Vera obeyed in silence. She took the petition and went towards a table placed in a deep embrasure of a window in front of which a trellis of gold covered with climbing plants, made almost a perfect screen.

As soon as she was here, where she could no longer be perceived and before commencing the letter which had been dictated to her, she opened the petition eagerly, and ran it over. A single glance sufficed to show that her suspicions were well-grounded. She grew deadly pale; her face, usually so composed was all at once transformed by the most violent outburst of hatred and anger. She crushed the paper in her hands, and remained motionless in the chair into which she had fallen, incapable of action, of thought, scarcely conscious where she was or what she was to do.

Finally she recollected herself, and made an effort towards self-control. The minutes were passing; the empress would be surprised at the time spent in fulfilling her command. She took up her pen, but scarcely had she written a line with her trembling hand, when a noise rarely heard at this hour was audible in the court-yard; the drums beat, the guard presented arms. Vera rose surprised and looked out of the window. The emperor had arrived in his sledge alone and without escort, as his custom was, although this was not the hour at which he usually came. Soon after, the doors were thrown open. This was the signal for Vera to leave the room. She tore up the letter, put the petition in her pocket, and, at the moment when the empress advanced to meet her husband the maid of honor vanished through the little door behind the tapestry, and hastily retreated to her own room which closely adjoined the apartment of her sovereign.

A full hour passed away, how, she could not tell. She had been able to act a part, to disguise,—and in the eyes of almost everybody to conceal entirely—the violence of a passion which vexation had but feebly combated, and which seemed to itself sure one day to conquer all obstacles. What indeed were these obstacles?—George, the husband selected for her from childhood, had he not once plainly enough shown the attraction that he felt for her?. This future, prepared for them both from the cradle, had he not, as well as she, seemed to regard it as the fulfillment of all his wishes? Since then, it is true, a shadow had come over this brilliant horizon, and when she had seen him again, George was no longer the same.—Why? She had striven to understand it; but all that she could learn was merely this, that a young girl, an obscure young person in his mother's service, had for a moment fascinated him; and she had heard whispered the name of *Gabrielle;* but the haughty Vera would have scorned to trouble herself about a trifle such as that. The future was hers, and she awaited it without fear, when news of the crime and ruin of Count George came upon her like a thunderbolt, and taught her, by the keenness of her grief to measure the depth of her affection for him. From that moment, she had had but a single thought; to prevail with the emperor, to obtain pardon for George, to bring him back to herself once more; and her first ill-success had not destroyed her courage or her confidence. But while her influence, her love, her efforts, all as yet remained without result, another—and what another! (Vera with all her pride was neither vain nor foolish enough not to appreciate the dangerous beauty of her against whom she must contend!) another, young, as beautiful—more beautiful than herself—eclipsed in an instant, by one heroic act, all of which her own devotion had ever dreamed, and went far beyond the limit of what she had esteemed possible. Could any one doubt with what sentiment George would receive her when she came to him in his prison? How could she contend against this adverse fate? What could she do? Who was this person, this young girl who had thus suddenly come between them? this girl who had the face of an angel, and whom she hated as though she had been a fiend? Suddenly like a ray of light came a thought: "Can that be Gabrielle?" she exclaimed aloud. But before she had time to linger over this suggestion, and to calm the new tumult of feeling which it had caused, the sound of the little bell interrupted her agitated reverie. Vera rose, with some surprise, however, for the accustomed signal which announced the emperor's departure had not been heard, and it was rarely that she was admitted while he yet remained; but her hesitation lasted only an instant, for the little bell ringing loudly repeated its call. Vera hastened to answer it, and whilst at the sight of her sovereign she stopped embarrassed, at the door, and made a profound salutation, she heard the empress, with mingled kindness and impatience, exclaim:

"Come, Vera! The emperor wishes to speak with you, and it is *he* whom you keep waiting!"

LIV.

While these scenes had been taking place in the palace, the Marquis Adelardi was on his way towards the fortress, considering as he went, what, under present circumstances, it would be best to say to Count George.

After mature reflection, he decided not to announce the arrival of Fleurange until he had learned the result of her interview with the empress. It was needless, in his misfortune, to torture George by vain hopes; above all things, fresh disappointments must be spared him. Moreover, it would be to postpone this communication, but for a brief time, since the young girl was to have her audience that same day, and on the morrow he could act in full possession of all the facts in the case.

To these thoughts was added a very serious anxiety, in thinking of the new circumstances in which his friend found himself. Now that his fate was decided, now that the strife of the long prosecution was at an end, now that the hour for resignation had come, in what mood would Count George be found?—George, with his rash and ardent nature, fastidious, a rebel against every form of restraint, sensitive to excess in regard to physical well-being, how would he endure the horrors of this new position, he, the one object of whose studies, whose tastes, whose passions had been enjoyment,—through his intellec, through his heart, through his mind, through his senses,—to enjoy! This had been the sole spring of his actions, even the best of them; and even in the dangerous chances which had brought him to his ruin, he had been seeking to satisfy his thirst for new and unknown emotions, far more than he had sought the realization of a chimerical but generous dream. He, for whom the words, duty, sacrifice, restraint, had no meaning at all, what to-day would be his attitude, in presence, no longer of danger, but of misfortune, under this pitiless aspect?

The marquis put these questions to himself, with an anxiety founded perhaps upon some resemblance between his own nature, and the one which he so well understood. Both were men of the world: the one more polished, more accomplished, more fascinating: the other, more subtle, more clear-sighted, more judicious. Both of them generous and honorable, and, saving these political errors into which both had fallen, incapable of any base or unworthy act. But in the human soul there exists one chord whose vibration echoes the voice of God, and it was this which was mute, with both these men, in all things else so admirable, or if not quite mute with the elder of the two, at least in the language of the great poet of his native land, inert and feeble "because too long silent." This mysterious, hidden chord never resounds very loud it is true, and all the noises of the world and of life, passions, pleasures, intellect, talent, glory, often smother it, and we fail to know that it exists; but when the silent hour of adversity comes, then it can be heard distinctly, and its sweet, strong music can transform all the atmosphere which is filled with it. Then, too, is the time when its absence is felt and produces a horror whose cause often remains a mystery to those who feel it!

George was not detained in a cell, but in a narrow room whither daylight penetrated only through a lofty grated window. There was no other furniture but his bed, a table, and two straw chairs. Upon his preceding visits, the marquis had found his friend sad, but always brave and calm, and, so to speak, scornful of the danger. Until this time, although paler and thinner, his features had retained all their noble and high-bred distinction, and the disorder of his hair, and even of his garments, had in no degree impaired that aristocratic look, which in the best sense of the word—had heretofore characterized him.

But to-day, it was so no longer; the work of years or of long illness seemed to have been accomplished since their last meeting.

Seated near the table, in an attitude of gloomy dejection, he scarcely raised his head at the approach of his friend, who grasped his hand in silence and sat down by his side, too much overcome with emotion to utter a word.

George waited until the steps of the jailor had died away in the distance.

"You are here, Adelardi!" he said, in an altered voice. "I have been surprised that you have not been here before since—since all is decided."

"I have not been able to obtain permission earlier; as a compensation, however, I am now allowed to come every day until—"

He stopped.

"Until the day when I shall relinquish the luxuries of this abode for those which await me elsewhere!" said

George, with a bitter laugh. "Adelardi!" he continued, changing his tone, and rising suddenly, "can it be that a friend such as you are, comes to me to-day with empty hands! Can it be that you have not thought of what I need, and that you are here without having brought me the means of escaping from my fate, and giving myself that death which they have the barbarity to refuse me?"

He paced the room in a sort of frenzy.

"Answer me, Adelardi," he cried in a violent tone. "Why have you not rendered me this supreme service? You, in the same situation, would have expected it of me, and I swear to you, you would not have looked for it in vain."

The marquis was not ignorant that there were principles in whose name he might reply, but he had long since lost the habit of appealing to them. He contented himself with saying:

"You are aware, George, that what you ask me is impossible."

"Ah yes! I forgot!—it is true. They take precautions to prevent a victim making for himself another exit from these walls than that which the hangman prepares; but they do not think," he continued, excitedly, "of all the resources of despair, and when a man is resolved that he will die, it takes more skill than they possess to hinder him from it, and to force him to accept the odious existence that they design for him."

Adelardi suffered him to go on thus for some time; finally he said to him with sudden firmness:

"George, until this day you have been calm and resolute; but at this moment, you oblige me to listen to words unworthy of your courage."

A slight color came in the prisoner's face, and he returned to his seat near the table.

"You are right, my friend, I acknowledge it; I am no longer what I was;—I may well surprise you, for I no longer recognize myself."

He remained silent and thoughtful for several minutes; then he said, "This is strange; for, Adelardi, I can say truly that till now I never knew what it was to be afraid; danger or death could not make me recoil; it is no extraordinary merit, I know. Nearly every man possesses it. Yet, such as it was, if any virtue has fallen to my lot, it seems to me it was this. Why then am I so weak to-day? Courage," he repeated, after a short silence, " is that true? is it really so? Had I *courage?* or was I only *brave?* It seems to me that is not the same thing. What is this difference?"

"I do not know," said the marquis, thoughtfully, "but there is one, certainly."

Neither possessed at the moment the true key to this enigma, neither, at the moment, thought of seeking it. But Adelardi, charmed to see the desperate mood in which he had found his friend soften ever so little, continued the conversation in the direction towards which George had led; he saw in it also, a way to touch upon the subject which he was not prepared as yet to speak of openly.

"Yes," he replied, "bravery and courage are two different things, and what proves it is that the most timid women often know how, on occasion, to be as courageous, —more so, even,—than ourselves."

"Yes, it is true; I know it."

"For instance," continued Adelardi, watching his friend attentively, "this courage of which we speak,— more than one of your companions makes signal proof of this, to-day."

"How is that?"

"You did not know that their wives, fearlessly and without hesitation, have asked and obtained the favor of sharing their fate? Some will accompany them on their sad journey; others will go a little later."

"And their husbands accepted this sacrifice?"

"Men who inspire devotion like this generally know how to understand and to accept it. Yes; one of them said yesterday, speaking to a friend admitted to visit him, as I am to visit you, 'I accept everything patiently now, I can undergo my punishment without a murmur; I am not to be separated from her! The only intolerable affliction in life is spared me, I no longer murmur, and I am grateful to the emperor.' It must be added that he is only lately married, and that he adores his wife."

"The only affliction," repeated George, slowly,—" the

only one! frankly, that is something impossible for me to understand! To love a woman to the extent of feeling that her presence alleviates a fate like ours, and that never to see her again is misery surpassing that which awaits us! No, that I cannot understand, I confess!"

"And yet," said Adelardi, with a good deal of earnestness.

But he stopped; the heroism of love may be felt, may be admired, but not suggested.

"And yet," pursued George, with a faint smile, "how many times you have seen me in love; this was what you were about to say? Yes, I admit it; although perhaps I have never been sincerely so but a single time, once only. And yet—what shall I say about it, Adelardi?—love, even such as that, was but a festival-day in my life,—one pleasure more, that is all. That beauty! that frank, rare intelligence! that virtue even which added an unwonted charm to the passionate tenderness that, sometimes, in spite of herself, her pure, sincere eyes betrayed! Oh yes! that time I was truly in love, and I could have easily been guilty of a folly which to-day I rejoice that I have avoided! Poor Fleurange! if I had married her, what a fate should I have reserved for her—and for myself!"

"For her, yes; I see that; the destiny your love offered to her, at the time when you did not scruple to testify that love was something very different; but if she—she, charming, devoted, courageous,—if she were near you now, do you not imagine that she could alleviate the rigor of your fate?"

"Mine? my fate? my actual, frightful destiny?"

George put this question with his bitter laugh, and resuming the same tone in which he had spoken at first, he went on:

"No, no; I am not one of those men to whom love can suffice, by itself alone, despoiled of all that makes its ornament and its value. In a word—think of me as you please, Adelardi—I resemble in nothing this companion in misfortune, whose case you have just cited. No human affection could make me endure the life that I lead here. Judge what it will be elsewhere!"

He rose, and began to walk up and down the room,

whilst Adelardi was silent, a prey to troubled and distressing thoughts. Soon George resumed, in a sort of frenzy:

"Come, Adelardi; talk to me of only one thing,—give me but one hope! death!—death!—I desire nothing else." And, raising his hand, with a desperate gesture, to the black silk cravat knotted about his throat: "At the worst, this will be my last recourse," he said, hoarsely, "if, during this coming week, I can find no means more worthy of a gentleman, to escape from their hands."

His friend preserved a sad and gloomy silence. What could one say, what answer could one make, when all on earth fails, and the heaven is shut? At that moment, Adelardi had the full knowledge, the keen apprehension, of what he lacked. He belonged to a land where the first impressions are always Christian ones, and rarely does the longest period of indifference and forgetfulness ever quite efface them from a heart where in childhood they have been profoundly impressed.

"My dear friend," he said, with a melancholy gravity, not at all habitual to him, "to be useful to you at this moment, I ought, I know, to be very different from what I am. Yes, George, against this gloomy temptation which overpowers you, against the despair that the prospect of your frightful fate causes in your mind, there is but one way, one only, a single remedy, and I feel myself unworthy to suggest it to you."

His voice faltered, and he continued with much emotion: "George, one must pray!"

George, for an instant, was surprised and touched, and, after quite a long silence, which neither one nor the other sought to break, he said, more gently:

"Well, Adelardi, it may be at least permitted me, in my prayers, to implore a favor which has not been denied to a man much more guilty than I,—Fabiano is dying."

"Yes; I know that his wound was mortal."

"He would not die so soon, perhaps, had it not been for the typhus fever, which attacked him day before yesterday with great violence. I was hoping something for myself from the contagion, when, for fear, no doubt, of diminishing our dismal chance in this way, they took him away the same evening, and carried him off to die in some hospital, I do not know where."

At this moment the key was heard to turn; the hour had gone by; they must separate; it was with an effort scarcely lightened by the thought that it was not a final adieu, and that the sad meeting would be repeated more than once.

At the moment when the jailor was opening the last gate to Adelardi, he offered him a letter: "Sir," he said, in a low voice; "I believe I am doing nothing wrong in giving you this. The dying prisoner who was carried away from here gave me this letter, one day, begging me to send it to its address, after his departure for Siberia. He is now on his way to another place, and I should like to fulfil the poor fellow's wish."

"Certainly," said Adelardi. "I will take charge of it willingly."

When he was outside the gates, he looked at the letter which had just been entrusted to him, and his surprise was great on discovering that it was addrssed to "*Mademoiselle Gabrielle d'Yves, Care of Professor Dornthal, Heidelberg.*"

LV.

The Marquis seated himself in his sledge, but he could not decide what order to give his coachman. Fleurange must, by this time, have returned from the palace. Should he go at once to find her, as they had agreed the evening before, to learn from her the results of her audience, and, also, to place in her hands the letter which he had just received? This was evidently the most natural thing to do, and when he asked himself why he hesitated, it seemed to him that it was because he had brought away from his interview with George, a sort of dissatisfaction, or, at least, a sort of disquietude, whose traces he feared she might perceive. In the singular mission with which he was charged, he began to be aware that the courage and affection were not equal on the two sides, and he would have come to asking himself anxiously whether it was absolutely certain that there would be gratitude equal to the devotion, had he not re-assured himself, in this regard, by many reflections.

It was not, indeed, perhaps, very surprising that George should speak lightly of a happiness which he must necessarily regard as beyond his reach. But if she, whom he was so far from expecting, appeared suddenly in his prison, would he complain then that the bride was too beautiful? The marquis thought not. He knew, better than any one else, what a fascination Fleurange had formerly exercised; no woman had ever held such sway over the fickle heart of George, and Adelardi was certain that it was only necessary for his friend to see her again, for an instant, to bring him under the same powerful influence once more. In this respect, Adelardi's perfect knowledge of his friend's character left him no room to doubt; he came, therefore, to the conclusion,—although he had felt wounded by the coolness with which Count George had spoken of Fleurange,—that, as soon as she appeared, this coolness would vanish like snow in the sunshine, and that there was no reason to fear that Fleurange would perceive or ever suffer from it. This was to him the one point of importance.

The interest which Fleurange had inspired in him was one of the best and purest sentiments he had ever in his life experienced. Without being aware of it, without striving for it herself, she had exercised a beneficial influence over him. A thousand remote impressions, crowded and almost stifled by the world, revived in the pure atmosphere which surrounded this young girl, and he welcomed them with a degree of feeling that surprised himself. And so, since meeting her again, in the interest of her happiness, far more than of George's, had he taken up the semi-paternal *rôle* which the princess had enjoined upon him, in relation to them both.

The considerations which we have enumerated having, however, completely reassured him, if not upon the present sentiments of George, at least upon those which he would be sure shortly to feel, he resumed his earlier intention, and ordered his coachman to drive to the Grand Quay. He had already alighted, and desired to be admitted to the presence of Mlle. d'Yves, when he perceived

Clement, who was crossing the vestibule. The idea occurred to his mind at once, that he had better address himself first to the cousin of Fleurange, rather than to herself.

Clement was sombre and pre-occupied. He had just seen Fleurange return from the palace radiant in her superb toilette and more radiant still in the joy of success. But the marquis had not time at this moment to observe the young man's face, nor the effort with which Clement replied to the first questions which he addressed to him, as soon as they were alone together in a reception-room on the ground-floor.

"I have to speak with you concerning an unexpected occurrence, Dornthal. But first, has your cousin returned from the palace?"

"Yes."

"Do you know whether her audience proved satisfactory?"

"Yes, the empress has promised for to-morrow the response which Gabrielle desires."

"I had no doubt of it. The empress is always glad to grant a favor, and even if that had not been so, it was impossible but that the sight of her who presented this request, should have secured its success."

Clement made no reply to this remark.

"You were saying, did I understand you, that an unexpected occurrence—"

"Yes, I am coming to it now. First I will tell you what you perhaps are not aware of: this miserable Fabiano Dini, who has so cruelly compromised George, and was in prison with him—"

Clement, surprised, interrupted him, in a tone of suppressed emotion:

"This unhappy man lies at the point of death: he has been removed—"

"*Parbleu!* I know it, for that is exactly what I was about to tell you. But you—how did you hear of it?"

"I have ascertained the fact."

"You knew him then, this Fabiano Dini?"

"Yes, a little; and I was interested to know what had come of him."

"And now, do you know?"

"Yes, I know in what hospital he is, and I am also aware that, thanks to the possibility of contagion, which keeps everybody away and renders flight impossible, he is guarded only by the nurses of the hospital. To-day I hope to be able to see him."

"You know him?" repeated the marquis, after a moment's reflection: "that makes something plain which was very incomprehensible to me. Your cousin Gabrielle knows him, in that case?"

"Yes, she knows him—as I do."

"Then all is explained, and, since that is the case, Dornthal," said the marquis, placing in his hands the letter of which he was the bearer, "take charge of this, and give it to her, yourself."

At the sight of his cousin's handwriting, Clement was unable to hide his emotion, and remarking the keen and questioning eyes of the marquis fixed upon him, it seemed useless to seek to conceal the truth. Without hesitation, therefore, and in as few words as possible, he related to Adelardi all the circumstances in the life of him who was now expiating his faults by a miserable death.

"I do not fear to entrust you," Clement said, "with the secret of this sad existence. You will keep it, I am sure;—you will never forget that it is *Fabiano Dini*, and not Felix Dornthal, who thus escapes by death, the fate of a criminal."

The marquis grasped his hand. "Count upon my silence, Dornthal," he said. After a moment, he continued, "This unfortunate man has shown much courage during the prosecution; an absolute contempt of danger for himself; he seemed to me absorbed only in the desire of saving him whose ruin he had caused, God forgive him!"

"Indeed, yes! May God forgive him!" repeated the young man gravely.

Adelardi held out his hand to him again, and was about to leave the room, when Clement detained him:

"Suffer me to ask you one question."

"Assuredly."

"Permit me to ask if Count George is informed of the arrival of Gabrielle?"

"Not yet."

"Without doubt he has been made aware of her resolution?"

"No, my dear friend, he knows nothing of it as yet. I had no doubt whatever of the success of Gabrielle's errand to-day; at the same time, before announcing so great a surprise to George, I desired to be absolutely certain that there was not the slightest possibility of any disappointment."

"Yes, I understand you. To lose a hope like that after having formed it, would be indeed more frightful than death itself!" said Clement, with a degree of intensity that struck his companion. Then he resumed in a calmer tone: "Suffer me now to ask one question more,—an absurd question, I acknowledge, and yet one which I must at this moment ask. As you know, my position towards Gabrielle is that of a brother. Can you assure me that he whom she loves, he for whose sake she thus sacrifices herself,—can you, upon your honor assure me that he is worthy of her?—that he loves her?—that he loves her as much as ever any man loved any woman? I cannot doubt it, of course, but—in compensation for so much suffering, I must have her happy—I must!" he repeated passionately, "and to this question which I have just asked you, I beg of you a sincere reply!"

The marquis hesitated for a moment. The vehemence of Clement made him thoughtful, and, under the impression of his recent interview with Count George, he, at first, knew not what answer to make. Should he betray his friend?—should he deceive him whose noble and loyal gaze rested fixed upon him at this moment?—He remained for some seconds uncertain, then at last decided to be sincere, and to reply as frankly as the question had been asked.

"You ask me for the truth, Dornthal. Well then, at this moment it is impossible to affirm that the affection of George for Fleurange is all that you say. In my opinion Gabrielle, at this present time, is for him only a beautiful dream of the past. But be very sure of this, my dear friend, so soon as this dream becomes a reality, as soon as she is there, before him,—his own,—oh then, do not have the slightest doubt, the half-extinguished fire will blaze brightly again, and nothing will ever hint to this charming creature that any shadow of forgetfulness has ever veiled her image. What can you expect, Clement,—in point of tenderness and constancy, the women far surpass us, and they are not to be commiserated for that. Adieu, my dear friend, until to-morrow."

Clement made no reply save by accepting the hand which the marquis once more extended to him. He had listened, pale and agitated; as soon as he was alone, he exclaimed, striving in vain to stifle a sob which forced its way from his breast: "Ah, good Heavens!—is *that* loving!"

LVI.

Fleurange, to the great regret of Mlle. Josephine, had laid aside the attire which had seemed to realize to the good lady her dreams of the preceding night. She had just reappeared, wearing the simple house-dress of dark cloth which was her ordinary costume, when Clement, who had said to her that he should not return until late in the evening, re-appeared suddenly in the apartment which he had left but half an hour before.

His design had been to consecrate the remainder of the day to his sad duty toward Felix, and he had thought it useless to mention this to Gabrielle, as he had concealed from her until now all that he had learned regarding their unhappy cousin; but the letter which had just been placed in his hands had changed the aspect of the case, and it seemed to him that she ought to know of it immediately.

He explained to her therefore at once and frankly, the situation of Felix. He explained to her his plan in relation to visiting him; finally, he repeated to her what he had heard from the Marquis Adelardi, and delivered to her the letter of which he was the bearer.

It was not without great emotion that Fleurange broke the seal, and read aloud and rapidly as follows:

"My cousin Gabrielle:
I am condemned to the mines for life, but as, at the same time, I am dangerously wounded, I suppose that I shall have long since ceased to live when this letter reaches, if indeed it ever does reach you. I regret my wrongdoing towards all, and especially to my last benefactor, and I regret this chiefly for your sake, for you perhaps, may suffer in consequence of it. I ought to have thought of this sooner, but one evening in Florence I saw you unexpectedly pass in a carriage. I waited about the door of the hotel where you alighted, then I yielded to an irresistible temptation to make you think of me, by throwing a few lines to you, hidden in a bouquet. A few days later my patron who was a thousand miles from thinking that the model was some one whom I knew, imprudently showed me his beautiful *Cordelia*. I confess it, from that day, a keen desire urged me to pluck him from that contemplation of your picture which so irritated me, and Lasko arrived at the right moment. But I did not think it would go so far. For the rest, Gabrielle, believe me, my love that you repulsed (and you did well, I admit it) was perhaps more worthy of you than his; for, I feel it, had I met you earlier, and had it been possible for you to love me, it would have made me better, whilst he——. But it is no longer the time to speak of him or of myself. All is over. It is to you, you only, my cousin, that I address these last words; you will repeat them for me to all to whom they are due, and from your lips, they will be heard: *Forgive me, and farewell!* F. D."

Fleurange's eyes were full of tears. This letter had touched her in more ways than one, and Clement, it may be easily believed, had not listened to it with indifference. But, at this moment, one thought had sway over all others. So, after a moment of silence, he said:

"This letter was written when he believed himself dying of his wound. Since then, fever has hastened his end, and, it may be, at this very moment while we are speaking, he is no longer alive. This evening, at all events, you shall know whether I find him dead or living—"

Fleurange interrupted him: "Clement, listen to me

first. If, as is not impossible, Felix is yet alive, I should like to see him, and to accompany you on this visit."

"You!—No; it is out of the question, the risk of contagion is serious. Besides, this hospital, you have no idea what a place it is! It is destined for malefactors and the most miserable of paupers. I cannot expose you to these horrors, and I will not!"

"But," said Fleurange, "if possibly, this preference, this kind of sympathy which he has always manifested for me in his way, gives me now the power of consoling the last hours of his unhappy life? Who knows if my voice might not cause to reach his ear, some word which could console his dying moments! Clement! Clement! would you dare to tell me I ought not to attempt this? Would you truly dare to deter me from this, because there is some danger for me in doing it?"

"Gabrielle!" said Clement, with a sort of anger, "you are always the same! Do you not understand that you are pitiless toward those who love you?"

"Come! Let us think it over for a moment, and then answer me, Clement!" she persisted.

A moment of silent agony followed these words, and then Clement said: "Come at once, lose no time. It is possible you have an influence over him which no other could have. Make haste, I will wait for you."

Before the words were finished, Fleurange was out of the room. In less time than it takes to tell it, she had returned, wrapped in a cloak, her velvet hat on her head, her face covered by a veil. They went down stairs together, without exchanging a single word. A sledge awaited them at the door. Clement placed her in it, seated himself at her side, and they were off, at the almost frightfully rapid pace that characterizes this equipage.

It was no longer daylight, for it was past four o'clock, but the brilliancy of the night, and the white reflections from the snow, lighted their way and permitted the horses to go as quickly as in broad day. The place towards which their course was directed, was on the opposite shore of the Neva, and much lower down than the point where

the river diagonally therefore, following a road marked by the fir-branches which, from point to point, indicated its course through the deep snow. They were thus transported in the twinkling of an eye, from the splendors of the city into the midst of what seemed a vast, white desert. As they descended the river, the palaces, the numerous and gilded cupolas of the churches, the immense and regular edifices, whose shadows rendered their effect more imposing, disappeared in the distance; and when they stopped at last at the remotest extremity of a suburb situated on the right bank of the river, they found themselves surrounded by low wooden houses, among which, here and there, were a few buildings of greater extent, but all of the poorest aspect and none above two stories in height.

Clement aided his cousin to alight, while he looked about for the person who was to meet him there, and serve as his guide.

A man approached them. "Monsieur Clement Dornthal?" he said in a low tone.

"Yes."

"You are not alone?"

"What is that to you?"

"I have no orders,—and a woman—it is impossible."

"I suppose however that more than one person can enter this place?"

"Oh, yes! but there must be permission, or rather—"

"Here," said Clement, in a low tone, "mine is enough for us both."

The guide seemed to find it satisfactory; he pocketed the gold which Clement offered him, and said no more.

They followed him, at rapid pace toward that one of the buildings just referred to, which seemed most lighted. Approaching, they perceived that this light proceeded from a great bonfire burning in front of it, and around which a number of individuals were warming themselves, some crouched upon the ground, some standing, others asleep in a radius near enough to the fire to make sure that the sleep would not be fatal; all lighted up in a grotesque fashion by the flame, which revealed their bearded faces, the angular form of their fur caps, their sheep-skin *caftans*, and, here and there, some vendors of brandy who were offering them, against the cold, a defence more effectual than even the blazing fire.

Clement and his companion passed rapidly before this crowd, not, however, without being assailed by some rude language, and Clement having hurled to some distance, by a well directed blow, an intoxicated man of inquisitive disposition, who attempted to lift the veil which Fleurange wore; but this lesson sufficed, and they arrived without further disturbance at the door of the building, complimented with the name of hospital, which was, in reality, nothing but a long, broad, wooden gallery.

They entered. In passing thus suddenly from the light of the great fire and the keen out-door air into the warm and dark interior of this shed, their first impressions were of total darkness, and a stifling temperature. Fleurange in haste, threw back her veil; then took off her hat and unfastened her cloak, for she could not breathe, and grew almost faint from this sudden transition. But she resumed them almost instantly. Clement, alarmed at first, soon saw that she was able to pursue their sad exploration. Indeed, as soon as their eyes became accustomed to the uncertain light which surrounded them, they could perceive a long row of pallets, upon which lay, in all the frightful variety of suffering, nearly two hundred human beings, whose mingled groaning arose on all sides like one sad and ominous cry, suited to freeze with terror and pity the firmest and most resolute heart.

That of Fleurange was beating fast, as they made their way slowly down the crowded space. Clement was asking himself remorsefully how he could have consented to bring her into such a place when suddenly a groan somewhere very near them, followed by words apparently spoken in delirium, arrested all other thoughts, and held them motionless, upon the spot where they were. Which of these sufferers had uttered those words? They looked around them as much as the imperfect light permitted; but among all these miserable creatures lying crowded together, they perceived not one whose face resembled his whose voice they believed themselves to have there heard.

"I beg you," murmured the young girl, in a voice of

entreaty to one of the attendants, whom she had just heard speak a few words in German, and who brushed past her roughly, a little lantern in his hand, " for one moment, lend me that light."

The man stopped, upon hearing his own language, and looked at her with surprise; then as if softened by the aspect of her who uttered this prayer, he handed her the lantern, saying:

"I leave it with you while I go down the hall. When I come back I shall take it."

Clement took it from her hands, and the light for an instant shone full upon the face and uncovered head of Fleurange. At the same moment a cry, an almost convulsive movement, and the name of Gabrielle in the same voice they had heard before, revealed to them upon which of these miserable beds they were to seek him whom they had discovered.

They drew near with hearts full of emotion; by the aid of the light, they were able to distinguish the face of the dying man. Was this indeed he?—Was it Felix?—His voice and his words left no room for doubt, and yet nothing in this face, disfigured by agony and lacerated by a frightful wound, recalled him whom they had seen for the last time, in all the fulness of health, and in all the pride of youth.

After the cry which he had uttered, he had fallen back as if dead, and Clement bent over him anxiously to ascertain whether he yet breathed.

The beating of his heart, feeble and irregular, had not ceased.

"Felix," he said, "do you hear me? do you recognize me?"

Felix opened his eyes.

"What a strange dream!" he murmured. "It seems as if they were all here. Just now, that vision, and now, this voice!—Oh my God! I would never wake!"

Fleurange had taken the hand of the dying man, and leaned over him to hear what he said. The light once more shone full upon her face. This time the eyes of Felix were fixed with frightful intensity upon those of the young girl.

"It is impossible!" he said. "But what is this illusion which makes me see and hear that which cannot be?"

"Felix," said Fleurange, with a tone of penetrating sweetness, "this is not an illusion; we are here. God has led us to you here, that you may not die alone, without a friend, without a prayer, without asking and obtaining peace and pardon!"

A ray of perfect intelligence came across the eyes of the wounded man, which, till then had been fixed, or wandering. He seemed to have understood, but he made no reply.

Clement and Fleurange hesitated to break the solemn silence. Soon Felix looked from one to the other, and taking the hand of the young girl and that of his cousin, he pressed them together to his heart, saying: "Oh, thank God, what miracle is this!"

Then he added, in a feeble voice: "What happiness that it is he, and not the other!"

Both alike understood his mistake, but both were not equally troubled by it; for while the young girl, blushing slightly, drew her hand away with a faint smile, the face of Clement grew as pale as that of the dying man. Yet a graver thought absorbed them both at this moment. After a short interval of silence, Fleurange spoke again to Felix; but he made no reply, and soon his head, which she was seeking to support, fell back upon her shoulder. He remained for a few minutes, fainting; then opening his eyes and seeing her still near him, "God be praised!" he said, "this vision is still here!"

"Yes, I am here, Felix," said Fleurange, fervently; "I am here to pray with you. Listen to me," she went on, speaking gently and very distinctly, "say after me that you repent of all the sins of your life."

"Of all the sins of my life!" repeated the dying man.

"And that if strength were given you, you would make full and complete acknowledgment, accompanied by hearty repentance! Do you still hear me?"

The hand that she held closed tightly upon hers. A tear stole down the cheek of Felix. A voice, which was but a whisper, repeated:

"Yes, a hearty repentance—"

A new fainting fit seemed to forebode that the end was very near.

"Oh God!" cried Fleurange, lifting her eyes to heaven, "if words of holy absolution could now fall upon his head!"

At this moment, the attendant came back to take the lantern roughly from Clement's hand.

"I must have it now for some one who has come to visit one of my patients!" he said. And as he spoke, along the narrow passage that separated the two rows of beds, a person made his way, imposing, majestic, whose long beard and floating hair, the full silken *cymar*, and cross of gold betokened sufficiently his character; it was a priest of the Greek church. He did not come for the exercise of his priestly office, however; one of the sufferers here had been an object of his charity, and he came simply to visit him.

He was passing without looking around him, and even turning away his eyes as much as possible from the sad scenes on every side, when the hand of Clement was laid on his arm, and detained him, just as he was passing the spot where Felix lay.

"What do wish with me, young man?" he said, in a tone of surprise.

"I entreat you," Clement said, "draw near this dying man; he is dying with sincere contrition for his sins, in full desire to confess them, if he had strength to do so; deign to give him sacramental absolution."

In spite of the place, the hour, the supreme solemnity of the moment,—the young Catholic girl started as she heard these words; her large eyes opened wide, with an expression of the most extreme surprise, and questioned Clement silently and anxiously. He understood her, and while the attendant translated his words to him who had heard them without understanding them, he replied to her:

"We are here, Gabrielle, before a priest clothed with all the power of holy orders. In the presence of death we must remember this, and this only!"

He knelt, and Fleurange did the same. The dying

man joined his hands, and while the word "pardon" for the last time escaped his lips, the Greek priest, raising his right hand, with a solemn gesture, pronounced above him the divine and compassionate words of holy absolution.

LVII.

FLEURANGE had been at home for some hours: the anxiety, horror, sadness, and emotion which had followed one another in her heart, during the affecting scene which we have just described, now gave way to a calm and deeply-felt sense of gratitude.

Ah! no one understands who has not experienced it, what faith alone can give, that mysterious joy which penetrates the soul, when the salvation of another soul seems to it assured, when in a tangible manner, so to speak, the abyss of misery which surrounds us opens and we are permitted to sound its depths; when, in return for a tear, we see heaven open; when in answer to pardon asked, it is given us to understand the ineffable significance of these two other words, sweet as mercy, grand as eternity: *pardon obtained.*

Fleurange felt herself then, if not happy,—the experiences of the day had been too solemn not to have left a veil of sadness over her soul—at least composed and serene; the sight of this bed of death had put to flight some of those visions to which she so often abandoned herself now without hesitation, visions where imagination mingled with the rapture of her present self-sacrifice the prospect of a brighter future, in which happiness with George would be consecrated and heightened by the suffering they should first have shared together; a cherished dream on which her heart loved to linger, believing as she did in the power of sacrifice, and making it the basis on which her hopes were built. All of this was now silent. It might be said that a graver, purer, more religious harmony made itself audible, and that this other mingled music, half heavenly, half earthly, died away in the distance. Until now the idea of self-sacrifice with and for another, had seemed grand to her; but in the hour of silence which followed this agitated day, a thought of something greater dawned within her, as if against her will: it was that of a sacrifice offered unknown even to those for whom one gives up everything!

The ideal sacrifice, indeed, the model sacrifice, was not this its nature? Had it not been offered for the sake of those who knew not of it? And this very ignorance, had it not been transformed into an excuse, by eternal compassion, offered to disarm eternal justice?

These confused ideas which Fleurange did not frame in words even to herself, were suffered by her as it were to float about her, while she neither offered nor denied them entrance to her soul. She was in one of those moods when, unknown to oneself, sometimes, there is forming in the depths of the soul a latent disposition whence may spring in an instant, efforts and sacrifices, which seemed impossible but an hour before.

Fleurange was sitting alone beside a great fire-place where now blazed a brilliant fire. This had been the attraction to her, in this little room beyond all the other drawing-rooms which were heated invisibly.

Clement after having brought her back had returned to the sad place which they had visited together, to seek to obtain for the remains of their unfortunate cousin a burial, not honored at all, but at least, separate.

Mlle. Josephine, at her accustomed hour, had retired to the splendid sleeping-apartment which she occupied now with less surprise than on the first day, and had been for some time, comfortably ensconced in the great bed where she had learned to enjoy the same tranquil repose as under the chintz curtains which formerly sheltered her sleep.

It was nearly eleven o'clock, and Fleurange had just resolved to leave her position by the fire, when the sound of a carriage was heard. The bell rung, and in a few minutes a card was brought to her. She read

"*The Countess Vera von Liningen.*"

and, underneath, these words written in pencil:

"*Will Mlle. Fleurange d' Yves have the kindness to see me a moment?*"

"Vera! Countess Vera!—"

Fleurange repeated the name twice. Since Florence,

this was the first time it had recurred to her mind: she remembered hearing it during the consultation of the Princess Catherine with the marquis, the first time she had seen the latter; since then Vera had never been named in her presence. Adelardi had instinctively avoided it in speaking to her, as, in speaking to Vera, he had avoided the name of Gabrielle: and that day at the palace, it had not been mentioned.

The surprise of Fleurange was therefore, inexpressible; she remained with her eyes fixed upon the card, until the servant who had brought it in, ventured to recall to her that the Countess Vera was below, in a carriage, and awaited a reply.

" Certainly, ask her to come in," Fleurange said hastily.

Then she awaited with embarrassment and curiosity her who was coming. Without well knowing why, her heart beat so violently that it almost took her breath away; but when the door opened, and she saw the beautiful maid of honor, she felt a sudden and extreme sense of relief.

" What, is it you, *Mademoiselle?*" she exclaimed joyfully. "Forgive me that I had not guessed it at once; but this morning I did not know the name of her who received me so kindly."

The idea which now crossed the mind of Fleurange was that sooner even than she had hoped, the empress had sent her, by her maid of honor, the favorable reply she had promised; but the pallor and silence of her who had just entered, struck her, and the words she would have added died upon her lips.

" You did not know my name this morning," Vera said at last; "but had you never heard it spoken before today ?"

Fleurange blushed.

" Never would be scarcely exact—" she began,—then stopped.

" No matter," resumed Vera, " I do not care to know when or how you may have heard it. I can easily understand that very little has been said to you concerning me; but, permit me, *Mademoiselle*, in turn to ask you if you, yourself, have not another name than that under which I had the honor to present you to Her Majesty?"

"My name is Fleurange," replied the young girl, simply, "but that is not the name which I bear habitually."

"And that other name?" asked Vera, in an agitated voice.

Fleurange was astonished at the manner in which this question was addressed to her; but she was still more so at the effect produced by her reply, and at the frightful change in the face of her visitor.

"Gabrielle!" she repeated; "I had guessed it, then!"

An embarrassed silence followed this exclamation. Fleurange knew not what to say, and awaited the explanation of a scene which became more and more strange.

And yet, as the silence lengthened, and she looked at Vera with ever-increasing surprise, a sudden apprehension seized her, and a fugitive and remote glimpse of the truth crossed her mind.

Nothing in the world was more vague than her recollection of the name murmured a single time in her presence; but that once was in a conversation of which Count George was the subject, and she remembered that she had then believed that they were talking of a marriage desired by the princess for her son.

Was it regretfully now that Vera brought to another this permission to accompany him?

Such was the question that Fleurange asked herself. Then approaching Vera, she said to her gently:

"If you have been entrusted with a message for me, *Mademoiselle*, how can I thank you sufficiently for having taken the trouble to bring it to me yourself?"

But Vera hastily withdrew her hand, retreating a few steps as she did so. Then, as if she were a prey to some emotion which she could not conquer, she fell back in an arm-chair placed near the table; and for some minutes remained pale, panting for breath, her expression gloomy and wild, from time to time brushing away fiercely the tears that, in spite of all her efforts, escaped from her eyelids.

Fleurange, motionless with surprise, looked at her with mingled terror and interest; but soon the frank decision of her character conquered her timidity. She went straight to the point.

"Countess Vera,," she said "if I have not conjectured rightly the motive which brings you here, tell me the truth. There is going on between us at this moment, something which I do not understand. Be sincere, I will be so, too. Let us not remain like this toward one another. Above all, do not look at me as if I were, not only a stranger, but an enemy."

At this word, Vera raised her head.

"Enemies!" she repeated: "Well,—it is true,—at this moment, we are so!"

What did she mean to say? Fleurange folded her arms, and looked at her attentively, seeking to find an explanation to this enigma of her words; to the still more obscure enigma of her face, which expressed by turns the most conflicting sentiments; to the enigma of her eyes which now regarded her with hate, now with the gentleness, and almost the humility of a suppliant.

At last Vera seemed to decide to go on:

"Yes, you are right," she said, "I must put an end to your suspense, and explain to you my strange conduct, but I need courage to do it, and to come here as I have done, to address myself to you, as I am about to do, there must have been—without my knowing why—"

"Well," Fleurange said, with a smile, "what else?"

"There must have been in my heart a secret instinct which assured me that you were good and generous!"

This conclusion, after this beginning, did not clear up the situation,—on the contrary, rendered it more involved than ever.

"This is enough by way of introduction," Fleurange said, with a certain tone of firmness. "Speak clearly, Countess Vera; tell me all without reserve; you may believe me when I beseech you to have no fear. Though your words were to do me a harm which at this moment I can neither foresee nor comprehend, speak; I require it of you, hesitate no longer."

"Well then,—here!" said Vera, throwing suddenly upon the table a paper which till then she had held concealed.

Fleurange took it, looked at it, and, at first, blushed; then she grew pale.

"My petition!" she said, "you bring it back to me? It has been refused then."

"No, it has not been sent."

"You mean to say that the empress after having shown so much kindness towards me, has changed her mind, and refused to undertake it?"

"No. She has given orders to me, on the contrary, to send your petition, and to add to it her own recommendation."

"Well?"

"I have disobeyed her orders."

"I await the explanation which you are no doubt intending to give me. Go on without interrupting yourself; I shall listen."

"Well then, first of all, answer me. Did you know that George von Walden was the husband who was promised to me,—for whom my father destined me from childhood?"

"Who was promised you?—from childhood?—No, I did not know it. But no matter; go on."

"It is true, it is no matter; this is not the question, although I was obliged to refer to it. It is no longer a question of his misfortune, of his fearful sentence, of that frightful Siberia, to which you propose to accompany him—to share a fate which you can neither alleviate, nor, possibly, endure yourself. The question is now, to save him from this destiny. To give back to him life, honor, liberty, all that he has lost. His estates, his fortune, his rank, all may yet be restored to him! This is what I have come to tell you, and to ask you to aid in its accomplishment."

"All this can be restored to him!" said Fleurange, in an altered voice. "By what means. By whose power?"

"That of the emperor, invoked, and of his clemency obtained through my entreaties; but upon two conditions, one of which is imposed upon George, the other of which depends upon me. To these two conditions, is joined a third, and that one rests with you, with you only!"

The great eyes of Fleurange were fixed upon Vera,

with an expression of profound astonishment, mingled with anguish.

"Finish, I implore you!" she said. "Finish, if you are not dreaming, in saying such words to me, or I, in hearing them,—if we are not both mad,—you and I!"

Vera clasped her hands together and cried passionately:

"Oh, I beseech you, have mercy upon him!"

She stopped, suffocated by her emotion.

Fleurange continued to look at her, with the same expression, and, without speaking, made a sign to her to go on.

She seemed to concentrate her attention to understand the words that were said to her.

"I am listening," she said at last, "I am listening quietly and attentively; speak to me with the same composure."

Vera resumed in a calmer tone:

"This morning, at the moment when I had just read your petition, and learned, for the first time, who the exile was whom you desired to follow,—at this very moment the emperor arrived at the palace, and sent for me."

"The emperor?" said Fleurange, with surprise.

"Yes. And do you know what he wished to say to me? You do not guess what it was, and I can understand readily why you should not, for you do not know with what ardor I have solicited pardon for George, how eagerly I have brought together, to this end, all the facts in the case which might disarm his sovereign's anger against him. What the emperor wished to say was this, that he deigned to grant me this favor—to grant it to *me*, Fleurange! do you understand?–but on two conditions."

"His pardon!" cried Fleurange. "Go on, I am listening."

"The first, that he should pass four years on his estates in Livonia, without stirring thence,—"

Vera had ceased suddenly. Fleurange looked up. "And the second?" she said.

"Then," said Vera, slowly, and speaking with difficulty,—"that the wish of my father, and of his, should be fulfilled before his departure."

Fleurange shuddered. An icy chill crept towards her heart, and her head grew dizzy. She remained perfectly motionless however.

"His pardon is upon that condition?" she said.

"Yes. The emperor has taken an interest in me from my childhood. He loved my father and it has pleased him to attach this act of clemency to this fulfilment of my father's wish."

There was a long silence. Vera trembled herself, as she saw the pale lips and colorless cheeks of Fleurange, and her eyes, gazing fixedly into space.

"And he?" she said, at last, "he will accept his pardon, with this condition—without hesitating, will he not?"

"Without hesitation?" repeated Vera, coloring with a new emotion; "that is what I cannot say; this very doubt humiliates and alarms me, for the emperor would regard the least hesitation as a new ingratitude, and perhaps might retract this pardon."

"But why should he hesitate?" said Fleurange, in a voice scarcely audible.

"Fleurange!" said Vera, in the same passionate tone she had used more than once during this interview, "let us break each other's heart, if we must, but let us go to the very end of this. It has been permitted you to see George, since you have been here?"

"No."

"But he is expecting you, he knows that you have come, and what devotion has brought you to him?"

"No; he knows nothing of it as yet, and is not to know until to-morrow."

A flash of joy shone in the black eyes of Vera.

"Then, it rests with you that he does not hesitate, that he is saved!—Yes, Fleurange, let him never know that you are here, let him never see you—never again," she added, looking at her with a jealous terror that she could not conceal "and life will once more become for him, beautiful, brilliant, happy,—what it was,—what it ought always to be,—and the memory of these few months will fade away, like a dream!"

"Like a dream!"—Fleurange repeated mechanically these two words, passing her hand across her forehead as she spoke.

"I have now told you all," Vera said. "I have done you an injury that I understand better than any other person can. But," she continued, in a tone which went to the very depths of her listener's heart, "I wished to save George! I desired him to be restored to me! and I have believed—I know not why, for it seems most unreasonable, and I am ordinarily distrustful—yes, I have believed that you would be willing to aid me, against yourself!"

Fleurange, her hands clasped and resting upon her knees, her eyes gazing steadfastly before her, had seemed for a few moments past, not to have heard what was said. She was listening,—but it was to that clear, distinct voice that rang so true, in her own soul, that voice she had always so well known how to recognize, and to which she had never denied obedience.

If George were free, if he recovered his name, his rank, his former position, would she not at once find herself in the same position toward him which she had formerly occupied?—would it not be treason, to avail herself, in this case, of his mother's permission, and that, too, to the detriment of her who sat there, the wife chosen for him from his childhood? Would it not, still further, be a treason towards him, to present herself before him as a danger, as an obstacle, which might perhaps, at the very moment when he recovered his liberty, cause him to lose it anew, with that momentary favor which had restored it to him!

She laid her cold hand upon the hand of Vera, and lifted to hers her gentle and steady gaze.

"It is enough," she said in a calm voice. "You have done right. Yes, I have understood, be tranquil."

Vera, astonished at the look and tone, gazed at her in wonder.

"Act fearlessly," pursued Fleurange. "Act as if I were far away,—as if I had never come."

And, taking the petition which lay upon the table, she tore it across, and threw it into the fire! The paper blazed up for a few seconds, then went out. She watched the cinders fly up the chimney.

Vera, with an irresistible impulse seized the hand of

lent and abashed. She had come, resolved to overpower her rival, to convince her, to struggle against her at every point, if she failed in her first attempt; but her victory had taken a character which she had not at all foreseen.

Certainly it had been an easy victory, and yet Vera understood that it had been a cruel one. She felt at this moment more pain than joy, and her attitude no more expressed triumph than did that of Fleurange express defeat. While the one remained with drooping head and downcast eyes, the other had risen to her feet, a fugitive color lingered in her cheeks, the effort of the sacrifice had lighted up her face, and given it unwonted brilliancy.

"I think," she said, "you have nothing more to say to me."

"No,—for what I should like to say I cannot, and I dare not."

Vera rose and went towards the door, but a recollection brought her back.

"Pardon my forgetfulness," she said, "here is your bracelet which you dropped this morning, and which I was desired to return to you."

At sight of the talisman, Fleurange started, her unnatural color faded, she became deadly pale, and as she looked at it in silence, a few tears, the only ones which she had shed during that interview slid down her cheeks. But it was only for an instant. Before Vera could think what she was about to do, Fleurange had attached to the arm of her rival the bracelet which the latter had just restored to her.

"This talisman was a present from the princess Catherine to her son's betrothed; it would bring happiness, she said. It is mine no longer. I give it up to you; it is yours."

Fleurange held out her hand. "We shall never see each other again," she said; "let us not remember each other with bitterness."

Vera took the hand without looking up. Never had she felt herself so touched and humiliated, and her very gratitude was a wound to her pride. The grave and sweet voice of Fleurange was, however, irresistible at this moment, and spoke to her heart in spite of herself.

hesitating between these two feelings, when Fleurange resumed:

"You are right, it is not my place to wait for you, at this moment, for you have nothing now to forgive,—and as for me, I forgive you all."

And while Vera still stood motionless with bowed head, Fleurange bent towards her, and kissed her.

LVIII.

The marquis Adelardi was accustomed to say that he had seen in his life so many extraordinary things happen, that it was very rarely the case that anything could surprise him now. The day which was now beginning was, however, destined to cause him this sensation in the most lively manner and twice repeated, in the space of a few hours.

He had risen, as usual, quite late, and was breakfasting at his fireside, when a note was brought him whose first effect was, to bring to an untimely end this scarcely commenced repast. After having read it, he fell into the most profound meditation, then rose, and paced the room in an agitated manner. Finally he drew nearer the window and read a second time the following lines:

"MY VALUED FRIEND:

I have changed my plan. I beg you earnestly when you see Count George, do not mention my name to him, and especially, take the utmost precaution that he shall remain forever ignorant of my design in coming hither, and of my journey itself. It will be easy, for no one knows me, and to-morrow, before the close of the day, I shall have left St. Petersburg. All shall be explained to you, but for the moment I write you this which is most necessary and urgent that you should know without delay."

It was useless to read and re-read. These were the words, signed *Fleurange*, which he had before his eyes.

For once, the marquis was completely at a loss. Nothing, absolutely nothing, occurred to his mind as the reason for this abrupt change, when the success of the petition offered the day before to the empress was assured, and with his recent conversation with Fleurange fully before his mind, in which, having no longer anything to conceal, she had let him see frankly the depth and sincerity of her affection for George. Her firmness and her courage he had long known, and the idea of seeing her shrink back from the trial at the last moment, never occurred to his mind. There was, therefore, an impenetrable mystery about it, and he awaited with impatience the hour when he could go and seek the promised explanation. But first, he must be faithful to his appointment with George. Poor George! a new compassion awoke in his heart for him; after having doubted the day before if he were worthy of the consolation which was to be offered him, it seemed now to the marquis that his friend could not live without her, and he was overwhelmed with grief at this new and fearful calamity overtaking one already too wretched. He was preparing to go to the fortress, thus more sadly than ever to fulfil the painful duty of his powerless friendship, when another letter was brought to him.

This time the mere sight of this second missive made him start, and he examined with extreme astonishment the envelope of the letter, the seal, the faint perfume which it exhaled, all was to him a new cause of surprise; and, in that case at least, it was not unreasonable, as it often is to weigh carefully all these exterior indications before seeking their explanation by opening the letter: for, in the address, the Marquis. Adelardi had recognized the handwriting of his imprisoned friend. Now, since George had been a prisoner, he had had neither the permission nor the materials for writing; in the second place, the paper, the arms emblazoned on the seal, the perfume, all these things belonged to another epoch; surely none of these past elegancies had been conceded to him in the prison. The mere external aspect of the letter, then, was inexplicable; and when at last he opened the letter, to seek the solution of the enigma, this is what he found:

"VERY DEAR FRIEND:

"At the mere sight of this letter, have you conjectured its contents? In case you have not, learn that I am free, or, at least, shall be so to-morrow! But, in the mean time, I have already emerged from the frightful place in which you left me yesterday, and here I am, thanks to the kindness of the governor of the fortress, established in his own suite of rooms, and surrounded already with all the delightful accessories of civilized life, from which I believed myself separated forever,—accessories which are the dawn for me of the bright day which is about to begin. Yes, Adelardi!—free!—by the emperor's pardon, against whom—I swear it faithfully—I will never again conspire; free, on two conditions, the one, to go and live at home, in Livonia, for four years; the other—guess it!—It is no more severe than the first; it is to return to my early love for her to whom I owe my pardon; in a word, to end where I began, and to become the husband of Vera von Liningen! What say you to that?—Is it not a *dénouement* worthy of a romance? You foretold it to me, one day, do you remember? *You will renounce the folly which tempts you, and will keep the promise that binds you!* I was far enough from believing it then, and even now, it is well perhaps that that fair siren is seven hundred leagues away, for I cannot say what I might do, if I found myself once more under the fascination of that glance which made me lose my head,—while now I am entirely given up to the happiness which awaits me. Vera has always loved me; she also is beautiful in her way; but above all she possesses a charm which, at this moment, is powerful enough to efface every other; she is radiant with the *liberty* which she offers me, and that I owe to her. So I am not tempted to refuse to her this hand, which she is willing to accept, nor this heart, slightly *blasé*, but which

It would be difficult to describe the strange mental condition into which the reading of this letter, following so quickly upon the other, threw the man to whom both were addressed. It would have been impossible for him to say whether he was gratified or sorry, indignant or affected, consoled or overwhelmed, by all this which he now learned at once; and although he was but partially enlightened in regard to some points which he desired to understand, it was now plain to him that, in some way or other, Fleurange had learned, before he had, this news of George's pardon, and the conditions thereto attached. From this resulted a very simple explanation of her note, and yet an explanation so generous, pathetic, sublime even, that all his interest turned towards this lovely and noble girl, whose letter, lying before him, side by side with that of George, seemed to make more glaring, by the greatest possible contrast, the cold and selfish levity of the other. At all events, he had nothing further at this moment to do for him, upon whom every thing seemed to smile, but only for her who, without his knowing it, sacrificed herself for him, to-day the same as yesterday, with a devotion a thousand times more disinterested and more generous than ever before.

At this moment his door opened, and he uttered an exclamation of joy and of welcome, in hearing Clement announced. It was precisely the person of whom he had been thinking, and with whom he wished to speak at once. As soon as he saw him, he perceived, however, that the young man knew nothing of what had occurred. Clement, in fact, having returned to the house very late the preceding evening, and having gone out before daylight, had not seen Fleurange again, since leaving her on their return from the hospital. He was now on his way home, after attending the obscure and far-off burial of his unhappy cousin, and had come to see the marquis to beg the latter to use his influence to obtain permission for him to place a stone cross over the sad grave.

But he had not time to enter upon the subject which brought him, for the marquis was anxious to discuss that with which his own mind was filled, and, with a degree of animation which at first hindered him from observing the effect which he produced upon his auditor, he explained to him that pardon had been granted to George, and the conditions upon which the favor was bestowed. Clement remained motionless, and, for a few minutes, the excess of his surprise prevented him from making any reply. This news changed so abruptly for him the aspect of every thing, that his mind refused to comprehend it. He looked at the marquis with an expression so singular that the latter was struck by it, and suddenly became conscious that he had imprudently touched upon a more hidden and more vital fibre than he had supposed.

" Pardon me, Dornthal; this is a surprise which you feel more deeply than I had supposed."

"Yes," said Clement, in an altered voice; "but does she already know what you have just told me?"

By way of reply, the marquis handed him the note just received from Fleurange.

He read it, it may well be imagined, with an emotion even more intense than that which he had just experienced, but he knew better how to conquer it.

" Poor Gabrielle! This was evidently a first generous impulse, worthy of herself. But," he said, in a different tone, where trembled the indignation which he scarcely knew how to repress, "I cannot yet understand how this —how Count George can consent without hesitation to the condition *proposed;* for, definitively, I shall never believe that this condition could be rigorously exacted by the emperor, still less that it could be accepted by her who is its object, if he knew how to represent with their true value those feelings which, on his side,—or, at least, I so suppose,—will hinder him from agreeing to it."

The marquis paused, for a moment, as if in hesitation, then he said: "Well, Clement, we have but very little time; you may as well know all the truth at once."

And he gave him Count George's letter.

As he read, contempt and anger flashed so vividly in Clement's face, that the marquis watched him with surprise. He crushed the letter in his hands, and threw it upon the table.

"That letter," he said, "is nothing, more than I ought to have expected from the man of whom you told me yesterday! Oh poor Gabrielle!" he continued in a voice broken by emotion, " is it thus that the dear treasure of her love has been lavished and lost!"

He leaned against the table, and hid his face in his two hands. For several minutes neither of the two men cared to break the silence.

Finally Clement returned to himself. "Pardon me," he said; "in truth I do not know what you will think of me, after having seen me as I have just shown myself to you. However, this is no matter, it is only of her that we must think. There is one point which I suggest to you, and upon which I do not need to insist: she must never know the contents of that letter; she must never know—*never*, understand me,—of what description this love was which she believed worthy of her own."

The marquis looked at him with amazement.

"And it is you, Dornthal," he said, "who are so anxious to spare your cousin's recollections of Count George."

This complete absence of common-place exultation and selfish hope added one notable surprise the more to those of the morning.

Clement neither observed Adelardi's tone, nor the kind and cordial good-will of the look which accompanied the words he had just spoken.

"I desire that she should suffer as little as possible," he said briefly; "this is my only care, and I have no thought beyond this."

He rose to go.

The marquis grasped his hand with an earnestness rare for him, and after Clement had gone, he remained a long time thoughtful.

Perhaps at that moment he was thinking that to know and study one noble heart was worth more than much which had hitherto engrossed his interest and his thoughts.

LIX.

Upon his return, Clement learned that his cousin had several times inquired for him. He went immediately to the room where she was. His emotion upon seeing her, although he had in a degree prepared himself for the interview, was greater than he had expected, for he was not prepared for the change produced in her by the few last hours. She was however calm and resolute as on the preceding evening, but during that interval she had gone through what one might call the mortal agony of the sacrifice,—that hour of ineffable suffering, which is not the one in which the soul accepts its work of self-immolation, nor yet that in which this work is achieved, but that intermediate hour when repugnance yet struggles desperately against the will. And it is indeed at this very point in the order of his sufferings, that this agony was endured by Him who is the Master of us all, when " He was made like unto us."

Fleurange had slept for a few minutes, just before day. The remainder of the night she had spent struggling with her suffering. The emotion suppressed with difficulty while she conversed with Vera, had broken forth without restraint when she found herself alone in the night, and she had given herself up to the vain solace of tasting deliberately all the bitterness of the sacrifice, of silencing all consolation, and letting the waves of despair rise to her very lips, if not break quite above her head.

The room which she occupied, even larger and more sumptuous than that of Mlle. Josephine (for it was the Princess Catherine's own room), was lighted but by a single lamp which burned before some holy images carved in gold and silver, and placed according to Russian custom, in one corner of the room.

Fleurange had thrown herself down upon a sofa, and for a long time, her head buried in the cushions, she had lain there sobbing, shedding torrents of tears, giving her grief the fullest utterance, without making one effort for self-control.

Once before in her life had she given way to such a

passion of grief. It was—with far less reason doubtless —two years earlier, during the first hours that had followed her departure from Paris, when it had seemed to her that she was alone in the world, and that all the happiness of life was henceforth at an end for her. On that occasion, the reader may remember, the sight of a star, which appeared suddenly, as the clouds broke away, had brought her a message of peace. When He pleases, God knows how to give a voice to all things in nature, and to speak to his creatures by the works of His hand, or even of their own.

An impression of a similar kind brought at this moment its first lull to the storm which had swept over her soul.

Lifting her head suddenly, after having remained long in the attitude we have described, her eyes were attracted towards the lighted corner of the room where the lamp was burning before the sacred images. In these Greek figures it is well known, the heads painted on canvas are detached from the gold and precious stones which surround them. The one which at this moment drew the attention of Fleurange was the figure of Christ, that sacred countenance whose type is well known to all who have seen representations of Byzantine art. This serious oval face, these gentle eyes, calm and deep, produce an impression far more profound and intense than any mere reproduction of human beauty. This impression which a religious love of art makes comprehensible, was accompanied in the case of Fleurange, by a vivid recollection of her childhood. She well remembered a picture like this in the Church of Santa Maria al Prato. She now fixed her eyes upon these divine eyes which seemed to gaze upon her, and by degrees, the sweet and powerful influence stole into her heart, and brought her sudden consolation, marvellous and inexpressible. She remained as if spell-bound, and, by degrees, rising from the attitude she had till now retained, she sat with folded hands for awhile. Soon, her eyes still fixed upon the sacred figure, she fell upon her knees, and remained long absorbed in meditation. Her immoderate grief seemed be appeased and to change its character. Her tears, without ceasing to flow, ceased to be bitter, and it was for another reason that she now wept, for, in the sweetness of that majestic look, she had read a reproach, and had comprehended its meaning!

"Oh my God and Saviour! forgive!" she cried fervently, bending her head till it touched the floor.

Pardon!—Yes, notwithstanding the purity, the devotedness, the uprightness of her soul, Fleurange had also need of this word, and had need to know that it meant peace and consolation.

At this moment she saw it for the first time. A light, never before seen, began to rise in her soul, like the pale white dawn which precedes the day, and her grief seemed to her now a punishment, her tears an expiation.

These thoughts were still confused, but their influence was already blessing her, and very soon she felt springing up in her soul, in reality, that strength and courage—of which during her interview with Vera, she had had only the external appearance. She had always been capable of action, even amid her suffering. Now, she began to understand her pain and to endure it willingly.

The night was already far advanced, but she no longer felt the need of repose, and before seeking sleep, it seemed best to her to give to heart and soul, a thousand times more wearied than the body, that of which they had need. Under the influence of all the varied incidents and emotions of the day, she wrote to Madre Madelina a letter containing a faithful recital of them all.

Her happiness at morning, her self-surrender of the evening, her despair, scarcely-pacified, of the night, nothing was hidden or suppressed, not even a new and ardent aspiration towards that cloister whence she believed that now she could not be repulsed, and which seemed to her at this moment the only refuge for her broken heart.

There is a certain art in reading the heart of another, but it is one no less great to make others read one's own, and this Fleurange possessed in the highest degree towards that great soul who, from afar, watched over hers.

This disclosing of her inmost thoughts consoled her. She slept for a little while, and, on awaking, the letter

But a night like this had left its traces. The reddened eyes of Fleurange, her altered aspect, her pale and trembling lips, the sadness in her eyes,—were all to Clement indications of a suffering which was to him an intolerable punishment. He would have spared her from enduring it at the expense of his life, and it is not too much to say that he had proved this. But now that the difficult duty was no longer laid upon him of invoking for her the happiness which she expected from the affection of another, the impetuous cry of his own heart made itself heard with almost irresistible power, and never had Clement shown himself more master of himself than to-day when he must check the impulse which would have thrown him a thousand times at his cousin's feet, and when he was able to control the passionate desire to tell her that he whom she loved and lamented was most ungrateful, and that she herself was even more ungrateful than he!

Instead of that, they clasped each other's hands in silence. Fleurange saw that he knew all, and it was a comfort to her that she had no need to tell him anything. In a few words they had arranged what concerned their departure, and Clement promised her that in twenty-four hours they should be on their way.

In the meanwhile, Mlle. Josephine had made her appearance, and Clement, too pre-occupied to use circumlocutions, announced to her, quite simply, without any explanation, the change that had occurred in his cousin's intentions. But when, at the very summit of joy, Mlle. Josephine exclaimed: "She is going back with us!—Oh what happiness!"—Clement frowned, and grasped her hand in so expressive a fashion, that the poor lady stopped quite short, and, according to her custom, shut up her delight in the most complete silence, saying to herself that a day perhaps would come when she should understand all these inexplicable things, this among the rest: that, when she wept at the departure of Fleurange, she had to strive to conceal her regret, and now that she was to return with them, it was forbidden her to express her rejoicing.

"All this is very odd,—I seem to make some mistake whatever I do. And yet, Clement, permit me to tell you, I suspect that as to this Count George, I was the only one o had the right of the matter."

This last reflection only escaped her some time later on one of those occasions, when, alone with Clement, she delighted to give full expression to her thoughts, and the smile which received these words, quite consoled her for his previous frowns.

The evening passed almost in silence. The Marquis Adelardi passed it with them, and the calm and simple manner of Fleurange,—while the frightful change in her face did not suffer him to doubt the extent of her sufferings,—redoubled the enthusiasm he felt for her, an enthusiasm which by degrees became a firm and lasting friendship, having its beneficent influence upon all his after life.

Before separating, Clement and his cousin exchanged a few words upon the sad burial of Felix. No religious act had been permitted to accompany it, but the Marquis Adelardi had promised that he would obtain the last favor solicited by Clement, and that a cross of stone should mark the place where he reposed; and on the morrow, mass should be celebrated for him in the Catholic church.

"We will attend the service together," said Fleurange.

"Yes, Gabrielle, that was my wish."

The following morning at an early hour, Fleurange and her cousin were kneeling before the altar of the great Catholic church in the Newsky Prospect. After all that had troubled and distracted the young girl the day before, it was a moment of sad consoling repose.

This long journey, after all, despite the bitter disappointment, the grief, the sacrifice which awaited its close, —she had not made it in vain! He whose last hours she had consoled, he for whom they prayed at this moment, had carried the blessed traces of her presence into those regions whither repentance had opened to him the way. Repentance! salvation of the soul that feels it, benediction of the soul which aids it, mysterious joy of the angels who inspire and welcome it, as one of the joys in their eternal beatitude!

Fleurange, absorbed in her own thoughts, walked on without looking about her, and Clement, on his part, was equally absent-minded, when a thrill like an electric shock, made them both start at the same instant:

"The bride and bridegroom are coming out," a voice said.

"The bride and bridegroom?—the two convicts you mean to say," said some one else, laughing, "they are to go into exile together, you know."

They heard no more.

The sudden effort of Clement to remove Fleurange was in vain; she resisted it, and letting go his arm, before he could prevent her, had taken a few rapid steps which brought her in front of the crowd, near a tree against which she leaned, and looked before her, pale and silent. She saw the gate open,—she saw the carriage emerge and soon pass before her,—she saw *him*, at last! Yes, she saw Count George's noble face, his smiling mouth, his radiant glance. For an instant she saw the brilliant dark eyes, the golden hair of the bride. Then she felt as if night came on suddenly, and everything vanished from her mind, as well as from her view.

EPILOGUE.

—"No, my Fior Angela, I tell you no, once more, just as when you asked me at Santa Maria, that beautiful evening in May, while from the top of the cloister we watched the sun go down. What has changed?—How has God called you now, in this solitude, if He had not called you then?—Because you suffer more?—But, poor child, you were suffering then. —Life, you said, is empty and desolate, unsatisfactory and imperfect! And indeed you were not wrong; this is its true aspect, compared with the better country which awaits us. Regarded thus, nothing certainly can give it the slightest charm; but this causes one no sadness; you are not sad when an object seems ordinary and worthless only because it is compared with another object, wondrous and divine, whose possession is assured. This is, as I have already told you, the disgust for earth whence springs the joyous and irresistible call to the cloister; but, I have told you also, this divine voice when it sings through the soul, sounds there alone, to the exclusion of all earthly voices. A flame kindles which absorbs and annihilates all others, even those whose terrestrial light is sweet and pure. This divine call has not been addressed to you: the earthly happiness that you dreamed of has escaped you, that is all, and for the second time, this disappointment has inspired in you the same wish; but I believe now as I did then, that if God had reserved for Himself your life, He would not have permitted that a heart like that of my Fleurange should be for a single day shared by earth!

This time, it is true, all is over, and you are parted irrevocably from him to whom this heart has been given, and, let me tell you so now, unreasonably given! You start, my poor child, you think me cruel, and all the false brilliancy which fascinated you, shines at this moment around the image which is still so dear to you. I must go on, nevertheless.

There is an earthly love which, though it lengthen our road to God, does not turn us away from it, and even by the virtues it requires, by the sacrifices it imposes, by the sufferings which accompany it, often seconds the soul's noblest efforts.

Have you not to-day recognized this, Fleurange?—the foundation of such a love was wanting in yours. I knew it well when first I listened to your story at Santa Maria, when you told me all that was in your heart. I then understood how it was that God was raising an obstacle before you, and imposing upon you a sacrifice, and your suffering seemed to me then the expiation of an idolatry which you could not yourself recognize in its true aspect. If I had found you uncertain or hesitating in regard to the path to follow, if I had found you weakly desirous of sparing yourself, and escaping from the sacrifice laid upon you, I should even then have used language severer, but you were acting firmly and uprightly, and I postponed, till a moment when time should have brought you peace, the duty of showing you the deep and secret error in your heart. Meanwhile, that which you suffered then seemed

But it was not so to remain; the temptation was to be renewed, and under a form which it was impossible for my poor child to resist; she yielded to the generous and impassioned impulse of her heart, and found in the very excess of her self-devotion that satisfaction to her conscience of which she felt confusedly the need; but this was not enough, she must suffer again, and suffer more than before: the idol must be broken, and with it her own heart, as she believes!

It is not so, Fleurange; across the distance, I would that my voice could reach you, and speak to you with divine authority, saying "Arise, and walk." Yes, go on still in the life God has ordained you; lift first your eyes to Him, and thank Him bravely that He has snatched you from the snare of an affection of which He was not the bond, and whose emptiness would sooner or later have revealed itself to you. Then, look about you, see whom you can console and succor; see also whom you can love; see, above all, who there is who loves you, and silence in your heart the thought, guilty and profane, which you express to me in these words: ' My life has been deprived of all that can give me a desire to live.'

You will re-read this, some day, Fleurange, these bitter and ungrateful words, and I assure you, you will find them false. If God has not created you to love Himself only, to the exclusion of these permissible affections which a ray of His love illumines, still less were you made to find repose in a love deprived of that light, a love whose perishable nature has only failed to be experienced by you because its sudden rending away has spared you that grief, in giving you for the moment, an acuter suffering.

Once more, Fleurange, to your knees and give thanks! then up, and act! No flagging energy, no self-pleasing thought of what you have lost, what suffered! Courage! —your heart has yielded, but your will has stood firm, and however rough was the path of duty, it has been enough for you to see it, and you have walked in it without faltering. Courage! you will live—you will do something better than merely live,—you will be healed, and you will remember this hour which seemed so dark, as that which

At first, this letter will but add to your sadness, and you will find yourself deprived of everything, even of the consolation you expected from me, but do not yield to the temptation to burn these pages when you have read them. Keep them to read again some day, and be sure of this, sooner or later the day will come when a sweet promise of happiness will respond from the depths of your heart as you read. You will understand then what are my wishes for you,—for that day, my Fleurange, they will have been granted !"

This reply to the letter written by Fleurange, during the agitated night which had followed her interview with the countess Vera, we do not place before the eyes of the reader at the period when, upon her return from her sad journey, it came to her at Rosenhain ; but two years later when, one summer morning, seated by the river, the young girl re-read for the first time these pages.

The aspect of her whom we now see again, was a little altered. A cruel illness, the result of the emotions and the fatigues endured two years earlier, had endangered her life, and to her long convalescence had succeeded a malady, slower, deeper-rooted, more difficult to cure, against which all remedies, even that of a will courageously resolved to aid them, had long remained ineffectual.

During this phase of weakness, till then unknown to Fleurange, her life became new and difficult. Long was she obliged to deny herself the solace of an active performance of duties, to support inaction without rendering it for herself and others, one discomfort the more ; compelled in a word, to constant and silent effort for self-conquest ; but she accomplished it, accepting, with grateful sweetness, the kind care of those who surrounded her, sparing them the knowledge of her sufferings, and striving to convince them that their tenderness sufficed her, and that, at home with them again, she needed nothing more. By degrees, this came easier to her. As the sun in springtime first melts the snow, then warms the earth, then covers it with flowers, she too felt, that under the influence of this beneficent tenderness, all things in her heart and thoughts, slowly came back again to life. Surely it was pleasant and sweet to her, as she lay on a sofa for hours, half-asleep, to hear, like the notes of birds, Frida's caressing voice, mingled with those of the little children of her two cousins, whom she loved to hold in her arms and to caress, when they had awakened her; it was consoling to lean her head against an almost maternal breast; it was salutary to talk with her uncle Ludwig when, after having been rolled to her side in his great chair, he spoke to her of so many things worthy of fixing her attention, without ever turning it away from the highest of all. And Frida? and Clara? and Julian and Hansfelt? did not each bring his share of steady and faithful friendship, a flower, so to speak, adding its perfume to the air she breathed? Was it nothing, finally, to meet the loving gaze of that dear old friend who, having thought to see her die, could now never weary of watching her, alive?

And now what shall we say of him whose name we have not mentioned as yet, of him whose solicitude for her was no greater, apparently, than that of his parents and his sisters, and who, however, during her long convalescence had come to occupy towards her a place which no one dreamed of disputing to him? The character of Clement has been ill depicted if, after the unforeseen catastrophe which gave him once more leave to hope, the reader supposes him prompt to express, or even admit that hope. And yet, since severe and constant self-control had ceased to seem to him an absolute duty, since the fear of betraying himself no longer obliged him to a constraint which, in the presence of his cousin, extended to all subjects, and ended by concealing in part from her the superiority of his mind and the rare beauty of his intellect; a change, of which he himself was not aware, had taken place in him, giving to his face, the tones of his voice, to his whole appearance, a character quite different from that of other days, in the eyes of her to whom he thus appeared for the first time. She observed it with surprise, and when he interrupted their hours of reading aloud by thoughts which sprung spontaneously from his heart or from his intellect now free in its flight, and touching upon a thousand subjects which he had heretofore denied to himself, she grew thoughtful, contrasting, in spite of herself, this eloquence of the soul whose source was so deep, and whose impulse so genuine, with that other eloquence which had once dazzled her and of which polish and culture made all the charm. Every day she looked forward with more and more impatience to the hour of these readings and conversations; she had already learned to appreciate the devotion, the genuine goodness of her cousin, his loyalty, his energy, his courage; to all these qualities, she had done justice, and yet it seemed to her suddenly as if she had never before known him, she even asked herself one day, if ever before she had really looked at him,—so much did the expression of his face, whence radiated all that is divinest here below, the double nobility of heart and intellect, so much did look and smile compensate for that irregularity of feature which the passage of years had already modified to his advantage.

And Fleurange thus soon became aware that, with all her friendly regard for her cousin, she had been unjust towards him, and had never appreciated him as he really deserved.

But what was the day, the hour, the moment, which taught her to see that she had been not only unjust towards him, but ungrateful, even to cruelty? This is something not easily told something concerning which she was perhaps, herself ignorant.

Was it the day, when after having read with a voice which half betrayed his emotion, a passage expressing what he dared not say in words of his own, he raised his eyes suddenly, and looked at her, as he had never done before?

Was it that other day when, with his violin, passing from one melody to another, he played that romance without words which Hansfelt had called "Unrecognized Love," and stopped suddenly, unable to go on?

Or, indeed, was it when, towards the close of the second spring after their return, she was entirely restored to health, and he saw her for the first time out of doors, standing near a great rose-bush, her hands filled with flowers? Was it when he knelt to pick up one rose which had fallen, and so remained until she held out her hand, and blushing, bade him rise?

It is of no importance. That day came, and had by a little preceded the one which found her sitting on the bench by the river attentively re-reading the letter which had, two years before, been addressed to her by Madre Madelina.

The young girl, as we have said, was no longer just the same that we have so often described. Her long illness had left some slight traces, but only such, as, in youth, give almost an additional charm for the moment. The figure of Fleurange, more lithe and slender, her complexion of more transparent delicacy, her long hair cut during her illness, now first growing again, and framing her girlish face with thick and silky curls; all, at this moment, gave her something of the grace of childhood, and seeing her to-day with her cousin, whose height and strongly-marked face had always added in appearance some years to his real age, no one could have believed that she was not the younger of the two.

She read, sitting motionless under the trees, and from time to time her face expressed the varied emotions of her heart. But when, after having read the words once written by herself, " My life has been deprived of all that can give me a desire to live ;" she came to these : " you will re-read this, some day, Fleurange, these bitter and ungrateful words, and, I assure you, you will find them false," she stopped suddenly, and lifting to heaven her tearful eyes, " Ah yes !" she said, " yes,—you were right."

She covered her face with both her hands, and remained for a long time absorbed and swept away, as it were, by a flood of thoughts.

In the depths of memory, vague recollections cleft the past, like flashes of lightning, and brought before her, as in a confused dream, many a forgotten scene.

That violent outburst of grief, those sobs which he could not repress, when he learned that she desired to accompany George : later, those murmured words upon the ice, at that moment which he believed the last of his life, scarce heard, and quickly forgotten then : to-day they revived, like those invisible writings brought out by an approach to the fire. This sentiment which she had discerned but a few days since, had Clement indeed felt it sooner, had he felt it always?—And, if this were so, oh! then, what had been his affection, what had been his constancy, what the sufferings endured for her?—Alas! what had she herself inflicted upon this noble, faithful friend!

"Ah!" she cried aloud, "who has ever been blinder, more ungrateful, more cruel than I?"

She silenced herself with a start, and raised her head, for she believed that she recognized her cousin's footstep. It was indeed he; he came to find her at her favorite seat; and now he was there, standing before her, in the same place, where, three years earlier, he had watched her while, unknown to herself, she had made him suffer so. It was the same place, the same season of the year, it was also the same hour; the daylight was fast fading, and now as then, the moon, already risen, threw a ray of silvery light upon the lovely face questioned by the same eyes. But this time, the question was understood, and the silent answer as expressive as any words, sent to the heart which heard it, all that happiness which is reserved here below for those alone who are capable of a pure, constant, only love : a love worthy to be called after that of God.

We might here end our story, and lay aside the pen, without seeking to describe the joy of the household, when, later, these two, the only ones absent from the family circle, returned together, and everyone guessed from their faces, what the conversation had been which, on this evening, had so long detained them by the river-side.

However, towards the close of this happy evening, Mlle. Josephine brought about, without intending it, a communication which we must not omit.

"Now you see," she cried, in the enthusiasm of her delight not unmingled with a secret pride in her own penetration, "how right I was in thinking that Count George—"

She stopped with a disconcerted air, remembering suddenly all the precautions of the past, and fearing to have been imprudent even now in neglecting them.

But Fleurange unhesitatingly exclaimed : "Go on, my dear friend, go on, do not hesitate to speak a name

And whilst as he listened, the memory of his past torture came over Clement, making him feel more intensely his present happiness, she asked him calmly:

"Is he still exiled from court, or have they pardoned him?"

With a smile Clement rejoined: "No, he has not been pardoned; he still suffers the full rigor of his penalty."

After a moment's silence he added, "I received a letter from Adelardi this very morning, which speaks of him. Will you read it?"

Upon an affirmative gesture from her to whom he addressed this question, he drew his pocket-book out to look for the letter. As he opened it, a bit of myrtle dropped out.

Fleurange recognized it at once.

"What! you keep this still?" she said blushing.

Clement made no reply. He looked tenderly at the little spray; it was part of that treasure so carefully guarded, so long the only solace of his hidden love.

"*Never! oh! no, never!*" he murmured. "That was my answer, Gabrielle, that night when you promised me a beautiful *fiancée*. You remember it?"

"Yes, for I had said the same an hour earlier, and the coincidence struck me."

"What can I think of it now, now that you stand here before me, the betrothed of my impossible dream?"

"That our presentiments often deceive us,—and our sentiments, too, Clement," she added, lifting to his her tearful eyes which seemed to implore pardon.

We will not say what Clement's answer was. We will say only that it made both of them completely forget the letter of Adelardi.

This letter, however, we will lay before the reader, less indifferent, perhaps, to its contents, than was, at this moment, he to whom it was addressed.

It was dated Florence. The marquis, whose visits to Rosenhain had become annual, announced his speedy arrival. Then he continued:

"The poor Princess Catherine, for whom you inquire, suffers again from her often-cured malady, which is aggravated by discontent and *ennui* even more than by age. No one succeeds in pleasing her as she once was pleased, and each new trial renews regrets which are not at all compensated by the gratification of her wishes in another respect. I have observed that there is nothing in the world like realized desires for driving from the mind all memory of the ardor with which they were pursued, and even the transport with which they were hailed, when first accomplished. It is true that there is nothing very satisfactory in her relations with her son, and that they are greatly influenced by the discontent of both. The exile imposed upon George would seem enviable to many, for the place where he lives possesses all possible attractions, save the liberty to leave it. But this terrible corrective spoils the rest; he can enjoy nothing, because every thing, he says, is obligatory. So I fear the future he is preparing for himself, and for his wife also, is very threatening.

"The Countess Vera is a noble and beautiful person, susceptible of devotion to a certain extent, but proud, passionate, and jealous to the highest degree. In marrying George under the circumstances in which he found himself, she believed that she had, by this great sacrifice, made sure of this volatile heart, and attached it to herself faithfully and forever, through gratitude. She has too soon perceived that this was all a mistake, and that the comparative liberty which was restored to him transformed itself promptly in his eyes into the hardest kind of slavery. Hence have resulted scenes between them which have, already, more than once disturbed an existence whose monotony they cannot break. In one of these, would you believe it, Vera, driven wild by irritation and jealousy, herself betrayed the secret, till then so carefully guarded, crying out desperately, that she regretted she had not left him to undergo the fate that another was so ready to share with him. Recovering herself, she found reason to regret her imprudence, for George insisted upon a full disclosure, and brought thus suddenly face to face with a recollection, clothed to-day in his eyes with the two-fold charm of the past and the impossible, he gave himself up in turn to the most bitter and unsparing reproaches; and it is altogether too probable that he had the cruelty to tell her that he would have preferred a thousand fold the destiny from which she had withdrawn him, to that which to-day was his, at her side.

"We know how much importance is to be attached to this glamour of his imagination; but after all this, you will not be surprised to learn that they both aspire with equal ardor towards that liberty which, for two years yet, is denied them, and which will, according to all present appearance, be equally dangerous to both. The princess sees and foresees all, since a visit she made last summer to Livonia, and in which I accompanied her. During her stay George was not sparing of his reproaches, and this was all the more distressing to her, because she has long since acknowledged to herself that she has sacrificed his happiness and her own comfort by an opposition which has resulted in removing from her at one stroke, her son and the only person whose services had ever been able to satisfy her. And as, when she is displeased, she must always lay the blame upon some other than herself, do you know who is now regarded by her as the cause of all her misfortunes?—Gabrielle! who she says, three years ago, did not know how to use and preserve as she should have done her empire over George! When she perceived that I in no degree, shared this regret—which will neither, I suppose, be shared by you, nor, as I delight to think, by her who inspires it,—she became vexed with me in turn, and declared sadly that all friends were unfeeling, and all children ungrateful!"

Clement's reply to this letter hastened the arrival of the marquis. He had seen his young friend's hopes revive and grow again, and he would not have failed on any account to be present at Rosenhain on the day when they were at last fulfilled. Wilhelm, and Bertha, who had known so well how to console the suffering of Clement without obliging him to recall it, were, with the marquis, the only friends who were with the family upon the day of rejoicing. The wedding was not less merry than Clara's, but the bride and the bridegroom were graver and more thoughtful, for a great trial had preceded this wedding-day, and it seemed to have added to their happiness that *something finished*, which is so often wanting ɔ the most joyful festivities in this life.

They also, in their turn, were to go to Italy, and one can readily believe that among the places they were to visit together, the first toward which their thoughts turned was that where awaited them the welcome and benediction of *Madre* Madelina.

Returning, Mlle. Josephine's house, enlarged and adorned, became their home, their old friend sharing it with them to the end of her days.

Was their destiny a happy one? We believe it safe to affirm that it was. Was it exempt from pain, from suffering, from sacrifice? This, even more safely, we can deny. It was enviable, however, for they possessed whatever is best of earthly happiness without ever forgetting that *" life can never be completely happy, because it is not Heaven, nor completely unhappy, because it is the road thither."*

THE END.

www.ingramcontent.com/pod-product-compliance
Lightning Source LLC
Chambersburg PA
CBHW030311240426
43673CB00040B/1134